The Route from
Neubrandenburg to Wittenberge

Showers on Thursday

By

John Bellamy

Maygog
Publishing

Published by:
Maygog Publishing
P.O. Box 452, Sorell
Tasmania, 7172, Australia
www.maygog.com

ISBN 0-975048-3-X

Printed by: Franklin Press
91 Albert Rd, Moonah, Tasmania, Australia

Cover design: Matt Pott
www.mattpott.com

To my wife Eddie

Acknowledgement

My most sincere thanks go to Maygog Publishing as a whole and in particular to those most closely involved in bringing this book to publication. I wish to thank Joan Carr for her help and encouragement leading up to the decision to publish and subsequently for her careful proofreading. No words can adequately express my gratitude to Helen Lawrence for her great work in editing my original manuscript - and in recommending essential changes so very tactfully.

My thanks also to Mike Shegog, without whose skills the photographs might not have been included and to Sue Cole for her preparation of the map, and to Matt Pott for the artwork of the cover. Nor do I forget the knowledgeable and kindly encouragement I received from Irene Parker, Patricia Ryecroft, John Hooper and Colin Pyefinch many, many months ago. I am indebted to you all. JDB

Foreword

As the events of the Second World War become dimmer in the memory of the veterans, it is I feel important that a permanent record of those times is kept. John (or Jack I as know him) has decided to record his life story in words and I'm sure many people will be saying Jack *who?* Well to me Jack is the role model for the typical airborne warrior as described by Field Marshal Montgomery, who said:

> What manner of men are these who wear the maroon beret? They are, firstly, all volunteers, and are toughened by hard physical training. As a result, they have that infectious optimism and that offensive eagerness which come from physical well-being. They have jumped from the air and, by doing so, have conquered fear. Their duty lies in the van of battle: they are proud of their honour, and have never failed in any task. They have the highest standards in all things, whether it be skill in battle or smartness in execution of all peacetime duties. They have shown themselves to be as tenacious and determined in defence as they are courageous in attack. They are, in fact men apart. Every man an emperor.

Jack qualified as one of the first para-medics in the British Army.

Perhaps it might be best to add a little explanation here: I think I became enthralled by military history when I was a small boy. I can remember going to the cinema in the 1970s as a schoolboy and watching "A Bridge Too Far" – the film account of Operation Market Garden, which would hopefully end the Second World War by Christmas 1944. Later like Jack I served in the Royal Army Medical Corps, and was stupid enough to volunteer for the parachute arm of the Corps, passed P Company and won a red beret and parachute wings. After serving my time I started to pursue my interest in the airborne medical services especially what happened at Arnhem in Holland – the infamous Bridge Too Far. In 1995 another veteran suggested I write to Jack about the 16th Parachute Field Ambulance. I tentatively wrote a letter explaining who I was and my research. Jack kindly sent me a 50-page account of some of his war time experiences in the airborne forces. I seem to recall writing in one of my letters that he had sent me some of the best material I'd received so far and I felt there was enough for a book on Jack's service alone.

He seems to have taken my comment to heart and we have remained in contact ever since. In 1999 I asked Jack to write a foreword for my book "Red Berets and Red Crosses", as he was one of the longest-serving para-medics left. He readily agreed to my request. I am now repaying the favour but feel I have no credentials for doing this except that I look on Jack, not as one of my airborne brothers but an airborne uncle. Even though we have never met (but we hope to meet in Arnhem for the 60th anniversary) we are members of the biggest and best union in the world – the airborne brotherhood. An integral part of this brotherhood has always been the medical services – often unsung and overlooked, we have never been far from the action. Jack was no exception, from North Africa, Sicily, Italy and then capture at Arnhem – he upheld the traditions of the Corps by being "Steadfast In Adversity".

I hope Jack will forgive me for using some words he wrote in his foreword for my book "the bond of the red beret though invisible was as strong as steel"" Jack has done an excellent job of illustrating this bond and has produced a most readable story of life at the blunt end in a parachute field ambulance and also of his life story. His work will be a welcome addition to any serious military historian's bookshelf and I hope it achieves the success it deserves.

Niall Cherry
Author "Red Berets and Red Crosses"
UK representative The Friends of the Airborne Museum
Oosterbeek Holland
Warton
Lancashire, UK,
March 2004.

Contents

Back, L to R: Audrey, Father,
Front, Lto R: Monica, Mother with Jack

Chapter 1

Hearsay

It is almost 8am on Thursday, 17th July 1919. A wet morning in the port of Prince Rupert, in the far northwest of Canada, just 50 miles or so from the Alaskan border. Dr. Kergin shows no surprise at the rain as he leaves the white painted weatherboard apartment block at the end of 2nd Avenue West. Hunching his shoulders against the veils of rain drifting in off the North Pacific Ocean, he hurries towards the comfort of his own home on 4th Avenue; for he has lived here many years and has become accustomed to the year-round rainfall of 90 inches or more. Behind him he leaves excitement and happiness in the Bellamy family household as father, mother and sisters, Audrey and Monica, greet the new arrival of a son, given the name, John Desmond.

Prince Rupert stands on Kaien Island, at the mouth of the mighty Skeena River that flows through the coastal mountain range of British Columbia. The island is only separated from the mainland by a narrow channel, bridged both by road and rail. Prince Rupert can now boast city status with 20,000 inhabitants, but is a far cry from being the rival to Vancouver its planner once visualised. Sadly, Charles M. Hays was one of the many who perished in the sinking of the Titanic in 1912. A young town, dating only from the first decade of the twentieth century, Prince Rupert had been a centre for centuries, a gathering point for two great Indian nations. For it was here that the 'Tsimshian' people of the mainland and the 'Haida' of the Queen Charlotte Islands met in conclave and it is appropriate that the giant carved cedar totem poles of these people should ornament the town today.

Perhaps the birth of a son was some compensation for the disastrous run of events that brought my parents there. My father was working as a clerk, the Registrar-General at the time of my birth. In our present day terminology this has become a rather grandiose position with political overtones, but in the prosaic world of far northwest Canada of that time, 'Registrar-General' meant just that. He was registrar of everything: births, deaths, marriages, mining claims and fishing licenses – you name it, my father had to register it! He was good at keeping books and figures and had been appointed to clear up the mess left behind by a somewhat less than honest predecessor; but he was not entirely happy with the work, always having a preference for the outdoor life.

Until a few weeks before my birth, our family had been living at Lillooet, or to give it its Indian name, Pap-Shil-Qua-Ka-Meen, the place where three rivers meet. Lillooet is set high above the banks of the Fraser River, 100 miles or so northeast of Vancouver and many hundreds of miles south of Prince Rupert. It is a small town now, but it was vastly different back in the boom days of the 1860s, when it was described as 'the biggest little boom settlement in the Caribou District'. The Caribou District was the old name for British Columbia. For some years, in addition to working in the assayer's office in Lillooet, my father, with his partner Walter Cox, operated a steamboat service along Seton Lake. This lake, like nearby Lake Anderson, is a long narrow glacial lake between extremely steep walls. Parts of these walls consist of unstable rock and scree and they presented a temporarily insurmountable obstacle to the railway pushing towards the little town. This steamboat service carried cargo, prospectors, miners, settlers and Indians along the 15 or so mile length of the lake from Portage to Lillooet. 'Portage' got its name because it was simply a portage, an overland carrying trail of less than a mile between the adjacent ends of Seton Lake and Lake Anderson.

My father told me many tales of his days with the boat. How it had been brought up in sections by ox-drawn carts for erection at the end of the lake. How slowly the old wood-burner progressed along the lake and how on calm days in summer he would trail a rope over the side and dive into the waters for a swim (having lashed the steering wheel to maintain his course) and return aboard via the rope. Inevitably he dived in one day and having forgotten to trail the rope, had to swim ashore and walk to where the vessel gently grounded itself on the gravelly beach! Needless to say, he never did this when he had passengers aboard. I believe the Lillooet days were generally happy ones for my father; perhaps not so happy for my mother, who would have been much more conscious of the isolation. Her beloved piano was her one luxury and indulgence in a world of basic self-sufficiency, where flour and sugar were purchased infrequently – in one-hundredweight sacks! Fish from the lake augmented fresh meat (rarely available in the town) and Indians from the reservation traded salmon and exotic meats such as elk steaks.

Disaster came to the partnership in the autumn of 1916. The steamboat service operated from a shed on the wharf that had become dilapidated. Walter Cox and my father decided to dismantle and rebuild it. Walter was removing decking from the front of the building, when suddenly, without warning, the shed section tilted forward and fell down, carrying Walter and the remains of the decking into the lake, where it pinned him head down in shallow water. Frantically my father ripped at the boards and timber holding his friend down. Years later he told me that it had taken weeks for his hands to heal and broken fingernails to re-grow, but he never did get over the horror of the sight of Walter's white rubber boots threshing above water before finally becoming ominously still.

The second disaster happened only a few weeks before my birth. Winter had passed, usually rather mild in Lillooet's surprisingly dry climate, and a pleasant spring gave way to a particularly hot early summer. The family walked down to the lakeside late one afternoon, clad only in their bathing costumes, taking light raincoats to wear on the return climb to their home. The evening meal had been left cooking slowly on the oil stove, when a sudden gust of wind must have fanned the flames and within moments the sun-dried timber home was fiercely ablaze. In a single dash through the flames my father rescued a black japanned tin trunk containing business papers, insurances, his beloved stamp collection and – explosives! His badly burned shoulders, singed hair and eyebrows were, apart from the trunk, all that he had to show for his efforts.

In the evening light they stumbled, stunned and tearful, along the mile or so of trail down to the Lillooet township. My mother, almost eight months pregnant with me, Audrey aged 9 and Monica almost 4, were clothed only in their bathing costumes and raincoats, and looked vastly different from the neatly dressed and groomed trio usually seen visiting the town. Mother's hair was black and curly and long, well below shoulder level. Audrey's was waist long, brown and like Father's, smooth and straight. Monica's was a mop of fair, shoulder length curls. Those curls never failed to amaze the local Indians.

The townsfolk of Lillooet were wonderful. Quite apart from the $200 that found its way unobtrusively into Father's bank account next day, my mother always remembered and treasured the comb pressed into her hand by the local storekeeper on the night of the fire. Large and black, with strong sturdy teeth on one half and finer teeth on the other, that comb virtually became a family heirloom. I remember seeing it on her dressing table almost twenty-one years later, on the morning of the 13th June 1940, the day I departed to report for my Army service.

With their home destroyed and the railway now able to serve Lillooet's needs, there was little future in the area for my father and after selling the boat, he took the job of Registrar in Prince Rupert and that was how they came to be .here for my birth.

But disaster was not yet quite over for the Bellamy family, for when the weather turned unseasonably cold a few days after my birth (and remember we were only 50 miles from Alaska) a hot-water bottle was provided for my infant comfort. It was one of those earthenware bottles, a horizontal cylinder, flattened along the lower side, with its serrated screw-in rubber-washered stopper on the top. Maybe it was an old hot-water bottle, perhaps boiling water had been used. Whatever the cause, when it was tucked in near my left hip, it burst! The resulting scald must have been an appallingly traumatic incident for an infant only a few days old and it would have been just as traumatic for my parents who no doubt felt responsible.

There was more to come! The state of medical knowledge in outback British Columbia in 1919 was by no means advanced. Little progress was made in the treatment of burns and scalds until the medical and surgical advances brought about in the wake of World War II. The prescribed treatment for my scald was the daily application of copper sulphate, commonly known as Blue Vitriol. This very probably prevented any secondary infection occurring,

4

but it led to unsightly scarring of that area of my anatomy for the rest of my life. Even today, eighty years on, running my fingers lightly over my left thigh I can feel the taut, raised edges of the scar through the fabric of my trousers. The one reassuring feature of the copper sulphate treatment was that it convinced my family and most of the nearby citizens, that there was nothing whatsoever wrong with my lungs!

For many years I was very conscious of this 'disfigurement' and can recall being at the local swimming pool and repeatedly pulling down the left side of my costume in a vain attempt to hide the ugly scar. Years later, with growing self-confidence, the thought came to mind that with a bit of luck, my scar might be mistaken for an honourable war wound!

But back now to Prince Rupert, where these successive calamities had made my parents listen more sympathetically to pleas from my mother's parents for them to return to England to take over the running of my grandparents' outfitting business in the English midlands town of Ashby-de-la-Zouch in northwest Leicestershire. Eventually they made the decision to do just that.

It was not until the end of September that I was considered sufficiently recovered from the scald to be baptised. So I was duly named 'John Desmond' by the Rev.G.A. Rix in the Church of St. Andrews, Prince Rupert, BC. Today that small church has become the basement of St. Andrew's Cathedral. The same font is still there, my name is in the parish records and the Rev. Rix went on to become the first Bishop of British Columbia.

Prince Rupert is now an important railhead for the Canadian National Railway, but in its earliest days it was envisaged as the western terminus of the Grand Trunk Pacific Railway. It may well have been on that line that I began my eastbound journey through Prince George, Jasper and Edmonton, arriving some days later at Montreal. Of course I recollect nothing of the long journey, but I can clearly remember two linen table napkins in our household some years later in Ashby. These napkins had a monogram CNR embroidered in red in one corner, indicating they were once the property of the Canadian National Railway. My mother told me she had been given these on the train when supplies of the more absorbent type of nappy had run short. At least that was her excuse for their presence in our home.

The train journey may have had nostalgic moments for my father. Before his Lillooet days he had worked on the development of these trunk railways and his duties often took him ahead of the rail line to organise camps and supplies for the hundreds of workers employed on the job. In this work he had known and worked alongside Pat Welch who went on to become one of the magnates of those transcontinental railways and made a fortune.

At Montreal we went aboard the Cunard ship SS Tunisia. My mother was quite an experienced sailor, having crossed and re-crossed the Atlantic Ocean three times previously. She used to tell us how she waited on the wharf at Liverpool for allocation of a passage on any available vessel during the 1914-18 War years. Her fear was that she and small daughter Audrey were about to be shipped on a rather dirty and disreputable looking cargo vessel and she was considerably relieved when she was directed to the luxurious White Star Olympic. She always said that Audrey refused to put on her life jacket during lifeboat drill until depth charges exploding in the water shook the great liner.

It may have been on this trip that she witnessed the devastation of Halifax, Nova Scotia, following the explosion of a munitions ship that was being loaded there. Perhaps her best story of these Atlantic crossings was in 1915 when, returning to England, she cancelled a booking on the liner Lusitania on the advice of her travel agent and transferred to the much smaller liner Georgic. Because, as she put it, "They had transferred gold bullion off the Lusitania to the Georgic – and what was good enough for bullion was good enough for me!" This was to be the last sailing of the SS Lusitania. She was torpedoed and sunk by a German U-boat near Ireland a few days later.

But of course in 1919 there was no longer danger from U-boats and our family journey in the SS Tunisia would have been as pleasant as any late autumn trip across the North Atlantic is likely to be. I have often wondered whether they saw the brilliant autumn colours of the maple trees on their long sail down the St. Lawrence River. Without doubt my father had seen it in all its glory at some time in his life as he spoke of it as one of the wonders of the world. Perhaps it was sights like this and the space and freedom of the New World that prevented him from ever being totally happy in the more intimate life of England. I feel sure we must have returned to the port of Liverpool, because my mother seemed to know and like Liverpool and revisited the city on a number of occasions. But in October 1919 our destination was Ashby-de-la-Zouch, at that time a small town of around five thousand inhabitants, many of them still coming to terms with the loss of loved ones in the 1914-18 War.

Ashby is a pleasant, historic little place, grouped just to the northwest of the ruins of a once massive fifteenth century castle – one of the castles where Mary Queen of Scots was imprisoned and which gallantly withstood a six months siege during the Civil War in the seventeenth century. People at Ashby are still anti-Cromwell. During the nineteenth and twentieth centuries the small mining villages surrounding Ashby had thrived on the coal and clay found beneath their land and Ashby had developed as the market and business centre for the region. Following the end of World War I, the mines were relatively prosperous. On the strength of this wealth plus that of the agriculture in the area, Ashby's economy was thriving and the shop that my parents took over assured them of a reasonably good income. The business could boast of having many of the best agencies – names like Wolsey, Jaegar, Aertex, Chilprufe, Dents and Folkspeare.

While the area remained prosperous our business continued to do well and in the early 1920s life for my family would have been as simple and as comfortable as might reasonably have been expected when sharing the home with my grandparents. But it must have been a very happy day for my father and mother when my grandparents decided to build a house for themselves in South Street, a few hundred yards away from the Market Street property. This would have been around 1924 or '25, for I have recollections of being taken down there and, with my hand firmly held, jumping over the narrow trenches of the foundations and drains of their new house. Little did I know then – or care – that this house would be the first home that my future wife and I would occupy, and for a short while we would run a café there. But that was not to happen for the next twenty years.

≈≈≈≈≈≈≈≈≈≈≈

Chapter 2
Early education

An old, rambling house built originally in 1486, 76 Market Street fronted onto the wide main street of the town, with its two front rooms on the ground floor forming the shop and showroom of our outfitting business. These rooms and those immediately above it were added in 1640 and this section had encroached on the main road. In fact the town administrators fined the builder eight shillings for his pains.

Everything in that house was on different levels. There was a step down from the shop to the showroom immediately behind it and a shallow, wide, very worn step led out of the showroom into the passage at the rear. This passage sloped a little and ended up in the kitchen with a further step down of about 4 inches. To the left of the passage, a small room that we used as a cosy sitting room was just about an inch lower. But on the right of the passage a wide low door opened into what we called the pantry and here great care was needed, for the single step down was at least 9 inches deep. A thin wooden rail was the only safeguard preventing someone from stumbling down a further flight of twelve brick steps into a brick vaulted cellar with a stone thrall on either side. The only light filtered meagrely through a cast iron grating capping a ventilation shaft at the cellar's western end. It was a dark, cold, damp spot and it filled me with dread. I shuddered to think of the foul deeds that might have been done in it. Legend had it that the Bull's Head, the very old public house directly opposite was, together with our house, connected by an underground passage to the medieval castle some 200 yards away. I was convinced that our cellar was exactly in the right position for this to be true and I imagined Cavaliers and King's men sneaking up out of our cellar to escape, while Cromwell and his army stormed the Keep of the castle. When workmen were digging behind the house to put in new drainage pipes, they discovered the remains of a brick arch lying in the right general direction. They considered this construction much too large for any known drainage or sewage system. So, did such a 'secret' passage once exist? It doesn't appear on any known plans of the castle – but then, it wouldn't if it were 'secret', would it?

The kitchen was the hub of the house. It stretched across the whole width of the rear of the older portion of the building, its natural lighting restricted to a small south facing window by the back door and a larger square window in the eastern wall. Beneath this second window was a long, shallow brick sink with one brass tap for cold water. An old iron pump painted green stood on the right hand side, slightly apart from the sink itself.

Vaguely I remember the old range, with its oven on the left and an open-topped hot water reservoir on its right, set deeply into a huge chimney recess on the south wall. It was eventually replaced by a new coal-burning stove, a 'Columbian', free standing on the opposite side of the kitchen. This new stove was the same type my mother had used so effectively in Canada, but most importantly it provided an almost constant supply of hot water and a new chrome tap appeared at the sink. But for some unfathomable reason, this was installed at the left hand edge of the wide sink – almost three feet from the cold tap. Ergonomics were not a strong point of this system, but the galvanised pipe rising to the ceiling and traversing the length of the kitchen to disappear through to the bathroom above was to revolutionise our lives.

Baths used to be a major undertaking. The copper in the washhouse, some distance down the yard, had to be fired up and a large quantity of water boiled. Then big buckets and lidded cans of steaming water were carried laboriously upstairs to the bathroom. Meanwhile huge kettles were standing on the range – these were to top up and warm the water in the bath as it cooled. A large, upright hot water tank stood, unlagged, in the corner of the kitchen close to the stove. When someone was having a bath, towels were draped round it and as soon as a call of "Towels, please," was heard, someone would collect the warm towels off the tank and hurry upstairs to the bathroom. Eyes were tactfully averted and a hand bearing a luxuriously warm towel would appear round the door.

There were three doors into our kitchen. One from the passage, another opening to the backyard on the west side, (it was the only door on the ground floor that had no step) and a third door on the kitchen's south wall. This third door opened to reveal yet another two steps that descended into what we called the coalhouse. The coalhouse was quite a large room with an oak-beamed ceiling and must once have been the living room of the original house. Half of its uneven brick floor was usually buried under several hundredweight of coal, while the remainder was hidden by a fascinating maze of tins of paint, old prams, hat boxes, travel trunks and general junk. The whole collection was covered in a fine film of coal dust that rose in a cloud when the large lumps were broken up with the coal pick before being taken in scuttles to burn in the household fires.

Just in front of where the doorway opened into this coalhouse, a flight of wooden steps led abruptly up into the workroom and the 'nursery'. The workroom deserved its title. In the workroom there was a long carpenter's bench – my grandfather's. I can still visualise the three wooden jackplanes that stood on their respective racks and smell the shavings of the deal and oak boards he often worked with. Saws hung from pegs on the wall, including a strangely shaped wooden bowsaw, a museum piece. We passed through one end of this workroom to gain access to the 'nursery', so called because it was a room where Monica and I could play on wet days. There were wonderful things in that room. Hatboxes bearing the famous name of Christies, with the Royal Coat of Arms and 'By Appointment' stamped on their lids. Inside them were genuine top hats, still gleaming brightly and with small shiny cockades on their crowns. There were other boxes with items of dress that had long since passed into history – lace-up corsets of indescribable complexity; some of them still in their long, slim, interesting boxes with 'Gossard' and 'Line of Beauty' emblazoned on their shiny white cardboard lids. A few years on I treasured those boxes around Guy Fawkes' Night for they were ideal for the pre November 5th garnering of fireworks. Even small rockets, with their sticks attached, could be lovingly stored in those corset boxes. A treasure house of old clothes was invaluable for 'dressing up' and provided long hours of amusement for us and may well have helped develop my sisters' love of theatre and ballet.

There were large tins in that nursery, full of apricot pulp and Chinese eggs. Where they had come from we never really knew. And there were small wooden packing cases, exceptionally heavy because they were packed solid with leaflets printed on thin white paper. These leaflets were aimed at breaking the Miners' Strike of the mid-1920s. They accused the miners' leader of being, amongst other things, a liar and of having misled the miners. Knowing nothing of politics, we children were just delighted to have the plain backs of these countless leaflets for our scribbling and lurid paintings. We folded them carefully, with sharply creased lines, into paper darts and aeroplanes that we launched from the nursery window. Fortunately, an iron bar, fixed vertically across the window, prevented our accompanying the darts to the cobbled path below. Two of the panes in this window were of 'bull's eye' glass with a round thickened lump in them where the glass had been poured and the outside world would assume weird and incredible new dimensions through these crude lenses. I could stand fascinated for long minutes as minor movements of my eye converted the ridge of the nearby stables into the sweeping curve of a Chinese temple roof, or the tall straight trunk of our pear tree into a gigantic contorted Bonsai creation. Antique dealers and their customers now actively seek this rare type of glass. Our nursery had two such panes and the coalhouse below yet another one and I don't think we ever knew or appreciated their true value.

The large tins of apricots or eggs made excellent stools and the wooden boxes of leaflets often served as tables, but at times they would be built into imaginative pyramids or bridges that crashed with resounding and satisfying thuds on to the lime-concrete floors.

These floors were a peculiar feature of the house. They were thick, six to eight inches or even more in places and they had been installed in every upstairs room with the sole exception of the workroom that had a wooden, deal plank floor. Linoleum or carpet covered most of the area, but round the edge of carpets in some rooms and on either side of the linoleum that ran the length of the upper passage, the concrete had been stained with permanganate of potash and then sealed with varnish. Through the varnish you could see the tiny particles of minute shells, almost like a mosaic, that made up this strange flooring. The large lounge room over the shop and the nursery were the only two floors that were remotely level and even on these floors a ping-pong ball would roll, slowly and erratically from one end to the other – to the great delight of our cats and their kittens.

My two sisters must have contributed freely to my very early education; Audrey was ten years and Monica four years my senior. This combination seemed to offer both the wisdom of an adult and the understanding of a near contemporary – although Monica would have been scathing in rejecting the thought that we were contemporaries. For years, even after I had grown taller than she was, she insisted on referring to me as "my little brother" when she was in a good mood and as "the little monster" when she wasn't.

I can remember nothing with real clarity before the age of four or thereabouts. Before this, there are vague recollections of cold, dark winter mornings and being taken from my bed (possibly wet) and bundled – quite literally – in a soft, loosely knitted woollen shawl and then being carried, only half awake, down the creaking Market Street stairs to the kitchen. There I would be propped against the wall at the end of the bench nearest the warmth of the stove. Huddled there, I would cogitate while my sisters had breakfast before they left for school. Then it was my turn and someone, usually my mother but not infrequently one of our maids would provide my breakfast. Don't misunderstand the use of the plural 'maids' – we only ever had one at a time, but among them I can remember a Rhoda and two Nellies and what wonderfully patient people they must have been – real friends of the family, never just servants.

My education probably began at these early morning breakfasts in our warm but dark and draughty kitchen, for I had a matching mug and an oversized eggcup all my very own. They were made of white glazed pottery and printed boldly in black on their outer surfaces was a jumble of the letters of the alphabet and the numbers 1 to 10. The oversized eggcup was used when I had my favourite breakfast – bread and butter, cut up into small squares and placed into the large cup and then a lightly boiled egg broken over them and the whole mass well stirred. It was easily my favourite and perhaps it explains my fondness for a poached egg on toast.

It was about this time that I developed a dislike for the smell of bacon and fried eggs. In my childhood days this seemed to be the daily diet of my grandparents and to a lesser extent, my parents also, but I don't think my sisters shared the adults' addiction. It is much more likely, if my own school days' experiences are any guide, that hastily consumed cornflakes (FORCE was the usual brand) or a plate of porridge would be the only thing that either of them ever had time for. But I had time to waste and must have spent long hours gazing at that mug and eggcup as I turned and twisted them in my hands to see the letters and numbers near their bases. In doing so, quite subconsciously I was learning to recognise all the letters of the alphabet. I think by the time I went to Kindergarten at the age of five I could basically read the simple readers provided. It seemed to me that there were several others among my fellow students who could do the same, for I don't recall being outstanding by any means.

St. Helen's Kindergarten, with its large and imposing pillared entrance, was really a feeder school for the girls' and boys' grammar schools in the town. However, its grand entrance was not for students, it was very strictly reserved for Staff Only. Situated at the top end of Market Street, it was only fifty yards or so from home and my father, the maid, or at times our shop assistant, would walk me across the wide road and right to the school door. The street was busy in those days and it became impossibly so by 1939. The kindergarten has long since closed and moved to a safer, quieter location. Thinking back, it surprises me that there were boarders attending this school. Seven to eight year olds, who went home each weekend. I went home for my midday meals, but often saw the meals for the boarders being carried in and was intrigued by the sight of a whole huge fish borne on a vast oval dish to the dining hall. The novelty of this attracted me and I longed to sample the boarders' meals – until I talked to them on the subject and they told me that they were horrid. They added that they couldn't wait for the weekend to get home for a decent meal.

In a year or two, when I had achieved greater reading ability, there were other aids to self-education at home. A large oilskin map of England and Wales, showing the myriads of railway routes that covered the country in those days, hung high on the kitchen wall above and behind the freestanding hot water tank on its low wooden stand. I would climb up onto the projecting corners of this stand and holding on to the water pipes ascending to the ceiling, press my body against the comforting warmth of the tank. This position gave me a good view of the lower two thirds of the map and I quickly got to know the geography of England and the English rail system as far north as Manchester and York. Further North was too high for me to read with any certainty.

There were always interesting books and magazines on our shelves. My father had a complete set of the Harmsworth History of the World magazines. These were beautifully illustrated and so fascinated me that long before I could read the full text, I knew exactly which magazine held the particular pictures that I loved. These included the Taj Mahal and the Eiffel Tower. I could find them and gaze at them whenever I wished.

My sisters' Wonder Books were another source of delight and soon I too was receiving books of this series as Christmas or birthday gifts. Several years later I acquired the Wonder Book of the Navy, The Wonder Book of Railways and The Wonder Book of the Wild. Of course there was lighter reading in the form of the ever popular comics. Tiger Tim's Weekly was my favourite, although I was quite partial to Rainbow and Comic Cuts if I could persuade my parents to purchase them. About the age of ten, The Children's Newspaper edited by Sir Arthur Mee was added to my list of permitted papers and that was very informative without being stuffily educational.

For the most part those were happy days. The school was well equipped for that era. It had large airy classrooms in the main building, a fine assembly hall that also served as a gymnasium and a fairly extensive playground. A small area of this was tarmac sealed, another larger area was gravelled and a much larger area still was lawn, for rounders and other games in the summer months. On the debit side the toilets were rudimentary and separated by a large stretch of yard from the school building. No one dawdled on the return journey on rainy days.

There were characters at that school. The Headmistress, Miss Hopkirk was an enormous woman who sailed majestically up to the dais for morning prayers, her long black dress brushing the floor. She must have been six foot and heavily built and to little titches like me, she was vast. Other teachers' names remain engraved on my memory. Miss Good, Deputy Head, extremely strict and I remember clashing with her from time to time. Miss Elliot, a teacher of mathematics who was so fierce in class and yet, until I was called up for Army service some fourteen years later, never failed to pass me in the street without asking, smilingly, how I was getting on. You remember such people with great affection.

The gymnastics mistress, Miss Spencer, met approving glances as she strode vigorously into the Hall we used for Gym. I think she was a good PT teacher and under supervision, we were encouraged to do quite daring exercises on the limited equipment available. Indeed, when I moved on to the Boys' Grammar School, I got into trouble for demonstrating one of the wall-bar exercises that Miss Spencer had taught us – and which seemed to terrify the much less progressive gymnastics master we had at the senior school.

St. Helen's School was close to a corner on Ashby's main street and the sounds of traffic could be clearly heard in all the classrooms on the front of the building. I would listen intently for one particular car hooter that I knew well. It was my father's Model T Ford and he would squeeze a rubber bulb to sound the hooter that emitted an unmistakable throaty 'honk' as he approached the corner. The school firmly believed that "Manners maketh Man" and Father was never slow to reinforce this point on me. When walking with him one day, my school cap was forcibly doffed with a swipe from his left hand when we met a teacher and I forgot to raise my cap.

My school cap was also removed unceremoniously on another occasion, this time by a horse. I was by then old enough to make my way to school on my own. I was walking on the pavement, passing Mr Radford's milk delivery float, with its large gleaming steel milk buckets in the back. As I passed the horse's head, it swung sideways, snatched the red and grey cap off my mop of hair and only dropped it on the road after discovering it was inedible. To say that I was startled would be a gross understatement. I was terrified. Fortunately the incident was observed, as otherwise no one would have believed how my almost new cap came to be so badly damaged so early in its life.

Leaving St. Helen's and starting life in the 'Big School', the Ashby Boys' Grammar School was exhilarating though also nervewracking. I was fortunate to live near a school of such high calibre. It was one of the finest country Grammar Schools in England. Founded in 1567 when Queen Elizabeth I was on the throne, it has produced some famous and infamous scholars in its time.

There was William Lely, born in 1602, a brilliant Latin scholar who was unable to take Holy Orders because his father was a drunken, penniless sot and an inadequate farmer. Instead William Lely went on to become an astrologer of some fame and was highly thought of by Oliver Cromwell and the Parliamentary forces. It is alleged that when Cromwell was addressing his troops before the Battle of Dunbar, he said: "Be of good heart, for Lely is with us!" Other evidence of Lely's activities indicate that he was a bit of a charlatan and duped a number of people, particularly women, in order to maintain a good income.

At the time I arrived in Form IIIc, the most junior class of the school, one of the senior students, Levi Fox, was showing great ability in the lofty heights of the Sixth Form. He went on to do brilliantly at Oxford and later became a senior administrator of the Stratford Shakespeare Memorial Theatre. And there was a class mate, Geoff Arthur (later Sir Geoffrey Arthur) who regularly obtained what the rest of us thought to be disgustingly high marks in all subjects, particularly Latin. He too went on to triumph at Oxford and finished up in the Diplomatic Service. I have often wondered how essential Latin was to such a position.

We had pleasant surroundings. Our main school building was an imposing one, mostly of stone, with a fine mullioned window that faced north and a small tower over the main entrance. But my early days were spent in a small timber building separate from the main school and referred to as the 'Reading Room'. This was probably because it had a number of glass-fronted cabinets containing a large selection of books. By no stretch of the imagination could it be called a library, but most of the books were well suited to our age group and I became a compulsive reader. The only time that we officially entered the main brick and stone building was for morning prayers in the hall and PT in the gymnasium.

There was one other part of the main building we frequented, but very, very unofficially; and that was the boiler room. Down the long flight of concrete steps we went as the invited guests of Dickie Leewood, who was to our minds undoubtedly the finest school caretaker there ever was. Handicapped by a malformed leg, he wore one boot with a very thick sole and walked with a pronounced limp. But that never seemed to slow him down as he almost trotted around on his duties. The school cat, attracted by the warmth, chose to have kittens perilously close to the coke-fired boiler. Dickie would invite us in to see them and dayboys like myself would bring scraps of food and even small bottles of milk to help the mother rear her brood. When our Mums were pressured into accepting one of the kittens, my home had its fair share.

Initially I was pretty successful academically, topping the class in my first year in IIIc. Competition increased in the subsequent classes, namely IIIa and 'Transition', but my undoing was being placed in a desk close to a wall radiator. The warmth made me drowsy (I earned the title 'dormouse') and I became inattentive. Of course my work suffered. In IVa and IVb, both arts and science subjects were studied, but in the next year's classes, strangely named 'Remove A' and 'Remove B', one studied either the Sciences or Latin and the Classics. My marks in Latin had been absolutely miserable, so from then on I was 'guided' to the science side of education and progressed through Remove B and the following year, Vb, to sit my matriculation examination in the summer of 1934.

In IIIc where it all began, my class master was 'Duggie' Goodwin, a small, kindly man who taught Scripture when not teaching IIIc almost everything else. 'Duggie' was in the choir of the local Parish Church as an alto, I think. He applied a lot of pressure to persuade me to join that choir. I resisted with all my strength, which included climbing into the thin topmost branches of a large ash tree on one choir practice evening and staying there despite the best efforts of some choirboy friends to get me to go along.

It was not all study at school, we had our sport and our sporting heroes. In particular there was an athlete named Bob Scott, whose running outshone all others. His best performance was at the middle distance events, 440 and 880 yards events. He competed at the prestigious Public Schools Sports Meeting at the White City Stadium in London and we fellow students were there to cheer him on. His greatest rival was a youth from Stowe Public School called Michael Bathurst. Both won their respective heats in both events and it was obvious that the final would decide the outcome between them. But they were destined not to meet in the finals. Bob scratched from the half mile to save himself for the quarter, Mike Bathurst did the reverse and both won their chosen events. Many years later I met Michael Bathurst in Tasmania. By this time he was a dentist and a colleague and he told me how much he regretted never having been able to beat Scott on the track. He also assured me that the vocal encouragement provided by the noisy Ashby students at White City had a great deal to do with Bob Scott's success. Due to Scott's outstanding performance at this Sports meeting, our Headmaster was able to persuade Harold Abrahams, an Olympic sprint champion of the 1920s, to visit the school to coach the more promising runners.

One of our fellow students was a rather simple lad who had learning difficulties. To our shame, we teased him unmercifully. Son of a farmer, he was certainly no dunce when it came to farm animals. At the age of fourteen his father entrusted him with the buying and selling at the Ashby cattle market and he never made a mistake. Another pupil, 'Puff' Leeds, was nicknamed for his explosive manner of speech. Puff showed remarkable aptitude for science and made it his career, but I will remember him for one invention in particular, the construction of the first television set I ever saw. I never quite understood the principle on which it worked, but I know that it involved a large rapidly rotating aluminium wheel with tiny holes precision drilled in its rim. It looked decidedly odd – but it did work. Puff took it to London and was able to receive one of the Baird TV transmissions, from the Crystal Palace if I remember correctly. He was once cast as Bottom in the school's production of A Midsummer Night's Dream and he was a triumph – virtually by being his natural self.

Most of our masters were devoted to the school and stayed with it throughout their working lives, as in Delderfield's novel To Serve Them All My Days. During my eight years there, only two masters moved on to other schools and with hindsight, most of us would have said that these two didn't fit in. Among the others, 'Lenny' Matthews, 'Scroggy' Scott, Jimmy Jones, 'Dosy' Woodward, 'Daddy' Marsh, 'Sam' Staples, 'Echo' Eckersley, 'Frankie' Addison and 'Gammy' Hill were the backbone of the establishment. Their teaching methods varied. Some cajoled, some threatened, all demanded high standards. Mr. Addison was a perfectionist in his demands of us in English literature. Mr Scott terrified us into achieving a pass at matriculation level maths. His temper was notorious. On one memorable occasion he tore my algebra exercise book in half and flung it over the open crossbeams of the ceiling. Two days later we had algebra again.

"Take out your exercise books," came the clipped northern accent.

My hand went up.

"What is it now, Bellamy?" His tone clearly showed early signs of exasperation.

"Please, Sir, I haven't got an algebra exercise book."

"Where is it? Lost it? Careless boy!"

"Er, no Sir. You tore it up last algebra lesson" – and of course I was in trouble again.

However, I can't remember ever being bored. The town of Ashby was lucky in having a benefactor, Sir Joseph Hood. Going on his accent he was probably locally born and brought up. His first major gift to the town was a much needed playing field area called, unimaginatively, Hood Park. The flat expanse of turf easily accommodated two soccer fields for our impromptu cricket and football games. It also made an ideal site for kite flying and for two or three summers in the thirties there was great competition in making and flying the best kites. We used good quality greaseproof paper and the lightest strongest twine (obtained from the local boot repairers). We checked the weather forecasts the night before, made an early start and arranged for a trusted friend to watch the string during meal breaks and calls of nature – very necessary as the flight endurance record was something like eight hours.

Sir Joseph's second gift was a swimming pool on the edge of the park. The pool was closed on alternate Mondays and emptied. After cleaning it was then slowly refilled from a gently flowing spring-fed pipe. Those in the know rarely went to the pool on Tuesday for it was invariably ice cold and not completely full, making diving hazardous. But one superbly sunny Tuesday I opted for the pool.

There was less water than I expected and only one other would-be swimmer was there – a girl of about fourteen – I was nearly fifteen at the time. Her name was Edna Banks, Eddie for short, and we talked and sunbathed and put our toes in, eventually having a wonderful afternoon running in the shallow water and splashing each other as if we were at the beach.

What a splendid summer that Jubilee Year of 1935 was! And what an auspicious Tuesday afternoon it turned out to be. Ten years and a world war later – this was the girl I married.

≈≈≈≈≈≈≈≈≈≈≈

Chapter 3

Interim

I have often silently thanked Mr. Eckersley's frequently light-hearted and innovative approach to History for my life long interest and enjoyment of the subject and perhaps I should blame – or bless – Jimmy Jones and his Geography lessons for making me an insatiable traveller. All in all, how fortunate we were with our masters and how lucky I was to be at that school – for I very nearly didn't go there.

It happened like this. My father was guardian for Peter Cox, a boarder at the school. Peter was the son of Walter Cox drowned in the tragic Lillooet accident when the wharf collapsed. The head master at that time had a reputation for being over harsh and severe and my father was considering removing Peter from the school, in which case I almost certainly would not have gone there.

However, about a couple of terms before I was due to change schools, a new head was appointed and this man, T.A.Woodcock, proved an outstanding headmaster. Firm, but scrupulously fair, he also had fine teaching abilities in the Classics, particularly Latin. Under his guidance the school achieved great things. Perhaps the most spectacular was the gaining of three Oxford Open Major Scholarships in one year (1936).

Our school had both dayboys and boarders. Boarders were accommodated in the large adjacent house that was also the headmaster's home. Day pupils came from the towns and villages that surrounded Ashby, as well of course from Ashby itself.

There was an internal system of 'houses' and we were assigned on the basis of where we lived. Ashby House (naturally the biggest and best), Coalville, Castle Donington, Donisthorpe and Woodville – all these houses competed keenly in sport and academic achievements. Some time after I left, the houses were changed and named after scholars who had made their mark in the world. From then on, students were randomly allotted to the new houses. It was a much fairer system, of course, but how sad it was to lose the passionate support for the house you belonged to by birth or residence.

For some of us, school holiday camps were a highlight and the Gower peninsula, a beautiful area on the South Wales coast near Swansea was a firm favourite. This was Jimmy Jones' home area and he was responsible for much of the organisation. But several other masters freely gave of their holiday time to come along and supervise forty or fifty boys and displayed a hitherto unexpected ability in camp cooking. Those masters who had seemed so fierce and heartless in class, proved to be great fun on these August fortnights under canvas.

Somewhat less popular were the Wednesday and Saturday afternoon cross-country runs. Our school week of Monday to Saturday had two official half-days – Wednesday and Saturday. In the Autumn and Winter terms these half-days were taken over by miserable cross-country runs which I loathed. Not least because I firmly believed it was breaking 'union rules' to have to attend a school activity on an alleged half-day. Also, I was a sprinter. Up to 220 yards I was fine, but no further. Another factor was that I would miss my midday meal and my mother was a very good cook. To have a heavy meal before a cross-country run was severely frowned on. Actually, I nearly always did have one and walked or trotted reluctantly – and slowly – well behind the others.

There was one such run that I remember painfully clearly. As I had complained of some back pain and my caring mother was convinced I had caught a chill, she insisted that precautions must be taken. These consisted of sewing a large square of 'thermogene' into the back of my running shirt. 'Thermogene' was medicated cotton wool, impregnated with cayenne pepper and other heat-producing agents. Standing in the chilly late autumn afternoon waiting for the run to start, the extra warmth under the cotton singlet was pleasant and I'm sure I shivered less than the other boys. But after about half a mile as I warmed up and began to perspire the effect was devastating. The perspiration must have leached out the medicaments and my back was suddenly on fire. I pulled the offending shirt up towards my head and only managed to extend the burning area up to my neck. How I finished I just don't remember, but when I got home and had a bath, my back was raw and red as the flames of hell.

By the summer of 1934 we were all swotting frantically for the great exam – the so-called 'matriculation'. Held in early July throughout Britain, the results virtually decided your ability to go on to University education or not. Much of my study was done in an improvised hammock I had erected under a large apple tree in my grandmother's garden. Not, I must admit, because it gave me peace and quiet for serious study, but because I could surreptitiously watch a very lovely schoolgirl, who regularly studied by an open window that overlooked the garden. Pat Johnson was a cousin of mine, but nonetheless delectable. What with that distraction and a hot summer that repeatedly drew me to the swimming pool, how I managed to pass those exams, I shall never know. It was a pleasant surprise that I did – even the headmaster said it was a surprise – but a gratifying one for both of us. My fifteenth birthday actually occurred during the examinations, but my age ensured that I have a further year at school – in the 'illustrious' sixth form. I think I gained greater satisfaction from having learned to dive during the examinations than of having passed the exams.

In the year that I spent in the sixth form I achieved very little. I failed to rise to the dizzy heights of being a school prefect or of winning the coveted school colours for playing in a First Eleven or Fifteen. The academic side was little better. Introduced to calculus in our mathematics course, I could never understand any of it – and still cannot! One year in the Sixth was more than enough for me. The headmaster said I should aim to study Law at Oxford, an idea that appalled me as I was an out and out Cambridge supporter. Anyhow, I was determined to leave as soon as I was sixteen and that date coincided with the end of the school year.

The last day of term came round and as usual I went home for lunch and sat in a daydream as I ate, possibly mooning over some girl. As a result I was late back for that last important afternoon. Living close to the school as I did, I can't remember ever having been late before, for not infrequently I was one of the first to get there each morning. When I eventually arrived, the whole school was in the Great Hall and the doors were closed. I could hear the joyous singing of our traditional end of term hymn:

Lord dismiss us with Thy blessing,

Thanks for mercies past received...

It was always sung well and with a great feeling of release from real or imagined tortures. But I heard it from outside the hall. I was not taking part. A pity. I would have loved to be joining in the singing of that tuneful hymn for the last time. I hung around outside until the short break-up ceremony was over and my fellow students came out. In the end of term excitement it was not surprising that no one had noticed my absence and yet in some strange way my regret was intensified by having missed the final 'Amen'. It was as though my school days had ended with a blurred smudge, rather than with a crisp, clean full stop.

The end of July 1935 was not a good time for school leavers. Britain was in the grip of the 1930's depression and jobs were very hard to come by, certainly so in my case, as nothing immediately presented itself. It was a period of great indecision; of applying for jobs in one line after another and not getting them. In one instance, at an interview for a position – any position – with Lewis's who had recently opened one of their big departmental stores in Leicester, I was really hopeful. Things had gone reasonably well at the interview and I was very surprised to be told that my success in the Matriculation examination had made me too highly qualified to be considered for the position of Sales Assistant! My close friend John MacNaughton left school at the same time and we were at a loose end together, taking many cycle rides and poring over the Situations Vacant in the local papers.

The months of late summer and autumn of 1935 were a strange twilight zone. We were neither one thing nor the other. We had left school but had not yet graduated to the workforce. And then my sister Monica, who had done a secretarial course at a Leicester College, suggested that I attend Louch's Commercial School, only a couple of doors up the street from home. It seemed a good idea and it also appealed to Mac and we were soon enrolled and involved in learning the mysteries of Pitman's shorthand and suffering the frustration of the early stages of touch typing.

It was a hole in the wall sort of school. A small, low-ceilinged room was tucked behind a front office that opened directly onto the street and also served as the local Employment Exchange. Almost bereft of natural light, a large single globe with a simple shade provided light over a big square table that Mac and I shared with two girls of about our age, Doris Harker and Pauline Swift. We all seemed to make reasonable progress and were soon taking shorthand 'speed tests' of twenty words a minute – which of course, can just about be achieved by ordinary long hand!

However, by the end of our second term there, we were up to 80 words per minute in shorthand and able to transcribe it with minimum faults. We were also alleged to be typing, error free, up to 30 words per minute. At least that's what our certificates stated.

This course probably provided me with one of the most useful skills that I could have acquired. My shorthand soon became rusty and almost forgotten, but the typing has been of inestimable value throughout my life. The fact that I had done a Commercial Course was instrumental in my obtaining a position as a very Junior Clerk in the Health Department of the Leicestershire County Council. And there I remained until call-up in June 1940.

But for a short spell before joining the LCC, I was taken on as an engineering apprentice at Austin's Motor Works. This was largely a result of my brother-in-law, Nick's influence. Audrey had married at eighteen. Nick was working in Birmingham at this time and knew many of the managers of Austins at Longbridge. No doubt it was an excellent opportunity and the work was fascinating. I had never done anything like it, nor even seen such work in progress. As apprentices, we were immediately set to work on milling machines. We worked in a team under the eye of an experienced foreman, producing specialised items required in motor assembly lines.

Not only were these foremen good at their job, they were also extremely talented in devising schemes to supplement their incomes and it was not only the foremen. Everyone (except the new apprentices) seemed to be involved in some undercover activity; a remarkable exhibition of the meaning of 'private enterprise'.

The leading hands happily combined responsibility for the output of their section, with a knack of making something extra on the side. Take Charlie, for example. He could never hang his coat in his locker for it was full of fitted shelves and these carried an

26

impressive array of Cadbury's products that he sold to all comers. I was one of his customers when I could afford it.

Another foreman, David, had a small bus, a fourteen seater, which he drove in from Smethwick every day with paying passengers who all worked at Austins. His bus was not only parked in the official car park, but it was also regularly and very thoroughly maintained in the Austin Service Department and I often wondered whether they filled it up with petrol for him as well.

Jim's sideline was less ambitious. He made and sold excellent wooden garden sheds. Sturdy and simple to erect, they were held together by 6-inch bolts. These bolts started life as lengths of Austin's brake rods. The trick was to cut a thread on them and complete them with a washer and nut. I made 20 or 30 for him one afternoon. But the man I had the greatest admiration for was the floor sweeper, Bill, who removed the swarf and metal filings from around our feet. He had the lowest paid job in the factory, with a wage packet that in 1936 would have been barely £4 per week and from that there would always be deductions for health and unemployment insurance stamps. But Bill always took home £5 hard cash week after week and his method was simplicity itself. He bought a good supply of cloak room ticket books, each of 100 tickets and every pay day afternoon he would raffle his unopened pay packet, still sealed in its envelope just as it had been handed to him. He sold a ticket for one shilling and made a point of never selling more than a hundred – except at Christmas, when his bonus was included in the unopened pay envelope and he then felt justified in asking for two shillings as well as selling a few more than usual. He never had a ticket left and probably could have managed to sell many more.

My greatest problem was also financial. As apprentices we earned only four shillings per week in the first year. We had to pay out more than that each week for the laundry of overalls that became heavily impregnated with oil and grease. The really crippling expense was living in lodgings. Mine were in a house at Bristol Road South, an immensely long road but not far from the main gate of the Austin's South factory. Our lodgings cost twenty-five shillings a week and it was desperately hard for my parents to find this money every week for the Ashby business was not thriving. I feel sure I could have done well at Austin's. Once through the first year, the pay improved and there were incentive payments for attending night school and obtaining good results. I could have stayed, but knowing the family's immediate difficulties I thought I ought to leave and did so. The deciding factor had been a cutting my mother sent me. It was an advertisement clipped from our local paper – a vacancy for a junior clerk in the Leicestershire Health Department. I immediately wrote an application, got an interview and landed the job.

I was there four years, working in a graceful Georgian building in Friar Lane, Leicester. Most of the staff consisted of friendly, easygoing people, but it was wise to mind one's Ps and Qs with the few who were not. There was an Assistant Sanitary Inspector, Fred Rodwell, who spent many very early mornings, winter and summer, collecting milk samples from farms in the remote corners of the county. It was Fred who persuaded me into becoming a 'real' cyclist, but more of that anon.

Workload varied at the Health Department. Usually it was reasonably placid, without great rush and hurry. We junior clerks took pride in the standard of the work we were involved in, particularly duplicating (there were no photocopiers in those days). The typist who had prepared the stencils would stand alongside us while we rolled off the first few copies to see that she had produced a good, clean, sharp, evenly cut stencil. In our turn, we watched the duplicators very closely, monitoring the ink flow to keep the finished product of clear uniform print density.

A lot of our work was production of minutes, proposals and reports for presentation to the meetings of the County Councillors and there was keen competition between the various departments involved to present the best work. We saw to it that the Health Department held its own against the Education, Roads and Bridges and Poor Law Departments.

On one occasion we had to undertake a mammoth task. There had been a new Government Act for the 'Control of Midwives' in Britain (I think it was 1936) and a copy of this act had to be sent to each doctor and midwife in the county. As copies of the Act had not been printed in bulk at government level, we had to reproduce and distribute them in duplicated typescript. It was a case of all hands on deck. All the typists in the sub-sections within the Health Department, such as School Medical, Tuberculosis, County Laboratory and Health Visitors cooperated. We were all pressed into service as proofreaders before the stencils were passed for processing. The other County Council departments allowed us to use their duplicators as well as our own as long as we did so in their own locations. This meant that Norman Freer and I were kept literally running between the various duplicator stations, checking ink-flow, feeding more paper, re-loading with fresh ink and collecting the completed sheets as they became available. Over five hundred copies of each sheet were required. This was more than a ream of paper, which of course meant re-loading the duplicators at least once for each stencil.

When all the sheets were completed, all the large tables in the general office were cleared and the neatly squared off piles of duplicated sheets carefully laid out on them in numerical order. Everyone who could be spared was then employed in walking in solemn procession, removing one sheet from each of the 60 odd piles and thus collating a full copy of this Parliamentary Act. It was a slow process and involved Freer and myself, as the most experienced collators, in some overtime. Of course the rule in local government service at the time was no extra pay for overtime. However, the Chief Clerk, Mr Burditt, did make a point of letting us get away early on quiet afternoons. Being a daily railway traveller himself, he was considerate enough to ask me what time my earlier train left. I told him quite truthfully, that it left at 4.20pm, which was over an hour before we normally finished. So he said I could leave just after 4pm, which gave me ample time to reach the station. Somehow I forgot to mention that I was now cycling into Leicester on fine days and as a result, I received a number of 'early starts' for my 17-mile ride home.

Our County Medical Officer was Dr. Fairer, an ex-naval officer from World War I and at this period of his career he had become friendly with the stage star Evelyn Laye. We often quietly joked, strictly among ourselves of course, that his wife had never been able to discover under what circumstances the two of them had met. The insinuations were, in all probability, totally untrue, but made a nice topic of conversation.

I was in the General Office one morning when there was a knock at the door and I was faced with a smartly dressed young man, with what I suspected was a lightly made-up face, who politely inquired, "Could Dr. Fairer spare the time to see Miss Laye, please?"

I asked him to wait while I phoned through to Dr. Fairer's office. "Could you spare the time to see Miss Laye, please sir?"

In his rather booming voice, Dr. Fairer said, "Who sonny?" (He called almost everyone who was younger or junior, 'sonny'). I repeated "Miss Laye," and the penny dropped.

"Oh, oh – show her up, sonny, show her up!"

There was a party of four or five including Miss Laye, very lovely of course, and wearing a short fur jacket. Dr. Fairer's office was up one flight of the graceful staircase and just a few yards along a passage. Not far at all, but when I arrived I was amazed to see that he had cleared his large mahogany desk, laid out glasses and two decanters and was standing there ready to welcome his guests all in the space of a minute or two.

The spring of 1939 brought the threat of war and our work changed to some extent. We were now involved in the planning of the Emergency Hospital Service that was intended to select and equip some of the large country houses to cope with the anticipated casualties from air raids. By mid summer of that year, we were already receiving and storing large amounts of equipment such as all-metal stretchers and bales of blankets. Storage was a great problem and all sorts of rooms in the complex of adjoining County Council buildings were pressed into service to hold them. This exercise provided its moments of humour. Norman Freer and I used an empty room on the ground floor of the Public Assistance Office for storing bales of blankets. These had been delivered to us in tightly compressed canvas-wrapped bales, each containing 50 blankets. They had 'Onkaparinga' stencilled on them – the first time I had encountered an Australian Aboriginal name.

Short of storage space, we had managed with great exertion to pile these bales four or five high, just fitting them in from floor and ceiling, so tightly in fact that we had to align the bales to lie between the exposed joists of the ceiling. We counted the bales, multiplied by fifty and this total agreed with the invoice. Weary but happy, we reported to Mr Baum, who was in charge of the Emergency Hospital scheme for the county.

"Have you checked the number of blankets?" he asked.

Yes, we had counted 40 bales and at 50 per bale we had received 2,000 which agreed with the invoice.

"Yes, but have you checked that there are fifty blankets in a bale?"

We had to admit that we had not.

"Let me have a look!" Off dashed Mr. Baum to inspect the bales himself. Before we could remind him how tightly they were compressed, he slit the canvas cover of one bale so that he could count the blankets it contained. Of course once released from their canvas prison, the blankets expanded upwards – with such force that they lifted the bales above them and also the floorboards of the room above.

And there was another storage fiasco. Norman and I were given the job of storing metal stretchers in an unused cellar under the Public Assistance office. They were brutes of things to handle in a confined space. All metal and non-collapsible, with a strong, unyielding metal mesh base, their design was intended to make decontamination simple should they come into contact with things like mustard gas. Their eight foot length made them difficult to get down the twisting steps to that cellar and we had to ease them, one at a time and turn them on their sides to get them round the corner. But we did it and some 200 of these green enamelled monsters were, eventually, neatly stacked in this musty old cellar.

The fun arose later in 1940, when local air raids called for the removal of the stretchers. No one could discover how we had got them down there – let alone get them out again. They eventually worked from the pavement at the front of the building, removing a grid and a small window that provided feeble daylight in there. They had to knock out some bricks before laboriously passing the stretchers through, one at a time, to be loaded on to a lorry.

I missed the fun because by then I was in the army, but when I paid my colleagues a visit on my first leave I was taken with great ceremony to see the new brickwork around that cellar window and hear about the trouble we had caused.

One of the things I enjoyed most about those Leicester days was riding my bike to work.

In retrospect I enjoyed my years at the Health Department, not only for the pleasant companionship but also for the awakening of a real interest in cycling.

Once I owned a lightweight racing machine, cycling became much more than a means of getting from place to place. It opened up a world of new companionship and of sporting competition and it became a passion that was to last for many years.

≈≈≈≈≈≈≈≈≈≈≈

Chapter 4

Wheels away

"A curly headed ten-year-old weaves a wobbly course down the gentle slope of the narrow, brick-paved path behind his Market Street home. His head and shoulders come just above the handlebars of the 'James' gent's roadster that is complete with roller lever brakes and a 3-coil spring saddle. His spine is strangely contorted to enable his right leg to pass beneath the cross bar and reach the right hand pedal, as he propels the bicycle somewhat perilously down the yard to South Street. Here, cautiously, he turns right. Earlier falls have taught him that right hand turns present more problems than left when riding in this manner. With growing confidence he rides down South Street and takes the left turn into Prior Park and here the contorting spine and legs work faster, propelling him briskly along the flat path to the railway line arch where a gate....."

So began my cycling days on my father's bicycle, soon to be exchanged for an old loop frame ladies' model found in the stables behind our house. There was an even older gent's model there that boasted a plunger brake that pressed a metal shoe down on to the tread of the front tyre as its only means of stopping.

Both my father's machine and the loop frame ladies' model were heavy. They had 28 inch wheels, heavy tyres and their sheer dead weight did not make for easy riding, but quite obviously I loved to ride either of them and there were many times when my father was infuriated to find his cycle missing when he urgently needed it. These two bikes saw me almost through my school days and were used to take me anywhere and everywhere around Ashby. Despite their somewhat battered appearance they were regularly cleaned with paraffin (kerosene), oiled and polished with loving care until, Great Day — as a reward for a school examination success, I was given a NEW bike — all my own! Expectations ran high and my eyes lit up on that July birthday morning at the sight of that black and chrome monster. Now I had a Royal Enfield, solidly built, shiny chrome handlebars, 28-inch wheels with Westwood rims, roller lever brakes, a Sturmey Archer 3-speed and just to add to the general tonnage, valanced steel mudguards. It weighed a ton but I was so proud of it. Quickly the range of my rides increased – Tamworth, Alrewas, Kings Mills, Market Bosworth and Nuneaton ceased to be just names on a map and became places, routes and roads full of interest and adventure.

Always I longed to see 'just over the next hill'. Father encouraged me in my wanderings, but my mother was fearful of accidents and her entreaty became a saying: "Look out for the other fool on the road!"

My father used to give me directions, a throwback to the years he had spent as a young man working for the Ind Coope Brewery in Burton-on-Trent. He would often give me advice that sounded like a road to certain ruin. "Take the road to Alrewas, keep on it until you get to the Dog and Partridge, turn right there and follow that road to the Bell Inn, then fork left and don't leave this road until you come to The Lamb." He certainly knew his pubs and the shortest routes between them. But then, so he should, for it had been his task to plan the deliveries of the casks and bottles in order to minimise the distance the carters had to carry the beer from the brewery.

It was not long before I explored Coventry with its cobbled streets and its lovely old Cathedral and a few weeks later we even rode on to the historic towns of Kenilworth and Warwick that lay a few miles beyond. The 'we' in this context sometimes means 'me and my bike' and at other times in company with my close friend John McNaughton.

At sixteen, school was left behind and despite strong pressure to go on to higher education, I chose Austin's Motor Works and then the Leicestershire County Council Health Department. Here I had my introduction to the world of 'real' cycling. This came about in rather a strange manner.

My salary at the Health Department for the first year, was the magnificent sum of £50 per annum! For good measure it was paid monthly in arrears. My daily train fare from Ashby to Leicester was 1/3d (one shilling and three pence) return and working a five and a half-day week, as I did, fares were a major slice out of my meagre budget. Anyway, I quickly got fed up with my frantic running to

34

catch (or miss) the 7.40am on six days of the week. The bus journey cost even more (2/4d), so not surprisingly, I opted for cycling the seventeen miles into Leicester, pedalling my Royal Enfield monster whenever I could. Up the steep Alton Hills, through the mining town of Coalville and then the joy of reaching the Field Head at Markfield and knowing that there was now a long downhill stretch when I could coast in the top gear of the Sturmey Archer 3-speed. If there was no stiff southeasterly head wind, I frequently found myself pedalling up Grey Friars and turning into the Health Department by 8.30am having left home a little before 7.30am. Senior colleagues in the office showed great interest and no little amusement in my exertions, although Fred Rodwell scathingly referred to 'your tank' as he called my Royal Enfield. But he was a real cyclist, riding a lightweight 'Sun Wasp' with a single speed fixed gear. Ernest Turner, a senior clerk, just did not believe that I could do the journey in one hour; so one morning, by prior arrangement, he phoned me at home at 7.30am and my father and I both spoke to him immediately before I set off for Leicester. Mr. Turner was in the Friar Lane office by 8.30am and could vouch for the fact that I was there already. Hot and sweaty certainly, but there within the hour. After this display of cycling prowess Fred really began to work on me. "Get a REAL bike!" And I began to examine the wonderful bikes displayed by 'Feakins and McIntosh' in their London Road cycle shop.

Catalogues were the next step. Hours were spent poring over the rival merits of 'Holdsworth', 'Raleigh', 'James', 'Sun' and of course the then Rolls Royce of the cycling world 'Claud Butler'. Slowly my mind was made up. It should be the 'Sun CTC' model, 21 inch frame of 531 tubing, Endrick rims, Sprite tyres and shallow drop Lauterwasser handlebars – all this with a wide ratio Sturmey Archer 3-speed! Knowledgeable cyclists looked askance at this last item, or laughed derisively. But we all have to learn and the miles slipped by so much more quickly and easily once my posterior anatomy adjusted to the narrow Brooks B15 saddle. It was a rather startling change after the coil spring 'hammock' fitted to my old Enfield. I bought this Sun CTC from an Ashby cycle dealer, Mr. Hemsley, and it was during these transactions that I first became aware of the Cheshire Cat smiling face of Eric Ellam, the shop mechanic. Later, when Eric had established his own cycle business, he was to become guide to cyclists of all types in the area and as a wheel builder he had few equals. He was a wonderful person to know, like countless other cyclists in that Midland area and I shall always be grateful for his friendship.

Shortly after having purchased my Sun CTC I happened to see an advertisement in the Burton Chronicle placed by the Stapenhill branch of the Cyclists Touring Club who were seeking new members. I wrote to the given address and one evening a few days later, a youth in the cyclists' uniform of corduroy shorts and white 'ice-cream' jacket, knocked on our door. It was Barry Williams, secretary of the Stapenhill CTC and he was my introduction to the joys – and problems – of club riding. The following Sunday, with bike extra well oiled and polished, I cycled off a little nervously to the rendezvous at 8.30am at the Stapenhill end of the bridge over the River Trent at Burton. There I met Barry and four others and promptly at 9am we set off in glorious sunshine for Rowtor Rocks. To be honest, I had never heard of the place. But it wouldn't have mattered if they had said we were going to Timbuctoo – I would still have gone along with them, for the whirr of the hard-pumped tyres, the occasional chatter of the changing Cyclo and Simplex gears and the sheer exhilaration had got to me. I was right in, up to my neck!

On that first run from Burton, our route took us through Tutbury and Sudbury towards Ashbourne, which we skirted by going through the park at Mapleton and climbing up to Thorpe to rejoin the main Ashbourne to Buxton road near Tissington. It was still a favourite route of mine fifty to sixty years later. We pressed on through Alsop-en-le-Dale, turning northeast for Youlgreave before swinging round for Birchover and finally, Rowtor Rocks. A little later, just for fun, we left the smooth surface of the Bakewell – Ashbourne road by way of a gate or stile and I had my first taste of off-road or 'rough-stuff' as we made our way along a grassy, stony track to Robin Hood's Stride. I can't remember where we had lunch or tea although it was most certainly one of the many CTC approved catering places. Perhaps I was too excited to remember anything as commonplace as eating and drinking, but I do recall that shortly after Robin Hood's Stride as we began our journey home it clouded over. A little later, inevitably, rain began to fall as we neared Ashbourne.

"Cape-up!" came the call.

I didn't yet possess a cape, only a very inadequate lightweight raincoat, far from waterproof. But by now, wet from head to foot, I was beyond caring and pedalled along delighted to find that I could hold my own with these experienced 'knights of the road'. Despite my odd appearance in a very unclubby waterproof, I was readily accepted as being one of them.

In an hour or so we were back in Burton saying cheerio to Barry and most of the other riders who lived in Stapenhill. But I had an additional nine miles to go to Ashby and I was glad of the company of a Swadlincote rider as far as the Bretby Arms. From Bretby, time stood still until I was wearily coasting down Burton Road hill into the Sunday evening emptiness of Ashby Market Street. A meal, a bath, then sleep – such luxurious sleep with wonderful hopes and dreams for the next Sunday run. It was curtailed all too soon and too suddenly by a raucous alarm clock that shrilled "Monday morning! Monday morning! To work! To work!"

Through the Stapenhill CTC I got to know members of the Burton Working Men's Cycling Club and rode with them all one winter. As most of their runs, even in winter, were of 70 to 80 miles and all of them seemed to be north from Burton, I probably achieved some remarkable mileage, as I was adding another 18 miles to their total with my extra journey from Ashby and back. Many times the battery of my cycle lamp would be on its last legs as I rode the final dark lonely miles home.

The dimming of cycle lamps reminds me of a rather funny episode that happened returning from Ashbourne with the Burton Working Men's Club one exceptionally cold and frosty January night. One of the riders had a carbide acetylene lamp that threw an excellent wide, white beam and despite their rather strange smell we were glad to have one or two with the large club. This night we were later than usual, it seemed extra dark and extra cold and his usually reliable lamp began to dim for no apparent reason. The trouble was eventually diagnosed as lack of water dripping on to the carbide to produce the gas, but our problem was just where to find water, on a dark night in the depths of the country, when every pond and puddle was frozen almost solid. Someone called a halt. The lamp was taken behind the nearby hedge and returned once more shining brightly and we thought it best not to enquire where the water had come from. It continued to work beautifully all the way home to Burton – although the usual smell changed to an even stranger one.

It must have been somewhere about this time that I encountered Sam Jarvis. I had seen him around, of course, for in a town the size of Ashby you virtually knew everybody. Sam's bike fascinated me. For a start it had a remarkably small frame that was all chrome plated. It also had abnormally straight forks. Sam always rode a high gear fixed cog, a mysterious contraption called an 'Os-gear'. It was through Sam that I met a wonderful local character, Frank Holden. Between the two of them, they persuaded me to give their cycling club, the Reynard Wheelers a try, rather than continue riding with the Burton club and as a result of that switch of allegiance, many outings were to follow with this club that was based on Coalville. In fact I didn't miss a Sunday ride with them for over eighteen months – which says a lot for my health and fitness but very little for my religious observance.

Botcheston was really only a hamlet, but we often finished up there when we were on a club run in that area because it had such a good tea-room. It was also the scene of my first race – the club Rough Stuff event, where one rode a hilly course, with a number of rough and unmade roads included together with a water splash which we were required to cross twice. Where the rough track passed through the stream, the water was invariably well stirred up by cattle. This meant you couldn't see the deep spots, nor any stones or boulders on the bed of the stream and yet it was considered very cowardly to slow down to any extent as you dashed through it. I managed to dash through, missed all the holes and stones, but my clean white shirt was anything but white when I got to the far side!

I did sufficiently well in that race to be encouraged to enter other races and from there it was only a short step to 'training runs' and '25s'. The '25s' were 25 mile time trials where you started at one or two minute intervals and rode alone and unpaced for 12 miles, turned around, calling out your number to the checker as you did so and pedalled back to your starting point. So, very soon, with my machine stripped down to the bare essentials, my legs reeking of 'Elliman's Athletic Rub' and clad, as the rules then required, in black tights and black alpaca jacket, I was being pushed off at some unearthly hour on a Sunday morning. The regular starting point for our time-trials was from beneath the clock on Alsopp's Garage on the Ashby to Tamworth road. I set off up the rise past Willesley Golf Course pedalling furiously. This turn of speed soon subsided to something more sustainable and I was on my way to that distant turn at Fenny Drayton. Then the return journey, past the bakery at Sibson, with its wonderful smells of hot bread and buns wafting across the road in the still morning air. Fork right at Twycross, through Snarestone, the lunge up the steep canal bridge (now alas, gone and the canal filled in) then the long uphill grind that sorted out the unfit, followed by that last half-mile sprinting descent to shout one's number to timekeeper Horace Cave just near Five-Lanes End. Oh those 'great days in the distance enchanted'!

By now I had sold my 'Sun CTC' model and purchased a Russell Woodward machine. These Russell Woodwards were really good bikes but they never became common, as Woodward lost his life in World War II. While I was waiting the arrival of this made-to-measure wonder machine, I had to make do with my second string, an old Raleigh Record Ace that had belonged to Dave Pearson, one of the Reynard Wheeler stalwarts. This bike had gained an unenviable reputation as being crash prone. It was true that the unfortunate Dave had come off it heavily on two occasions. Indeed my first contact with the bike had been to carry parts of it home from Marchington Cliff while Dave went off to hospital. However it always served me well, although for quite some time the club made me ride at the rear whenever I turned out on "The Killer" as it was affectionately known.

We entered a team for a Mass Start race that was to be held on the old Brooklands Motor Racing circuit. That day started pretty hilariously with a series of mishaps to a small car, Fred Candy's. It had a trailer attached containing our four precious racing bikes, spare wheels, tyres etc. We all presented promptly at 6am and the first delay was while Fred got sufficient petrol in his car to go and get the trailer that he was borrowing for the day. Eventually a half-full tin of petrol was produced and that was done. Then two of us climbed in the back, Fred settled into the driver's seat, with the fourth team member alongside him to act as navigator. The engine started and we were off for all of ten yards! An unpleasant grating sound occurred whenever we moved forward. Fred got out, walked around, looked under the car. He informed us that our combined weights were depressing the springs so much that the bottom of the tow bar barely cleared the ground and we could only advance in a series of jumps like a kangaroo. The prospect of our reaching Brooklands in time for the race began to fade. But ever resourceful, Fred phoned a friend and despite getting him out of bed on a Sunday morning, persuaded him by sheer force of personality to drive his car to Brooklands as well to lighten the load. Incidentally Brooklands in Surrey is not far from London and well over a hundred miles from our starting point. The friend said he would come and we set to work unloading the unusable trailer and reloading the bikes and gear on the two cars instead. Eventually, much much later than we had envisaged, we set off on our journey.

We didn't exactly fly along and we were hot and cramped as well as late by the time we drove through the competitors' entrance at Brooklands. Those of us who were racing hurriedly dressed in our black shiny shorts and the white shirts with their blue bands and running-fox insignia of the Reynard Wheelers on their fronts. Meanwhile the non-racing support team assembled our bikes as best they could. We had no time to check them and had to present them to the race officials immediately for their safety inspection, with no opportunity for a trial ride for personal adjustments. All too soon we were lined up and we were off.

Brooklands track was once a vast asphalt and concrete oval with steeply banked corners. Our race circuit took in only part of the full track, repeating laps of a course marked out by 40-gallon drums. Some of the turns around these flagged drums were sharp and would send us climbing up the steep banking, 80 feet wide in places, to yet another flagged drum near its top. The turn around this second drum would send us heading back in the direction from which we had just come. At one moment I was chasing hard behind the rear wheel of a rival, when his back tyre rolled off with a bang on one of the turns and he fell. Too close to stop, I rode over his back wheel and his leg and continued the race.

After 35 miles of the 75 mile event I was feeling far from fit. Two of my team mates had already dropped out and one of them, Fred Candy himself, had set up a primus stove right on the edge of the track and was cooking eggs and bacon in a very large frying pan. The effect on the riders was devastating. Their Bisto-kid noses twitched every time they pedalled past the pits and after resisting the temptation for two more laps, I became sharply aware that I had had nothing to eat since 5.30 that morning and it was now after 3.30pm. The fragrance was too tempting to resist and I was soon contentedly watching the remaining riders pedalling past, while I took large bites out of an egg and bacon sandwich.

Fred's aromatic cooking got a write-up in the Press on a par with the riders who finished in the first few, so that we believed, with some justification, that the Reynard Wheelers had made their presence felt – or should it be 'smelt'?

I vividly recalled the 1939 Annual Cyclists' War Memorial service at Meriden in the heart of England. Riders came from as far afield as Devon and Somerset and some had ridden through the night from the Scottish border. It was a superb May morning. The sun shone, there was little wind, the countryside looked as only England can in May and we made our cheery way south through Atherstone and the Bentley Woods where bluebells were still flowering.

Just short of Meriden we came upon some young lads pulled up by the side of the road, looking forlornly at one of their bikes. They were not club cyclists and they were not going to Meriden and most of the clubs riding by shouted some jocular remark and kept on riding. But not our Frank. "Hold on, Jack," he said to the leader and he opened his saddlebag that seemed to hold an unending supply of tools, bits of wire and spare nuts and bolts. In about twenty minutes the boys were riding again.

By now we were running late for the service, so we had to join the back of the 7,000 strong group of cyclists gathered around the stone memorial. Even as we hastily parked our bikes and joined those standing there, the choirs were processing to their positions for the service. That was to be the last Cyclists' Memorial Service for some years for it took place in May 1939 and 'the lights were going out all over Europe'. A fair number of club members out of the 6,000 there that day did not survive the war.

The weather remained delightful for much of that fateful summer. After the service we rode on the few miles into Kenilworth and sprawled on the grassy slopes around the ruins of the old Norman Castle. We talked and laughed as we waited our chance to get into one of the crowded tea rooms. We had a view over a flat low lying area of land with the odd pool of water and a meandering stream. There was once an ornamental lake on which Robert Dudley, Earl of Leicester, entertained Elizabeth I with a regatta offering stupendous meals in the adjacent castle. That was in the sixteenth century. Now in 1939, the occasional aircraft zoomed by from a nearby airfield. Spitfires? Hurricanes? This was the 'phoney war'. The real war was yet to come.

On our way home by a different route, we paused at Furnace End crossroads while one of our members called at a garage to have a faulty freewheel attended to. As we waited for him, an Austin 16, quite a big heavy car, approached the crossroads on the minor road and virtually halted to ensure that all was clear. Then, as it slowly started across, a motorcycle travelling very fast, flew down the hill and struck the rear of the car by its off-side wheel. The rider and his pillion passenger flew right over the top of the car!

The car was rolled by the impact and finished up on its roof – no seat belts of course. The elderly driver and his wife were just badly shaken, but their daughter cut her head on the glass roof light – and I have this image of a slight girl with white-blond hair and bright red blood trickling down from a wound on her scalp. Of course we assisted them and the two motorcyclists as best we could.

The driver of the motorcycle was wearing leathers and apart from two broken wrists and facial abrasions, he got away fairly lightly. But his pillion passenger was wearing only ordinary clothes and these had shredded away as he slid along the rough tarmac and he was in a poor way when the ambulance arrived.

And would you believe it, less than two miles further on, as we climbed steadily to Bentley Woods, a young heifer, driven frantic by the attentions of a persistent warble fly, suddenly dashed madly down the hill parallel with our road. She crossed two fields and leapt two hedges in real steeplechase style before crashing through a third and slowing to a halt almost half a mile away.

Although I fitted in happily enough, most of the Reynard Wheelers were manual workers; coal miners, pipe-clay workers or boot and shoe factory operatives and I must have been one of the very few clerical workers. I remember a man called Arthur Blaza, a giant of a man, with a badly misshapen left side of the head and neck, probably a congenital malformation. He had virtually no left ear, an undersized left half of the lower jaw and a shortening in the neck on that side, which made him tilt his head towards his left shoulder. He was well over six feet tall and his shock of black hair and dark complexion coupled with the misshapen face gave him an appearance of such ferocity that he could be intimidating on first acquaintance. His voice was little short of a bellow even in his quieter moments and he had no difficulty whatsoever in making himself heard when ordering a drink in a crowded pub. But his appearance completely belied his character, for he had a gentle nature despite his abnormal strength. Arthur lost his life in a mining accident, some say that he attempted to shore up a collapsing roof while other miners got out. Knowing the cheerful, unassuming man that Arthur was, I can well believe it.

One day, I was sitting next to him at a Botcheston tea stop on a Christmas Eve club run that I had joined direct from Leicester. Unknowingly I had a broken finger on my right hand after a spectacular spill in Leicester on a wet and slippery tramline. Although the finger was extremely painful, Arthur Blaza was such a riot of fun over that tea that I was barely aware of my injury.

Back at work after Christmas, I had one of the doctors on the staff take a look at the finger. "Severely bruised," was all he said.

But the swelling didn't subside, so about a week later I went to the Casualty section of the Leicester Royal Infirmary and a young medico in an unbuttoned white coat worn over a scruffy pullover and baggy flannels saw me. He immediately sent me for an X-ray of the offending finger. Half an hour later he had the X-ray results in his hands.

"An oblique fracture with partial healing." It was said with a good deal of satisfaction.

He asked me how and when it had happened. I told him I had had a spill eleven days ago and he looked at me sadly, "And you look almost intelligent!"

Knowing that my call-up was imminent, I took leave from work and made what I rather dramatically called 'my last cycle tour' of Somerset and North Devon. It was a totally wonderful experience. I remember a kindly lady at the bed and breakfast farm at Whittington near Bristol who apologised that at this time of the year she had no strawberries to accompany the clotted cream that their farm produced. She fished whole strawberries out of a jar of home made jam and presented them to me on a huge mound of cream. And I met a young farm worker in the Mendip Hills and asked him, "Am I going the right way for Blagden?"

"No, Zurr, you b'aint. I be going that way!" was the answer I received in the warm round tones of the Mendip Hills dialect.

At Lynton post office in North Devon, a letter from home was waiting for me. My call-up papers had arrived and as if to make my homeward journey more challenging and interesting, the local authorities, fearing invading Nazis, had suddenly taken down the town and village name signs and removed all the signposts.

≈≈≈≈≈≈≈≈≈≈

Chapter 5

Army days

From the moment Neville Chamberlain returned from his visit to Germany with his scrap of paper and the cry of 'Peace in our time', preparations for anything but peace went ahead quickly in Britain. Part of this process involved the registration, medical examination and categorisation of all young men prior to call-up for National Service. At the time of the medical, you could express an option for the arm of services you would prefer to belong to and to a limited extent your choice of corps. Of course the Army took a much larger number of men at that stage than did either the Navy or the Air Force. At my medical examination I expressed a marked preference for medical work, that is non-combatant duties. This choice was partly influenced by my involvement in health, but I had read a lot about the remarkable work done by the Friends Ambulance Unit in Finland and this greatly impressed me. Moreover, my friend and work-mate for the past four years, Norman Freer, had very strong beliefs regarding the morality of involvement in armed conflict and this must also have had an effect.

With my educational and employment background, my choice of the Medical Corps was readily accepted and approved. As I had anticipated, my medical category was A1, but I was intrigued and amused to find out many months later that they had entered 'Nil' under 'Any distinguishing scars, marks or features', apparently completely overlooking the large scar on my left hip. Some years later, the Germans were much more efficient for they noted it when I was examined after being taken prisoner.

Following the medicals, there ensued a highly unsettling period of waiting for call-up papers. Some received almost immediate call-up. For others it was so belated that it appeared to have been ignored altogether. In my own case nearly six months elapsed, so I had been able to take that short cycle tour in southwest England in late May of 1940. This was just before my 'papers' arrived in early June and so immediately after my return from this holiday, I was setting out early on the morning of 13th June, 1940, for a completely new lifestyle.

England was still reeling from the tragedy and the miracle of Dunkirk. Signs of worry about invasion were the complete absence of any indication of destination on the front of the bus. Armless signposts stood forlornly at cross roads and there were blank boards where nameplates of towns and villages had been until very recently. But I needed no signposts to know this land and as the bus climbed out of Ashby on its way to Leicester, I concentrated intently on every familiar detail. Once in the countryside, I looked fondly on every little hump-backed bridge, tree and landmark that I already knew so well.

But now, at twenty, fit and quite sun-tanned as a result of my recent solo cycle tour, I was off that morning to serve my country. It must be said that I went unwillingly. The uncertainty of the unknown life ahead didn't appeal to me in the least.

Entering Leicester, I left the bus at the old Roman remains known as Jewry Wall and my walk to the station took me through long familiar ways; Guildhall Lane, Grey Friars, the Market Place – now so very different with their sand-bagged doorways and their windows diamond crisscrossed with protective tape. Granby Street, the main shopping thoroughfare, was quiet and almost deserted save for one or two shopkeepers opening up at the start of another day. I walked down Granby Street towards London Road and the grimy gloomy Victorian-Gothic railway station.

A glance at the station clock confirmed that there was no desperate hurry and I dawdled, window shopping, peeping through the small apertures in the largely blacked out or boarded up windows, before joining the queue to have my rail warrant inspected.

"Platform 1," intoned the railwayman. So many times I had watched the long crowded London trains arrive and depart from this platform while waiting for my own small local train on Platform 4. Now, despite my love of travel and the evocative locomotive smell, I would have answered with a decisive "No!" to the question posed on nearby bill-boards, "Is your journey REALLY necessary?"

Occasional rapid snatches of familiar places flicked past the window. The smoky arched bridge near Market Harborough where we used to pause on the road and watch the main line monsters thunder by. A glimpse of Wickstead Park near Kettering, where I had spent hours and untold energy pedalling furiously around the cycle race track. Then came the June-warm countryside of the Southern Midlands, much less familiar to me. All too soon, the yellow brick fingers of the northern London octopus were reaching out on either side of the rail line, devouring more and more of the countryside..

London – St Pancras Station – one of many young men with a faintly lost sheep countenance, intrigued by the ease with which we were recognised by the red-capped Military Police and quickly, brusquely, directed to the appropriate Underground.

My Underground took me to Waterloo and here a crush of people, mostly male, stared up at the large direction boards in search of destinations, train times and departure platforms. Navy, Army and Air Force uniforms mingled with the 'civvies', many of us carrying, rather self-consciously, the mandatory brown paper and string. We had been instructed to bring this with us, its purpose being to wrap up our civilian clothes and shoes for return to our homes, once we had been inducted into the anonymity of army uniforms. We all carried one other item – a highly distinguishing feature. Our Budgie Boxes. This small cardboard box, roughly a six inch cube, was slung on a tape or string and was intended to be carried over the shoulder at all times. It contained a civilian gas mask, poor relation of the much more grandiose 'Respirator, Anti-gas, Services pattern Mark 2' we were shortly to be issued with.

We passed through Clapham Junction and Woking en route to my destination of Fleet in Hampshire. No name boards were displayed at the stations along the way and instead, raucous railway porters shouted out the name as the train pulled in. Some you could understand, while others depended on the interpretation of your fellow passengers for a translation.

On arrival at Fleet, the long platform of the simple little station became alive as large numbers of young men de-trained. Quickly, red-sashed sergeants packed us into waiting buses and we were whisked away to Crookham village and Boyce Barracks. In the bus came the first opportunity to look more closely at future companions. We did this surreptitiously, wondering whether we

47

would get on well with him or maybe with him, wondering, indeed about everything and everyone in this very new life that was just beginning.

There was no time to think of possible answers to the numerous unspoken questions. Loud voiced non-commissioned officers were urging us out of the buses.

"Line up here!"

"Stand up straight!"

"No talking in lines!"

It was quite obvious that once past the guardroom at the gate of Boyce Barracks, our civilian clothes and haircuts notwithstanding, we were in the army now.

Life in the barracks was, to start with, very much what I had feared and expected. Living conditions were clean but lacking in comfort. The beds were perhaps the most startling piece of equipment – it was said they dated from the Crimean War and I never doubted it. Solid iron, they had a number of iron straps running both the length of the bed and across its width. Quite rigid, they had absolutely no give in them at all and the three rectangular 'biscuits' stuffed hard with horsehair that inadequately substituted for a mattress were almost equally unforgiving and unrelenting. Three grey army blankets and a coarse pillow completed the bedding provided. The absence of sheets, a hopeless pillow, together with the hardness of bed-base and mattress, caused many of us some restless nights before fatigue and familiarisation brought us once more the blissful blessing of sleep.

C Company, comprising two hundred of us, occupied a network of huts that were called 'spiders'. This name arose from the fact that they consisted of eight individual huts connected together by covered pathways. Six of these huts were for accommodation, approximately twenty men in each, with a small separate internal room immediately inside the entrance porch for a corporal in charge of the Barrack room. The remaining two huts of the spider complex had washbasins and baths in one and toilets and urinals in the other.

A number of boy soldiers provided the buglers in the camp and at 6am every morning, they would sound the 'Rouse' or Reveille as it is more popularly known. It was decidedly unpopular, but some of these boy buglers were excellent and to hear the notes of their calls in the early morning from some distance away was delightful. But if they happened to be standing immediately beneath your window these same calls quickly lost their appeal. The rush to the ablutions area after Reveille was incredible – more than 120 men, all trying to wash and shave at something like 20 basins in the minimum possible time. It meant dashing back to our huts to get dressed and be ready to march up for breakfast at 6.30 sharp under the command of a corporal.

For many of us the wearing of unfamiliar army boots was an agonising experience. I had never previously worn boots, except perhaps the occasional football boot and the agony of the blisters produced was only equalled by the pain of our badly bruised ankles. Others of the Company had regularly worn boots in civilian life and quickly adapted to army issue. There were guaranteed 'cures' for the hard and unyielding footwear that were causing the rest of us so much pain.

One of these cures was to fill the boots with water and let that soften the firm but excellent leather. Others advocated donning the boots and standing in really hot water and there were other, more exotic, remedies that are perhaps best not described in detail. If caught by Company non-commissioned officers using either of the water softening treatments there was trouble and the threat of the direst consequences. In any case, we were spending long hours with black boot polish and toothbrush handles 'boning' the toes of our boots until they reflected like mirrors and the soaking in water treatment to soften them made it virtually impossible to get any shine on them at all. Gradually, sweat and constant brushing and polishing softened and moulded these boots to our feet. But we had hardly succeeded in getting a pair really comfortable when they were promptly recalled into store to have their soles reinforced with hobnails and we had to repeat the whole agonising procedure with a newly issued pair of the black monsters. Eventually I got on very well with my boots and discovered there was nothing quite like them for walking or marching. It was almost a tearful moment for me when the pair I had kept on demobilisation, finally fell to pieces, rotted by the acid peat bogs of the mountains of Skye.

A keen rivalry was fostered between the various huts and squads right from the beginning of our training, both on the square and in the perfection and orderliness of our barrack room. Our blankets had to be folded in such a way that no edge could be seen. Two blankets carefully and geometrically folded in this manner, had to be placed at the head of each bed and equally carefully surrounded by the third blanket – again folded so that no edges could be seen. Towels were hung over the foot rail of the iron bunk and kit and uniform not in use had to be hung or laid out in a perfectly symmetrical manner. Later in the course, when I was excused the morning parade due to sickness, I used to stay behind and expertly line up the lower edges of all the hanging towels to a uniform level. This manoeuvre was to result in our hut being declared the smartest for a considerable number of consecutive days. But I believed that the absolute end had been reached when we emptied the galvanised fire buckets that always stood just inside the door and polished the inside of these buckets to a brilliant finish with steel wool and brasso before replacing the water. One soldier always had a last minute duty before leaving the hut for the morning parade of removing the dust that settled on the spotless water in the spotless buckets. What it takes to win a war!

Much of our time in the first few weeks of training was spent in 'square bashing' and we learned very quickly that the parade ground square was a holy of holies. You never walked across it. Indeed, if you were on it officially, you never 'walked' but always marched, smartly at attention. In these weeks we also learned to stand properly at Attention, at Ease and Easy. We Advanced in Line and marched in Column of Route. We fell in on the Marker on the Right, we fell in with Tallest on the Right and Shortest on the Left. We Saluted to the Front and we Saluted to the Left and to the Right – but never to the Rear! We Halted. We About Turned. We Dressed by the Right. We Numbered. We learned the mysteries of the Blank File. But the greatest triumph of the British Army was to be ours when we finally mastered the intricate manoeuvre of: Forming forward into Line, at the Halt, on the Right, Form Squad!

Of much more immediate importance to us all was the fact that, at the end of June 1940, the Government in its wisdom, caused the Army Council to raise the basic pay of the private soldier from One Shilling a day to TWO shillings per day. We understood that this was the first rise in the basic rate since Waterloo, way back in 1815.

Great celebrations followed the day of the new pay rise. There was, however, no reason for similar celebration the night after Inoculations. The one referred to as TAB appeared to promote a very considerable reaction in just about everyone. Some fainted right away merely at the sight of the dreaded 'needle'. The injection itself didn't worry me, but the awful feeling of malaise that overtook me about four or five hours later, was one of the most depressing feelings that I can remember. Two days excused duty following TAB inoculations were well earned.

In addition to that holy of holies, the parade ground, much time was spent in the gymnasium under the none too gentle care of the Army Physical Training Instructors. Unlike some members of our Company, I had been taking regular exercise and indeed training (for cycle racing) right up until the day of my call up. As a result, once unused and unfamiliar muscles had stretched or strengthened a little, I was able to do the gym exercises with ease and thoroughly enjoyed them. The PT Instructors spotted this and I was soon out in front of the squad setting the time and pace of some of the various workouts they had us doing. Part of our duties in the face of the threatened invasion, was to leave camp in fatigue dress and dig anti-tank traps across the face of Surrey and Hampshire. This excursion into the countryside made army life much less irksome than I had expected.

But whether it was the dust and grime of digging, or the fact that we were sleeping in blankets of dubious cleanliness, without sheets or pyjamas, I don't know; but I was unfortunate enough to become infected with impetigo. Initially the sores were on my chin and lip and looked little more than nasty shaving sores. But the ointment I was given melted in the warm sun and spread the infection down my neck by day and up onto my cheeks when I lay down at night. I was excused shaving and in no time became a dreadful mess. The treatment alternated between starch poultices or Ung. ammon. dil, depending which medical officer happened to be on duty. Finally, one of them realised I was getting worse despite the M and B sulphanilamide tablets I was taking daily and I was dispatched to a hospital in Aldershot.

I do realise that there was a severe shortage of transport at this time, (shortly after Dunkirk), but I never have forgiven the army authorities for making me go to the Cambridge Military Hospital on public transport. My face looked terrible; a matted growth of 10 to 14 days' beard, caked with the crusting sores. I was given a bus warrant and a route that required three different buses to get there and I was nearer to desertion at that moment than at any subsequent time in my six years of army life.

At the Aldershot Military Hospital, a medical officer delved in the drawer of his desk and produced two razor blades (and razor blades were like gold at that particular time) and tossed them across the desk with: "Sorry! But go and get it off!"

Despite it being perhaps the most painful shave of my life, I was delighted to see it go and said so to the MO when I saw him the following morning. The first treatment prescribed was application of Calamine and Ictheol. It was pleasantly cooling and felt dry and clean in complete contrast to the feel of the oily oozy ointment previously used (that had done no good and absolutely nothing for my morale). Now, despite a ridiculously clown-like face of white or very pale pink, I felt healthier immediately and I feel sure my improved morale had quite a lot to do with the speed with which the bulk of the infection cleared up. The bulk of it, yes, but not the entirety. Two tiny stubborn spots of infection remained, one almost on my lip close to the angle of my mouth and the other on the lobe of an ear. These residual spots were treated by the skin specialist with everything under the sun, including silver nitrate solution which produced a fine black pigmentation but no healing. My treatment became prolonged and after six weeks, the skin specialist was sufficiently baffled to ask me what I thought was the best treatment. I told him nothing had helped me as much as the original Calamine and Ictheol and after some hesitation he agreed to give it another go. I was put back on that – and was discharged from hospital within the week, completely cured.

Life in that hospital for six long weeks could have been irksome, but for some delightful light relief. There was a nursing sister in charge of our ward during the day. Patti, an American girl, could be induced to sing for us when not too rushed. Her voice was good and she sang the popular songs of the day and we loved it and her. Another interesting aspect was the presence in the ward of some New Zealand troops. They had seen active service in North Africa and could be a real handful at times, but they welcomed me into their group because I knew how to play the card game 500. It was virtually unknown in England, but my parents had learned to play in Canada and I had picked it up from them. The New Zealanders taught me the song "Now is the Hour" and I was happily singing this well before it was popularised in England by Gracie Fields and Vera Lynn.

One of the New Zealanders, a short, stubby man named Banks, was immensely powerful in the arms and wrists and delighted in picking up the very heavy Windsor chairs in the ward with one chair in each hand holding them just by a front leg. One evening there had been some ragging with a great deal of disturbing of neatly made beds. Sapper Banks decided he was going to have a bath and carefully remade his bed before leaving the ward. Turning at the door, he warned everyone that if his bed was disabled while taking his bath, he would not bother to try and find out who was the culprit – EVERYBODY would be tossed out of bed! He had barely closed the door behind him when his best friend went across, pulled sheets and blankets apart and tossed pillows to one side. We awaited Sapper Banks' return with interest. When he opened the door the ward was completely silent. Sapper Banks strode down the centre aisle with beds on either side, grasping the corner of each mattress with one massive hand as he passed and flicking mattress, bedding and patient with contemptuous ease on to the floor. There was uproar of course and unwisely I jumped out of my bed to try and defend it. For my pains I was flung, mattress and all against the sharp metal edge of the adjacent bed – and I still have the scar down the front of my shin to show for it.

Of course the noise that erupted was deafening and brought down the wrath of the authorities. Next day our ward was emptied and we were all transferred to huts in the hospital grounds – a much less salubrious set-up than our cool, airy Ward 6. We also lost our singing Sister Patti and one of the ward perks – a daily issue of oranges and fresh milk. Or, to be exact, we should have lost it, but did not do so for almost three weeks because of a little opportunism on our part. While in Ward 6 we had been required to send two of our number daily, at 4pm precisely, to the kitchen, where they stated the number of occupants of Ward 6 for that day and collected the issue of oranges and pails of fresh milk accordingly. We calculated that the kitchen would probably not have been immediately informed of the closure of the ward and we duly turned up, right on time every afternoon, to collect our goodies. We were quite right, the kitchen staff were not informed of the demise of Ward 6 until the end of the month and we continued to enjoy the illicit privilege of these perks for over two weeks. There was hell to pay when it was discovered of course, but they couldn't recover the milk and the oranges!

When I returned to the Training Depot after my six weeks stay in hospital, I found my mates of C Company tanned and fit from their tank trap digging labours. They were also now considered fully trained and ready for posting to units in the near future. On the other hand, I was not considered ready. I had not received (or suffered) the requisite number of hours of square bashing, nor training in the basic duties of a Nursing Orderly Class III.

While my training companions departed to various Field Ambulances and hospitals, I was used by the C Company office initially as a Company Messenger and even got to use the heavy sit-up-and-beg bicycle, for transport around the large camp. My trouble was that I never really became adept at Cycling at Attention (as one was required to do when passing an officer). However one day a sergeant in the company office discovered I could type rather better than he could and from then on I was promptly employed on clerical duties in the office. Another large intake was about to arrive.

About this time, I happened to be playing table tennis in the NAAFI (the Navy, Army and Air Force Institute) when I noticed that one of the army physical training instructors was watching rather closely. The upshot was that he invited me down to the gymnasium where they had a match quality table and excellent lighting and I got a real game. I must have acquitted myself reasonably well despite lack of serious practice. With the help of the staff of C Company office, this instructor began to pull strings to keep me on permanently at the Depot, the idea being that I would work in the Company office and also be available to play in their table tennis team as well. But I already hated and rather despised the highly artificial life of the Depot with all its 'bull' and inflated disciplinary regime. So when I was asked how would I like to stay on at the Barracks, I made it very clear that there was nothing that I would like less.

Their response was masterly inactivity! Nothing was officially done about completing my training. Instead I was graded and mustered as a Clerk Class III and kept on in C Company office without anything official to say that I should be retained there. Admittedly, the office was very busy preparing for this next large intake and we were kept working overtime preparing for the arrival of the new recruits.

One Friday evening we had worked particularly late, returning after the tea meal and although nothing was said to me, it was clear that they were expecting to have to work on the Saturday afternoon. But I had already decided otherwise. Immediately after dinner on that Saturday, I cleaned up and as smartly as I could manage, took myself out of barracks for a pleasant afternoon at Farnham where I enjoyed myself immensely. No office opened on Sunday, so I was not required to work, but somebody must have been busy, for when I fronted up on the Monday morning it was to be told to go and get my kit packed. I had been posted to Haig Lines.

Haig Lines was an old and a rather dilapidated set of barrack huts, lacking many of the amenities of Boyce Barracks, but there was an air of informality about the place and its unsealed parade ground that I rather liked. There was a rumour about that parade ground that may well have been founded on fact. For years, it was alleged, soldiers had been employed collecting the larger stones that worked their way above the gravel surface and throwing them into the pinewoods that ringed the square. A new commanding officer to the camp decided that stones on the parade ground strengthened the ankles of the soldiers drilling there. As a result, soldiers now spent hours in the pinewoods throwing the stones back on to the parade ground.

The informality of the camp extended to the strange lack of system that existed for postings of the men. A young corporal from the office would make a physical tour of the barrack rooms when a request had been received for someone with a particular trade or skill. He would ask whoever happened to be in the barrack room at that time what army trade qualifications they possessed. One day, in my particular barrack room, he came in when only two men were there. One was a cook, the other a nursing orderly. The cook was told to pack his kit for overseas, the nursing orderly was not posted, because they wanted a cook and a clerk, not a nursing orderly. I was a clerk, but I missed this posting to the West Indies simply because I was washing my smalls in the ablutions block at that moment. On such curious chances hangs your fate in wartime.

A few days later, a short rather tubby man, S/Sgt Lattling arrived in the camp. He was an 'old soldier', with something like twenty years service in the Medical Corps behind him. One evening, in one of his less sober moments, he told some of us that we were to be posted with him to form up a new Field Ambulance. Sure enough, a few days later, kits packed, we were on Fleet Station catching the train for London. But it didn't get there.

This was just after the Battle of Britain and frequent bombing of railways was occurring. As a result of the line being blown out somewhere near Wimbledon, we were de-trained and bussed to Clapham Junction station to re-embark on another London bound train. Despite our early start, these delays made us more than hour late arriving at Kings Cross where we were to catch the Flying Scotsman to Edinburgh. The train was still at the platform long after its normal scheduled time of departure, but the ticket barrier was closed when we reached it. At S/Sgt Lattling's urging, we ran past the railway official and lurched, with all our kit, into the last coach, oblivious to its being already very much overcrowded. Although the train was already on the move, we expected to be able to pass along through the carriages to a less crowded part. However, we discovered that the last two coaches were not corridor connected to the rest of the train and were full of people who had been bombed out in London the previous night. Some had minor injuries that had not been properly dressed and as we were Medical Corps, albeit very raw recruits, we did what we could for them. At least it helped pass the time of that slow and tedious rail journey and those we helped were incredibly grateful.

We had breakfasted at 6am but there was no possibility of getting any food on the train. At stops along the route such as Peterborough and Grantham, there was a wild stampede for the refreshment buffets or the mobile tea bars on the station platforms. Either the crowds were too hectic, or we had not been in the services long enough to learn the not-so-gentle art of queue jumping, but we failed dismally and it was not until York and nearly 6pm, that we finally managed a cup of railway tea. The train was running very late with numerous tedious and unexplained delays. Its passenger load thinned out appreciably at Newcastle-upon-Tyne where many of the bombed out Londoners left the train and we slumped gratefully on to real seats from Newcastle through Berwick to Edinburgh – much better than standing in the corridor or squatting uncomfortably on your kit-bag.

It was nearly midnight when we finally reached Edinburgh and only the joker in our party asked if the canteen was open. We were told that the services' canteen should have closed almost two hours ago. 'Should have' were the important words. For when the Scottish lasses running this YMCA canteen heard that there were troops on this late train and that they had travelled all day without a meal, they volunteered to stay on and provide us with something. To be asked in that soft Edinburgh brogue, "Would egg and beans on toast be all raight?" when you had not eaten for almost 18 hours, was heavenly music indeed. The final touch was their complete refusal to accept payment, for, as they put it: "It's a wee bit after hours and we shouldna be sairving ye at all!"

Our destination was still some miles out of Edinburgh city and we climbed aboard an Army lorry for the remaining leg of our journey to Newbattle Abbey. Later on during the war, Newbattle was destined to become an ATS Training Centre where thousands of young women were trained in army ways, but there was certainly no sign of that future as we climbed out of the lorry at the Gatehouse to the Abbey.

It must have been around 2am when we arrived and rather than disturb other soldiers in their barrack rooms, the Guard commander had provided us with blankets and we were temporarily installed on the floor of the room immediately over the gatehouse guardroom. In the light of our hurricane lamp, we saw that three other soldiers were there already, but we were so weary by this time that we just spread our blankets on the floor and slept, barely exchanging more than a grunt with our room mates. In the morning, which came all too soon, we seized towels, soap, razor etc from our kit and set off to freshen up after the short, cramped night we had just spent. The resident troops stared at us with some surprise and hostility as we descended the narrow stone stairs from the small upper room, but when we went to step outside to make for the nearby ablutions, there was an infuriated bellow from the NCO in charge. "Where the bloody hell do you think you're going?"

We duly and sheepishly came back, but explanations were at hand. The guard commander who had bedded us down had just gone off duty and came back to explain to the loud-voiced one that we were newcomers to the Depot and had only arrived at 2 am that morning. Moreover, we were nothing at all to do with the other three inmates of our overnight room – who it turned out, were deserters, and were marched off to breakfast – in handcuffs!

After this, naturally enough, we were relieved to be out of the guardroom and delighted to be shown our own quarters. There was little or no preparation for our arrival and no beds available in the empty, bare barrack huts. Although S/Sgt Lattling had not had to share the floor of the guardroom with us, pressure on accommodation was initially so great that even senior NCOs had to share the same rooms as other ranks. Out of deference to their rank they were given the few available beds – the rest of us slept on mattresses or palliasses on the floor.

It was here that I had a strange stroke of good fortune. For a start we did not have S/Sgt Lattling in our room, but another senior NCO and while making up my bed one evening, I was quietly singing the song learnt from my Maori friends – "Now is the Hour". I didn't hear or notice that the Staff Sergeant sharing our room had come in (he often wore rubber soled boots and could move like a lynx) and I was startled when he abruptly demanded to know where I had learned the song. I told him and he asked a lot more. What had I done before the army? Where had I worked? What was my army trade? In return he told me that he had been a Sick Berth Attendant on P&O Liners in the Pacific and that was where he had frequently heard "Now is the Hour" or to be strictly accurate, the Maori version of it.

A few days later this man, S/Sgt Ellis, was promoted to Quartermaster Sergeant. The stores needed a clerk and he chose me (provisionally, for I had to be 'approved' by Lieutenant Quartermaster Alston). Lieutenant Alston was a sharp little man, with twenty odd years' service behind him; quick of mind, tongue and movement and I seemed to get on with him well enough. In fact I developed a tremendous respect for him over the two-year period I was to spend with this Field Ambulance. Soon the purpose of our posting to Newbattle Abbey was revealed – we were to form a new Field Ambulance – the 10th Light Field Ambulance – intended, eventually, to be part of an armoured (tank) brigade.

≈≈≈≈≈≈≈≈≈≈≈≈

Chapter 6
10th Light Field Ambulance

The time drew near for us to leave Newbattle Abbey. We gathered the 120 men needed to make up our Unit strength in medical corps personnel quite quickly and our Royal Army Service Corps section would soon be ready to join us with their vehicles. The winter months were cold and cheerless in eastern Scotland, for it was the start of the particularly hard winter of 1941 and I remember a bitterly cold commanding officer's parade held one Saturday morning. We formed up, standing in about two inches of fresh dry snow and a keen wind blew flurries of powdered snow along our ranks. We waited and waited and waited. One young soldier succumbed to the cold and we envied the men who carried him off to shelter. At last our colonel arrived and carried out his inspection – no doubt free of the ills that plagued us such as numb feet and chilblains on the fingers.

But if the weather was unkind, the good people of Edinburgh were the complete opposite. It was not at all unusual to be tapped on the shoulder by a total stranger after leaving a concert or the cinema and asked "Would ye like to come awa' haim for a wee bite of supper?"

We often cursed the rattly old tram back to Dalkeith and the rules that prevented our accepting these kindly offers. The ladies of the YMCA Canteen in the grounds of the Abbey were another ongoing source of joy. For a start their canteen offered food of a tremendously high standard. They were continually trying to help us by darning socks and making 'phone calls home and they always had trouble with the arithmetic of our bills, with the errors always in our favour. It was quite sad to leave, but many of us wished we could have departed before the debacle of our tragic Church Parade.

Newbattle Abbey was the Scottish and Northern training depot for the RAMC and there were usually two or three companies of raw recruits under instruction there. One Sunday, S/Sgt Lattling, (who in view of his long service had been promoted to Acting Sergeant Major) was in charge of our unit for an important Church

Parade. We had been warned that we were expected to turn out particularly smartly, as we had all had at least three or four months training, while the recruit companies also parading, had only three or four weeks. We formed up in the long driveway some little distance from the parade ground proper and briskly marched on to the square. Sgt Major Lattling shouted an order: "Right Wheel!"

The front of the column did so smartly enough, but our very long column had reached the far edge of the parade ground before the rear files had completed their wheel and reached the tarmac. 'Mark Time in front! Rear threes cover!' would have been the appropriate command to let the rear files complete their wheel and get into line. But acting Sgt Major Lattling lost his nerve and to our total embarrassment in front of all those raw recruits already drawn up in the square, he shouted out in his rich West country accent: "Field Ambulance! Field Ambulance – WHOA!"

We shuddered to a halt. And that inglorious moment was never lived down until we marched out of Newbattle to join a train at Dalkeith that was to take us to Nottingham. Tongues click-clicked and "Gee-up, Neddy!" calls added to the fun of our 'whoa-ful' departure as the trainee companies saw us off.

We arrived at Nottingham station on a cold foggy evening and marched out to Colwick Park Racecourse to spend our first night under the grandstands there. It wasn't as bad as it sounds, but it was far better when we were billeted on local people in the neighbourhood. I was placed with a Mrs Skellington, whose pride and joy was a large parrot (there was no Mr Skellington) kept in a cage on a table by the front window of the house. She had been warned of the injurious effects of blast, if bombs should land nearby and her air raid precautions for Cocky consisted of tying the cage to two hooks on either side of the window. She had used only thread for this purpose.

Cocky's imitation of the local coal vendor was first class. He would give just two cries of "Co-al? Co-al?" his voice rising on the second syllable. In that cold winter when fuel of all sorts was in terribly short supply, his mimicry was good enough to have nearby housewives out on their front doorsteps, purses in hand, looking hopefully for that elusive coalman. The parrot's second party piece was imitating the sounds of milk bottles clinking together and when he did this in front of his opened window in the early morning, he usually managed to fool a few into hurriedly putting out their milk bottles and change for an invisible milk man. After the sharp air raid that Nottingham experienced a few weeks later I went to check up that Mrs Skellington and her parrot were all right. They were, but Cocky had some explaining to do. Directly after the raid 'he' laid an egg!

Nottingham was just 22 miles from my home town and it was nearly Christmas and I had had no leave since joining up. It was overdue, so naturally I was elated. Besides, there were other possibilities. Eddie, my girl friend of school days was working there. In the few weeks that we were actually stationed in Nottingham, I managed to go out with her only once and that was to the cinema. After the show we walked back to the large house on St. Anne's Hill where she was living. I thoroughly enjoyed the outing and I hoped she did too, for as was to be expected, ten days later our Unit moved 35 miles away.

Much as I enjoyed being in Nottingham, I must admit it was very unsatisfactory for us as a Unit. We were scattered, our training areas and facilities were almost non-existent and it was no surprise when we moved to Market Warsop, a mining village some 25 or 30 miles north. Lying between Mansfield and the lovely country of the Dukeries, with the tank brigade that we were intended to serve dispersed around the town, it seemed ideal in all respects. When the locals of Market Warsop had recovered from losing the previous unit stationed there, (the 151st Field Ambulance), they took us into their hearts and we had a wonderful time.

We had been in Warsop only a few days when quite a heavy air raid hit Nottingham and the Colwick area suffered more damage than most. Although we were some 23 miles away, we could hear the bombs and see the glow of fires in the sky and the sky-probing pencils of the searchlights. Our Unit had put a consignment of boots in for repair in Colwick and as I now carried two stripes as a sign of my responsibilities in the Quartermaster's stores, I was detailed to take a driver and a lorry from Warsop to collect the finished repairs. We made good time down the Mansfield road, but as we entered the city area we saw the occasional shattered building and the wet charred woodwork where tiny wisps of smoke still curled into the crisp morning air where fires had been recently extinguished. There was more damage apparent as we neared our destination, but we continued on and swung off the main road into the side street leading to the boot repairers. Here there was a wooden barrier across the road, a single pole supported at either end, with steel helmeted police and Civil Defence workers standing by. Recognising our Army lorry, they lifted the pole to let us through. As my driver, Ronnie Gentle, drove slowly through the gap, someone called out "You are the Bomb Disposal aren't you?"

Until that time I had no idea how quickly Driver Gentle could reverse and turn round in an emergency! We made another journey to recover the boots three days later. I made an on the spot decision that they weren't needed all that urgently.

In Warsop, many of our lads were billeted in a large wooden building that rejoiced in the title of the "Empress Ballroom". Behind the stage were a couple of smallish rooms and these were taken into use as storerooms. Justifying it on the grounds of the need for security of the stores we had there, three of us were given permission to sleep in them. This had a number of advantages. We were separated from the large number of men sleeping on the floor of the ballroom area and that ballroom got very stuffy in the early evenings when all the blackouts were in position. Also, we had our own private back entrance and could come and go when we wished – as long as we were not caught doing so. We were able to establish some minor creature comforts, such as the makings for early morning tea. My particular luxury was an airbed that I was able to secrete, still inflated, amongst the stores by day and sleep on by night. Life was getting better all the time.

There was a church hall nearby that we irreverently called the "Silver Slipper Bar". No liquor was permitted there, just soft drinks and light refreshments kindly provided by local ladies, but we regularly used the hall for table tennis and dances two nights a week. I had never learned to dance, but with nothing else to do on those long evenings, I went along and that was where I met Lily Crookes. An amazing girl, she suffered patiently while I trod on her toes and tripped over her feet, but she managed to teach me to get around the floor without making a complete fool of myself. She was pretty too, a very good dancer and why she should have devoted so much time to teaching me, I just don't know. But thanks to Lily, I began to really enjoy dancing.

Market Warsop was about 40 miles from home. I could get there via Nottingham by bus, but had to make three changes to do so, all very time consuming. So one weekend I made the return journey on my bike and having my 'wheels' gave me mobility and independence in the district.

That graceful stretch of country was known as the Dukeries because of its stately homes. Our field exercises were carried out in the countryside and on one scheme we were sent out to establish a Dressing Station. After a due interval, a messenger arrived with a map reference telling us where we were could locate and collect a 'casualty'. The A section officer, Captain Ballantyne, a man I admired, gave me the map and the reference coordinates and told me to find the spot. On the figures given, I said that the casualty was about 50 miles east of us – in the North Sea. So we sent a return message to HQ: "Please confirm map reference."

A very curt reply from Captain Harrisson who had set the exercise and the map coordinates came back: "Map ref. confirmed. Get on with it! Patient dying!"

I still reckoned the casualty would have to be in the sea. So we returned to base without having found our wounded man. An inquiry was held into our failure to locate the poor patient. By the map coordinates given us, the casualty WAS in the North Sea! But Captain Harrisson, who had inadvertently put him there, never got on well with me from that day forward. The patient was actually among the trees of the Dukeries, quite close by.

It became clear that we were likely to move from Warsop before the summer was out, as some of our Tank battalions had already left, but before we did so I was able to have one wonderful weekend back home. I was given a weekend pass and took the bus to Nottingham and from there, travelled on the old familiar Midland Red X99 to Ashby. Once home, I wasted no time in getting out of uniform into slacks and my favourite old sports coat.

And after lunch I hurried off to see Eddie in her home in Prior Park Road. We spent much of a glorious sunny afternoon together and this was to be the last time I would see her until December 1943, but I didn't know that then. That weekend of the early summer was to stand out above all others.

Prior Park had happy associations for us for it was there, five years earlier that we had shared our first kiss. We must have been about fifteen at the time. It may have been a clumsy effort, but for each of us it was the very first romantic kiss and of course we knew the exact spot where it happened, in the shadow of a hedge by the railway embankment.

Our move became more imminent and Lt. Qm. Alston was detailed to take an advance party to prepare the new location for the arrival of the Unit. One of the problems in our field ambulance unit was the strange mixture of Regular, Territorial and National Service men in it. Some Regulars, such as QMS Ellis, were good at their job, but some of the Territorials had received promotion purely on length of service and they were far from competent. Others, both Territorials and National Service, had excellent educational backgrounds and considerable ability, but because of lack of length of service were of no higher rank than corporal. Lt. Qm. Alston, who didn't suffer incompetence quietly, refused to take

the Staff Sergeant and another sergeant proposed for the advance party. When told he couldn't have any of the other senior NCOs, he said that he would rather take two corporals – and that was really the first time that Corporal Howard Jones and I were closely associated. We were to become very good friends over the next few years.

When the advance party had been selected and agreed on, there was a last minute change of plan. It was decided that Lt. Qm. Alston would be needed for the marching out procedures at Warsop and that Captain Harrisson would be in charge of the advance party at Westmeston Manor near Ditchling in Sussex. It was a pleasant enough site in the warmth of the late summer months, about a mile from the village of Ditchling, alleged to have the highest proportion of millionaires per head of population of anywhere in England. Certainly some of the properties were very beautiful, but we missed the openhearted friendliness of the Warsop mining community.

Due to the fact that Captain Harrisson seemed to pay rather more attention to the establishment of an officers' mess than to our primary purpose as an advance party, we achieved little by way of preparation for the main body of men who were due shortly. Fortunately, I answered the phone one day when Capt. Harrisson was out and Lt. Alston asked what progress we had made and was horrified to hear how little had been achieved. He arrived in Sussex about two days later and things really began to hum.

And there was another frustration. Eddie was stationed in Lincolnshire, but I heard, to my dismay, that she had just got engaged to a RAF ground staff. The fact that I was far away in Sussex didn't help at all. There was nothing I could do, so I vowed to drown my sorrows in Ditchling, but it was a mortal blow.

In the meantime, friend Howard Jones and I had watched people in the fields immediately adjacent to Westmeston Manor where the harvest was being stooked and collected. It was hard work and they were grossly understaffed. So each afternoon as soon as we were off duty, a few of us joined the harvesters and coming to it fresh, we made a big impression. Part of the attraction of course, was that there were often two or three Land Girls working there too (Eddie was a Land Girl and this activity was a painful reminder of what I had lost). But the workers were friendly and grateful and by way of showing their appreciation asked us to join them in their 'local' in Plumpton Green. This village lay in the opposite direction to Ditchling. Introduced by the local farm workers, we were happily accepted and were soon supping Sussex cider with the best of them.

That Sussex cider was to cause a few headaches, both literally and figuratively, when the rest of the unit arrived. The majority of them were either Scottish or North Country lads weaned on whisky. When they discovered they could no longer get Scotch or McEwan's Beer – nor for that matter, any beer at all – they were absolutely disgusted. They openly regarded the local Sussex cider as "kid stuff" or "gnats' piss" and downed it in large quantities and in its turn, it downed the drinkers in equally large proportion.

For the first few nights after their arrival our guardroom, set up in the lodge at the gates to the Manor, saw some amazing sights. As the lads rolled and staggered back just before midnight, many of them had to be propped up to report in to the guard commander. By this time QMS Ellis had been promoted to Acting RSM. Lattling had left (mourned by nobody). However Ellis earned himself no popularity within the unit by making it his business to be down at the guardroom as the revellers returned. He insisted that the young guard commander put on charge all those returning who were improperly dressed or could not stand to attention and quote their name and regimental number when checking in.

The commanding officer's orderly room the following morning was huge and had to be deferred because of a further delayed effect of the cider. Many of those who had celebrated particularly heavily the night before, were again adversely affected as soon as they had anything to drink in the morning. These hardened Scots drinkers just could not believe that cider would do this to them!

We had moved into an area that was commanded overall by General Montgomery and he was a fitness fanatic. Very soon everyone in the unit, without exception, was engaged in early morning PT or runs. One morning when I was in charge of a party, we made a determined attempt to run to the top of the Downs immediately above us. I had quite underestimated how far the summit, Ditchling Beacon, was from the camp and we were very late back for breakfast – and most unpopular with all concerned. But those Downs did provide us with our first taste of real duty, as opposed to make-believe.

Some tanks, Matildas if I remember rightly, were exercising on the Downs one morning and on a particularly steep stretch, the tracks of the tank gripped the turf quite adequately, but the turf itself stripped away from the chalk lying just three or four inches below the surface. The tank sledged down the hillside, to drop about twenty feet almost vertically into a chalk pit that had been dug there goodness knows when. The driver and others in the tank were severely injured and members of our Field Ambulance were rushed to their assistance. It was fascinating to see who knew what they were doing and who didn't. Our second in command, Major Graham, a police surgeon from somewhere in Yorkshire, had obviously seen casualties before and gently pushed the flapping section commander medical officers to one side and got to work. Corporal Harrison showed his mettle and ingenuity in extracting the injured men from within the tank and his previous experience as a first aid worker in the mines enabled him to instruct others, senior in rank to him, in the best way to go about it. The Service Corps, determined not to be left out of the action, turned out three motor cycles and escorted their ambulances at high speed to the General Hospital in Brighton. In fact they made a real meal of it but overall this accident did much to make us feel a unified unit, rather than a bunch of medics and a separate bunch of drivers.

Our training continued, without the involvement of the tank battalions we were supposed to serve. In fact we had less association with them than we had when we were in the Warsop area, for there we had at least competed with them in rugby and soccer. It was rumoured that only one of the tank battalions making up our armoured formation was anything like fully trained and these trained battalions seemed to be continually posted away to make good the wastage in the North African campaign. As a result, the formation as a whole never reached a fully trained state and we, the Field Ambulance, continued to lead a boring repetitive existence of seemingly endless training.

We were involved in one huge exercise that appeared to mobilise everything in southern England. We drove miles and miles, a lot of this driving done in darkness with the absolute minimum of lights. There were accidents and casualties on the four days of this exercise. Our dispatch riders were exceedingly vulnerable on their motor cycles to sudden sideways lurches made by some of the tracked vehicles, particularly the Churchill tank. In its early days, this tank had a poor reputation for control and manoeuvrability. We would happily travel in convoy with a Matilda tank on our tail but would always keep a very respectable distance from any of the Churchillian variety.

There was one emergency that arose during Exercise Bumper that could have had tragic consequences. It taught us a never to be forgotten lesson. The weather was wet and we were sleeping rough – no tents, just a cab of a vehicle if you were lucky, or in the lee of a truck or tank if less fortunate. Some of our boys had spread their ground sheet and blanket beneath a stationary tank whose great width offered them good protection. About 3 am a startled shout from one of them roused us. He had tried to turn over in his blanket and found he couldn't do so because the base of the tank was pressing down on him. What was happening of course, was that the tank was gradually settling and sinking into the rain-softened earth. Two of the men were stuck and we dug them out rather frantically with entrenching tools and shovels and dragged them clear of the steel monster before it sank further and crushed them completely. Nothing would induce anyone to sleep under a tank after that close shave.

Local entertainment could be summed up as weekly dances at Plumpton and vigorous table tennis matches played with the Hassocks team. We also played cricket against local teams, made up of veteran cricketers and half a team of boys. All their regular, younger, players were, like us, in the Forces. We made occasional trips into Brighton, a pleasant enough place in normal times, but now with its beaches mined and wired off from public access, it offered little other than some extra good canteens. Mostly we had to content ourselves with walks on the Downs and visits to the little town of Lewes, rather than seeking our pleasures in the fleshpots of Brighton.

Unlike our move from Warsop, there were few regrets when we came to leave Westmeston Manor and so it was with great interest and high hopes that we arrived at our new location that rejoiced in the name of St. Nicholas-at-Wade, near Birchington in East Kent. We occupied two large houses that had once housed either handicapped or orphaned children and we used the village square in front of one of them (and the local public house) as our parade ground. In winter St. Nicholas was a chilly place. We swept a covering of snow off our 'parade ground', pushing it up against the wall of the pub, expecting it to melt and run away down the nearby drains. It didn't. For six wintry weeks that dirty off-white bank of snow stared back at us as we formed up for morning parades.

We had moved into Southeastern Command and this was now very much General Montgomery's own show. Physical fitness for all ranks became an absolute priority. Despite an icy winter, sports were encouraged and several of us marvelled at the ice that formed on the hairy stockings we were wearing while playing soccer on a pitch of long grass on the edge of the English Channel one Saturday afternoon. Monty's pièce de resistance was the introduction of cross country runs in which everyone from Brigadier downwards was compelled to take part and moreover, to finish the course within a time that was set according to age group. One of these runs took place in the country just inland of Dover. Over five hundred of us started, all in a huge bunch and we ran our five mile course over hills and valleys, to the finish, where we were steered into different pens, constructed of hurdles, according to the time of our finish. Our names, numbers and units were then noted before we were 'released' to clean up and dress in uniform once more. If you had satisfactorily completed the course within the time allotted for your age group, you were not required to run again for 3 months. If you had failed and taken longer than you should have, then you ran the following week and the week after that, until you achieved the standard set, or finished up seeing the medical officer and getting invalided out of the division. This did happen to a few, but to only one of our unit - a very pleasant hospital orderly who not only carried surplus weight, but as it turned out, had a heart condition as well. Just one of the cases strangely missed at the National Service Medical examinations, for he was officially in category A1.

For some of us, St Nicholas-at-Wade was a happy place. Our Unit had a Sergeant Wally Pitcher, a remarkable organiser of dances in our local village hall and he put on memorable impromptu meals with Land Army friends who lived nearby in Christina Cottage. These girls worked very hard indeed. The threshing they did was a filthy job and they would leave Christina Cottage before it was light in the morning and of course in winter it was dark well before their return. Wally organised a few of us to assist them. We had a key to their cottage and as soon as we finished duty, would pop along there, get a fire going, organise some hot water for them and not infrequently cook a meal too. We had a fine confederate in this, a private in the unit, who I'm sure must have been a poacher in civilian life, for he produced hares and ducks or geese that he trapped in the nearby marshes. It was a period of pleasant, simple companionship, epitomised by the long winter evenings we spent just talking in the tiny parlour of that cheerful little cottage.

At Christmas 1941, we were still at St Nicholas. I remember an early communion on Christmas morning. The ban on the showing of lights and the impossibility of blacking-out the large windows of the church, meant that the only illumination was little night-lights, sitting in saucers, at the end of every other pew. Later that day, as is traditional in the Army, the officers served a really good Christmas dinner to the other ranks. It may have been the excellent food or the drink that went with it, but something drove a group of us to propose a mad swim in the Channel. The air temperature must have been close to freezing and the easterly wind and dull grey sky were off-putting to say the least. But we took the plunge and were amazingly quick at getting out again. Strangely, no one seemed to be any the worse for this absolutely crazy swim.

New Years Eve was the officers' turn to celebrate and I happened to be the duty NCO in the office that night. Twice during their celebrations, individual officers came up to the office

71

'to see if I was alright' and to bring me a much-appreciated sample of their celebrations. Many of them were in a delightfully happy state, but the highlight occurred about 2am. Hearing a slight sound in the corridor outside the office, I opened the door to see our CO walking down the passage towards the toilet adjacent to the office door. He was very correctly wearing his hat and his swagger cane was tucked smartly under his arm, but the overall effect was sadly marred by the fact that he was not wearing another stitch of clothing.

Apart from the light relief of Christmas and New Year and the excitement of seeing the Scharnhorst, Gneisenau and Prinz Eugen sailing up the Channel to German ports, army life was pretty routine and rather undemanding. Several of us were feeling the need for more active involvement or more worthwhile work to do. Some had sought transfers to other units, but as we were part of an Armoured Corps formation and it was an army priority to maintain and strengthen such formations, no one was permitted to actually transfer out of them. We could have volunteered for duties as Tank Commanders and Howard Jones and I seriously thought about doing so. But it was at this time that Lt. Qm. Alston in his wisdom talked to us like an uncle. He told us that he believed that if we stayed with the Medical Corps and one day saw action with it, we would be proud of the Corps and of being part of it. We listened. He talked sense and 12 months later, when the North African campaign was behind us, as far as I was concerned he proved totally correct. By then I was very proud of our Corps.

Just a few weeks after talking with Lt. Qm. Alston, an Army Council Instruction was read out on parade and it called for volunteers from the Medical Corps for parachute duties. It expressly permitted those within armoured formations to volunteer. It was a way out. Howard and I didn't even discuss it. We were some distance apart on parade, but caught each other's eye and put our thumbs up – and that was that. No discussion before and none afterwards, until we came to fill in the necessary application forms.

≈≈≈≈≈≈≈≈≈≈≈

Chapter 7
Parachute training

After the application forms were submitted there followed a whole sequence of intense medical, dental and optical examinations. The fitness requirements for acceptance for training were very strict indeed. But once through these thorough medicals it was goodbye to the 10th Light and all our friends, a number of whom thought we were quite mad and others who confidently predicted we would be back with them very shortly. So one morning seven of us were taken by lorry to Canterbury, through the villages of Sarre and Sturry. It was in the river at Sarre approximately eleven hundred years ago that ships of King Alfred's English fleet had sheltered from a North Sea storm. But Canterbury was merely a breathing space and we were soon on the train for London on our way to Chesterfield in north Derbyshire and to Hardwick Hall, where our introduction proper to the Parachute Forces was to begin.

The gates and guardroom of Hardwick Camp were typical army and there was no sign of the magnificent Hardwick Hall. The camp spread out on the gently sloping hillside looking very much like any other army establishment, the colourful 'red beret' worn by the guard on the gate being the only obvious distinguishing feature (it was actually plum coloured). Soldiers gathered at Chesterfield station from medical units all over England. The reception was brisk but good natured and we were allocated to barrack rooms largely choosing our own companions and told to go and get a meal and learn our way about the camp. We were to report to Gymnasium No. 3 at 7pm sharp.

The meal was the first evidence that this unit was going to be different. There was butter, not margarine on each table, seemingly lashings of the stuff and all the food was much better than the fare usually provided. Complete satisfaction was evident all around the tables and we were similarly pleased with the sleeping facilities that were only army-comfortable, but extra well backed up by first class showers, baths and toilets. Eager now, we waited expectantly for 7 o'clock.

The introductory talk was also something of a surprise. We were brought to attention for the Camp Commandant, a major, with the coveted parachute wings on his arm, but from then on it was total informality. The CC welcomed us to Hardwick and hoped we would enjoy our stay. What had we come to? Could this be the army? He introduced some of the instructors, mostly warrant officers or NCOs. They also seemed to have friendly dispositions and we got the message loud and clear that they wanted to make our training good fun. It was certainly light-hearted at times, but physically very demanding.

Someone had told us that it would be like a military prison and we certainly did have to carry a large pack with a blanket in it at all times and move at the double during normal duty hours. We were double marched here, there and everywhere and always with this pack and blanket. But there was banter rather than abuse if you were panting rather harder than you should have been. Indeed the greatest disciplinary punishment was that of RTU (Return to Unit) the ultimate threat, enforceable for bad breaches of Army Regulations, the unwritten code of the Paratroops. It was this threat alone that enabled our commanding officers to control us all with minimum difficulty.

Many of the initial training lectures were designed to build our confidence in the actual parachute. We were told of the strength of the individual pure silk rigging lines – 28 to each 'chute. We had 5 a side tug o'wars with a single rigging line to convince us of its strength. The mysteries and strength of the harness which enveloped you and the flat metal 'box' with the shiny metal tongues that locked the harness on to you, were all explained and demonstrated with great care and detail. But we certainly did not sit around all day just listening to lectures. Every morning there was early morning PT before an excellent breakfast, followed by a short instructional period on parachute or aircraft equipment. Then we would either be in the gym, or on an assault course, on a cross country run, or swinging on the wires from high metal scaffolding as we learned to fall without injury. This last exercise produced laughter, lumps and bumps. Much of the laughter originated from

74

the 'punishments' dished out by the NCOs for repeated failures to land and roll properly.

A minor error would receive the command "Right! Over the top bar, now! Go!" and you had to swarm up 20 feet of steel tubing, swing over the cross bar at the top and descend the other tube. If you didn't execute the task quickly enough you repeated it immediately.

The tubes were rough and rusty and it was both dirty and highly strenuous work, but it was not feared as much as the 'bicycle' form of punishment. The 'bicycle' was nothing more than a set of handlebars, complete with bell. For repeated bad landings or other shortcomings, you had to take the bicycle handlebars and holding them in front of you, run up a hill and round the building on top, ringing the bell and chanting, "I am a bicycle – I am a bicycle!"

The building on the hill was the little camp hospital and on hearing the bell, the nursing sisters would come out on to the balcony to see just who was the bicycle-man this time and of course, laugh their heads off.

One day, a muscular member of our squad made a number of poor landings, but he obviously enjoyed being sent on the climb over the bar, so our instructor sentenced him to the 'bicycle'. Up the hill he trotted, grinning and embarrassed, as he rang the bell and chanted sotto voce "I am a bicycle". We were all dressed in denims without any indication of rank and it was customary for the instructor to call the squad to attention, but before dismissing us, invite the officers to fall out. On this day the instructor's face was a study when one of the officers falling out was none other than the repeatedly 'punished' man who had had to take the dreaded 'bicycle' ride – it was Lieut. J. McGavin, one of the finest medical officers in the Unit.

Another strenuous physical activity was to practise exiting through the 'hole' in the floor of the aircraft fuselage. It involved dropping through the 'aperture' on to a gymnasium mat some eight feet below and immediately running round to climb a short ladder back into the fuselage to continue the exercise ad nauseam. We now realised that the pack and blanket that lived on our backs was to simulate the parachute pack we would soon be harnessing up.

There were both indoor and outdoor assault courses at Hardwick. Our PT instructors loved to vary these, keeping us constantly vying with one another as they became more and more horrific. The outdoor assault course was kept secret until the day of our final passing out tests, when we found out that it had a great number of hidden surprises we had not suspected. But with the excellent food and the constant exercise, we were so fit that we delighted in the daily cross country runs and long run-marches around the countryside.

Some of the training was specifically designed to give the 'feel' of parachute descents. One of these was 'The Tower', a skeleton metal construction, some 80 or 90 feet high, with an arm like a gantry crane projecting from the top. From this arm a thin wire hawser suspended a mock parachute of about half the normal size and from this 'chute a standard parachute harness was also suspended and you hung there, in the harness. A small flat platform was our launching pad and from about seventy feet up you had to step off into space and trust that the man controlling the paying out of the cable would slow you up sufficiently to make your landing reasonably gentle. It was quite obvious that the 'chute had no effect whatsoever on your speed of descent. One of my descents from this tower was memorable and served me well on future jumps. I was on my way down, concentrating on locking my feet and knees together as instructed, when a stentorian bellow came up from the ground below: "Keep your bloody elbows in!"

On every real jump I made, save one, I 'heard' that voice once more as I neared the ground. The sole exception was my very first jump from the balloon and I was just so relieved and excited to be floating rather than plummeting down that I wasn't aware of anything else at all.

Accidents did happen of course. Some fell awkwardly and broken collarbones and badly sprained knees and ankles were relatively common. We had sessions controlling real full size parachutes on windy days on the grass of the parkland in front of Hardwick Hall. If the wind was right, you lay to windward of the 'chute that was still collapsed on the ground. A couple of your mates would then 'open' the mouth of the 'chute allowing the wind to inflate it. While being tugged along the ground, you were then expected to get to your feet and run very quickly to the leeward of the 'chute thus causing it to collapse. If you couldn't get to your feet, you might be towed along the grass in a strong wind. Then the technique was to roll onto your back, hit and release the metal box that secured your harness, hold your arms above your head and let the harness pull off your body. At times this technique did actually work, but not for our unit Regimental Sergeant Major Bagg, (I will leave you to guess what his four letter nickname was). In his case the system literally got bogged up. He was pulled face down along the ground and then through some soft mud that got packed into the quick release mechanism of the metal box. It failed to open when he rolled on his back and hit it as per the usual instructions. Unable to get to his feet and equally unable to get rid of the harness, he was towed across Hardwick Park at increasing speed. The turf was reasonably soft, but by no means level and over the undulating ground he was alternately lifted and thumped down again very hard indeed. We were in hot pursuit by this time, but no one managed to catch the 'chute until after he had been dragged unceremoniously across the hard driveway leading to the Hall. He had numerous bruises although he managed to escape serious injury. But despite the injuries, at the end of five or six weeks of intensive training most of us were considered fit enough and sufficiently trained to go to Ringway near Manchester, for the RAF portion of our training.

There was another full scale medical. Amazingly it weeded out two or three who had passed all previous such examinations. This last test required ten or a dozen of us at a time, completely naked, to run, walk, touch toes and lift weights. All this in a warm room under very strong lights, while about eight medical officers watched us from all angles. Under this 'activity examination' it was remarkable what was revealed. One fellow had to leave us because a spinal anomaly was revealed (he had been passed A1 in all previous tests) and another had a malfunction of a hip joint – he too was officially A1! But those of us who did get through it all began to think we must be super fit, and went off to Ringway brimming with confidence.

Sitting alongside the driver in the cab of the lorry, I could enjoy the springtime journey into the late afternoon sun through the high country of the Derbyshire and Cheshire Moors. Some of this country was familiar to me from my cycling trips, other parts of it were quite new.

As we approached the camp on the Cheshire plain, an aircraft flew over at about six or seven hundred feet and to our intense interest about half a dozen parachutes appeared beneath it. Then, to our horror, we saw that the rigging lines of the 'chutes were obviously badly twisted, some totally so, with the result that the figures suspended beneath the partly opened 'chutes plummeted earthwards with their unopened canopies streaming behind them in the dreaded 'Roman candle'. It was a great relief to see men on the ground pick up the 'victims' and sling them over their shoulders. They were quite clearly dummies, dropped with twists deliberately placed in their rigging lines for experimental purposes.

Medical Corps trainees were only about one quarter of the total number of troops arriving at Ringway to do the same jump training. The others were Infantry and Royal Engineers. We were divided into groups of twenty, (two 'sticks' of jumpers) and we would jump from a Whitley aircraft. Each group was in the care of an RAF flight sergeant and the total six groups came under the care of a squadron leader. This pattern was repeated for the Infantry and the Royal Engineers and a wing commander was in overall command.

Our army instructors back at Hardwick had made disparaging reference to the RAF instructors as 'The Brylcream Boys'. They gave us the impression that they were 'soft' and that we would find their training childishly easy in comparison with what we had been through already. Undoubtedly the RAF instructors were well aware of these comments. The commander himself had all of us, nearly 500 in all, out on the square in PT kit and he put us through a series of exercises specially chosen to create agony in muscles that had been stiffened by the army training and for twenty minutes we suffered hell! Then the Wing Co called a halt and said: "Right. That is just to show we can be as tough as the Army – but from now on, we'll be friends!" and that is just how it was.

The RAF training paid particular attention to the attachment of the 'strops' and 'static-lines' that pulled our 'chutes from their bags when we left the aircraft or balloon. We were taken for air experience flights in Whitley aircraft; their advantage for parachuting was that they could slow down to about 90 knots and habitually flew with their tails up – a characteristic that kept the tail well up out of the way of the developing 'chute. We were shown films of jumps from the aircraft, from the ground and even from another parachutist.

Just to make sure we hadn't forgotten how, we went on run-marches around the Manchester suburbs. Our RAF instructors were initially under the misapprehension that the RAMC trainees were less fit than the infantry and REs. To the delight and surprise of our six RAF instructors we completed the longest run without a single man falling out, the only group to achieve this. We then found out that they had had the impression until then, that if you were in the Medical Corps you were not A1 and had to be treated gently! We soon put them right on that score, but overall they were terrific guys.

Much of the time after the first few days training was spent waiting for suitable weather for our first jumps. Some of the waiting was done in a very good canteen where the cream buns were excellent – but not to be recommended shortly before you were due to jump.

The wind had to be minimal or non-existent for your first go. One reason for this was that we had to manhandle our own barrage balloon into position at Tatton Park before we ascended. We went up four at a time, plus our instructor, in a square wooden cage that had an ominous tapering aperture in its floor. Our instructor was a Flight Sergeant Johnson, a superb psychologist, alleged to be an insurance salesman in Leeds in civilian life. I expect he made a good living at it, but he never tried to interest us in any insurance. The four of us, two officers and two NCOs sat, tucked as tightly as possible into the corners of the cage well away from the gaping hole in the bottom. But Flt Sgt Johnson moved unconcernedly around, checking our harness and the attachment of our static lines to the steel bar that traversed the cage above the hole. He asked – as was traditional – which sort of jokes we wanted, Red or Blue? And got nothing more than a strained silence. The cable securing the balloon began to be paid out by the motorised winch; our fellow squad members released their hold on the stabilizing ropes of the balloon, while we swung slightly into the wind and began the ascent to 800 feet. For a while we could hear the purring of the motor through the rubber padding of our training helmets, then it went silent. We were at 800 feet and the nervous tension was palpable. For weeks now we had gone through this aperture drill. On the command, "Action Stations!" you swung your feet into the hole and balanced, buttocks on the edge, back arched, so that the 'chute on your back would clear the aperture as you flipped out by a thrust from your hands and arms. Then the bellowed command, "Number 1, GO!" and the first man was launched into the void.

I was number 4 in our balloon and sat watching the tense agonised expressions on the faces as the moment of departure arrived. The first to go was Captain Young and with contorted face, he murmured "God!" and flipped out of sight.

The cage jerked slightly as the static line tugged at the packed and folded silk of his parachute. Flt. Sgt. Johnson leaning nonchalantly over the side of the cage gave us a running commentary on his descent. We heard the Tannoy system far below take over and advise Captain Young that he had made a good exit. "You are drifting slightly. You should expect a side left landing."

Number 2 was not dispatched until number 1 landed safely and we heard the distant cheer of our fellow squad members as Captain Young picked himself up. Number 2 went through the same ritual, with the shouted commands that impelled him to jump, while my whole being was screaming "Don't do it! Don't do it!".

Then it was S/Sgt. Smith with "Number 3! GO!" He hesitated for what seemed an interminable second then slid rather awkwardly into the aperture, his parachute catching on the edge, tipping him forward a little so that the padding of his helmet brushed the far side of the aperture.

At that moment I just did not know whether I would go or not. Whether indeed, I could go! I sat on my hands, feet in the hole, nervously easing my weight from buttock to buttock. I think Flt.

.Sgt.Johnson realised my mental state and this was when his supreme applied psychology took over.

"That's right Number 4. Make yourself comfortable. I won't give you any commands. Just put yourself out in your own time."

All this in a normal conversational voice, none of the shouting that had accompanied the exits of the other three men and my tension left me just like the expiration of a deep breath. I flicked my body into the aperture and plunged two hundred feet before the tug on my shoulders reassured me that my chute had opened after all and that I was floating, not plummeting toward the earth. Dimly I heard the Tannoy talking to Number. 4, deaf to what was said. I did hear something about a "Side right landing" just as I swept into a sideways roll about fifty yards from the winch lorry that was already reeling in the balloon.

Gratefully rolling up the lovely silk canopy that had borne me so safely to earth, I became aware for the first time of the name 'Ginger' chalked on the empty pack on my back. "Thanks Ginger," I murmured to the shadowy WAAF whose skilful hands had packed that parachute and walked back to the waiting squad feeling six inches taller. I had done it. Or had the greater fear, of being seen to be afraid, overcome the lesser fear of the jump itself?

Captain Young and two of us had to go to Bulford to make preparations for our Unit's arrival after completion of our parachute training. We had to rush through our jumps as a matter of priority and before I had recovered from the excitement of that first jump I found the same four of us, once more with 'chutes on our backs, sitting only slightly less tense beneath the great grey balloon. This time they were kind to us. We climbed to 900 feet before the shouts of the dispatcher dinned in the ears of No. 1 once more. I was more aware of that awful void below my feet as I glanced down after the departure of Number 3 and it seemed to require just as much effort to make that second launch. Then came the sharp, crisp voice of Sgt. Johnson shouting "Action Station Number 4. Number 4 GO!" And I duly went. At his suggestion, I looked up as I dropped to watch the canopy develop above me – and turned a neat involuntary back somersault!

I heard the voice of the Tannoy from below. "Number 4, Number 4 – you are facing east and drifting in that direction. Take a good look at Manchester, you will never get a better view of it!" I never did get a better or longer look at Manchester from the air, but this time on the way down I 'heard' the dulcet tones of that Hardwick instructor: "Keep your bloody elbows in!"

Next day it was aircraft jumps for just the four of us who had managed to get in two balloon jumps in one day. We found ourselves at the airport drawing 'chutes from the store with complete strangers. They were not even army personnel, but the brave individuals who parachuted regularly into Europe to help organise the French Resistance. We didn't know their names, some spoke very little English and they had not been through the thorough pre-jump training that we had. I missed my companions and found those two jumps, the 'slow pairs' as they were called, very trying, for only two of us left the aircraft on each circuit over Tatton Park.

It was almost dusk as the four of us once more got together on the dropping zone out at Tatton and we all felt exceptionally tired. We climbed aboard a utility truck and settled on the 'washing bags' – used parachutes returning for re-packing. The vehicle bumped over the grass of the park and long before we reached the gates, we were all fast asleep.

Only one other jump of our magical seven is worth mentioning. The seventh not only earned you the coveted winged parachute to sew on your sleeve, but it was the point at which the actual jump ceased to be voluntary. Before your seventh jump, at any time, you were permitted to say "No more" without any recriminations and you could return to your previous unit. Two of our training companions did just this after their sixth jump. One explained that he had done his six jumps to show it wasn't fear that made him renege from the seventh, just a realisation that he was a little too old to cope with the physical demands that would be asked of him. Fair enough – but we missed him at the celebration party for the winning of our wings.

My sixth jump was an eye-opener. It was on a Sunday morning and should never have taken place, for the wind was far stronger than was recommended for 'learner' parachutists. Literally hundreds of Home Guard soldiers from all over Lancashire and Cheshire had come to see a drop and learn at first hand that paratroops are most vulnerable just after having landed. Our 'plane circled the dropping zone over Tatton Park. We were to be dropped in two 'sticks' of five and I was one of the first 'stick'. First time around the red light and the "Action Stations 1" came on, but we didn't get the Green.

Apparently the pilot thought that the gusting cross winds could sweep us off course. We went round again and this time got both Red and Green lights and jumped. The wind was still blowing at about 18 to 20 knots and the five of us had some spectacular landings. My own was fast – too fast. I was swinging in an anti-clockwise circle as I descended and also drifting with the wind and at the moment of hitting the ground the drift and swing combined to bring me down at about 40 mph, close to the trees at the edge of the Park. I don't recall much of the landing itself. I know that I rolled violently and little more than instinct prompted me to pull half the parachute in and collapse it before it towed me away. Ground observers ran towards me and to others scattered widely across the park. Two of my companions didn't get up and an ambulance raced towards them. On this occasion our landings were filmed and I discovered later that I had done three forward somersaults when I hit the ground. The cameraman caught the facial expressions of some of the Home Guard onlookers and they were quite incredible.

Of the five of us who jumped (they promptly cancelled the other five who were supposed to have followed us) two went to hospital, one with a fractured cervical vertebrae, the other with a damaged shin – he hit a tree trunk. A third was badly winded and kept under observation.

These were the only casualties experienced in our actual jumps – remarkable when you think that 120 of us made a total of over 800 jumps between us. I believe we actually suffered more minor casualties getting back to our quarters after the celebration night at the end of the course, which says a lot for both the training and the care the RAF lavished on us.

Geordie Hodgson, a Tynesider, chipped a cervical vertebra. He recovered, completed his jumps and rejoined the Field Ambulance. For the operational jump on Sicily, I was number 7 to jump, Geordie was number 6. As we stood waiting to jump, a piece of shrapnel hit Geordie in the leg. He still jumped when the light went Green.

≈≈≈≈≈≈≈≈≈≈≈

Chapter 8
First Ever Parachute Field Ambulance

Bulford should have had two l's in its name instead of one. It was severely army style and run on very regimental lines and full of 'bull', all of which came as quite a shock to us after the life of Hardwick Camp and Ringway. Some of us were fortunate enough to occupy unused married quarters instead of the typical barrack rooms that stood in drab uniform rows. But even the married quarters were cold, sterile, cheerless houses that provided little more than a roof over our beds. They were places to get out of at every opportunity.

There was a lot of work to be done before the 120 volunteers could be said to have formed into a cohesive unit. Our name was to be 16th Parachute Field Ambulance and we were part of the 1st Parachute Brigade, which included the 2nd Parachute Battalion whose members had already earned a great reputation for the Bruneval raid they had very recently carried out.

At the start, much of my work was done in the QM Stores. As ours was the first ever Parachute Field Ambulance there were no previous criteria on which to base our equipment entitlements, either in the strictly medical or in our day to day living requirements. The second category that dealt with everyday needs was the G1098 as the Army Ordnance Corps listed it, by far the simpler to assess and quite rapidly arrived at. As we were numerically very similar in strength to a Light Field Ambulance we were equipped accordingly. Of course special provision had to be made for our camouflage smocks, a coverall jumping jacket designed to ensure that no exposed buckle could catch and snag the rigging lines. Colt 45 pistols were included, for we were, to our surprise, to be armed. And last but by no means least, the fighting knives to be secreted in a special narrow hidden pocket by the knee of our khaki jumping trousers. In the hands of some of the more fiery tempered members of our unit, these knives threatened to cause more casualties than the enemy. It was a blessed relief when they were withdrawn from medical personnel.

The purely medical equipment posed a far greater problem. Our Unit was to have four sections, each in the charge of a Medical Officer and also two completely separate surgical teams, each with its own surgeon and someone acting as anaesthetist. These requirements represented a great deal of medical and surgical equipment and the powers-that-be finally decided that we should be issued with <u>two</u> sets; the first to the same scale as a light Field Ambulance, the second to the scale of a full Field Ambulance – a huge amount of equipment. We unpacked the lot, laying it out in two vast storerooms in long lines against the walls – the Light Field Ambulance equipment on the left and the full Field Ambulance on the right.

In the space down the middle we had a number of the cylindrical containers in which equipment was dropped. These were our allocation of supplies that would be dropped with us and they had a parachute packed in their 'tail' and wore a collapsible metal 'nose-piece' to absorb some of the shock of landing. Unlike us, containers could not 'bend at the knees' when they hit the earth. On the other hand they had no bloody elbows.

Each section and each surgical team was allowed four containers for their equipment and by trial and error and repeated consultation with the Section Medical Officers on what was absolutely essential, we discovered just what would pack into the container space available. We had to be ready to hold our casualties for a few days, as evacuation from behind enemy lines might not be immediately possible.

A similar process with the surgical teams and their equipment enabled us to arrive at a list, a very lengthy list, of what we would need. This list became the prototype for the medical equipment of parachute field ambulances that were to form up after us. Much of the credit must belong to Lt. Qm. Anderson, the speedy and efficient officer in charge of all our stores.

It quickly became apparent that the medical supplies carried with us would only last a limited period in action and that arrangements for re-supply in the field had to be agreed on as well.

A great deal of this work was done by trial and error. The infantry units were experimenting with containers, dropping them and checking their contents for damage. We were kept busy packing and re-packing our own containers many times, all four sections involved in the work. It also became obvious that each man would have to carry supplies with him on his jump if we were to have a chance of saving life on arrival in action.

Large kit-bags were strapped to the leg with a quick release pin system that allowed the parachutist, once he was clear of the aircraft and descending normally, to release the kitbag. It then dangled on 15 or 20 feet of rope beneath him. A lightweight folding stretcher was evolved and with a blanket wrapped round it could be carried in the hand when leaving the aircraft and similarly released on a rope once the parachute developed. When fully attired in camouflage jackets, small packs, over smocks, parachute pack, kit-bag on leg and stretcher and blanket in hand, we virtually needed to be placed in a wheel-barrow to get us out to the aircraft, let alone climb up the steps into it.

Aircraft for training purposes were in short supply and some of us undertook balloon drops to ensure continuing familiarity with parachuting. One of these nearly had an unfortunate end for a good friend of mine, Sgt. Arthur Davenport, known to all his friends as Dizzy. It happened this way.

All but three of those detailed to jump had done so. When the balloon cage was about to ascend with the last three jumpers for that evening, a spare unused 'chute was noticed and the instructor asked did anyone want a second drop? Sgt. Davenport won the race for the spare 'chute, picked it up from the grass where it lay and donned it quickly. The first three jumps and descents from the balloon were without incident, then came Dizzy's turn. He exited normally and dropped the 200 feet or so that it took for a 'chute to open from a balloon, but it didn't open! It streamed, extending for its full length but the mouth of the canopy remained closed. Onlookers stopped breathing, powerless to do anything to help. Fortunately when little more than 150 feet up, the 'chute suddenly snapped open and we breathed again while Dizzy completed a very rapid parachute drop from 800 feet. The 'post mortem' on its failure to open (which could so easily have been one on Arthur Davenport), came to the conclusion that damp from dew on the grass had been the reason for the malfunction. From then on we tried very hard to make sure that our 'chutes were kept dry at all times.

Part of our training at Bulford involved a Unit inspection by Lieutenant General FAM Browning and his staff – an inspection to end all inspections. Our webbing had to be fitted exactly as well as 'blancoed' to perfection. The Service Corps contingent cleaned their lorries until they gleamed beneath their camouflage, even preparing their tool kits for inspection. But they were caught out when General Browning's observation was, "In my experience, Service Corps are excellent drivers, but usually far from physically fit!"

They were promptly dispatched on a 45 minute run-march under the general's critical eye.

The Unit office did not escape close inspection either. All the record books that the army requirements said should be maintained but so seldom were in wartime were closely examined. We had Leave Books, Bath Books, Conduct Records and Inoculation Registers all laid out for one of the Staff Officers to peruse – and they did, thoroughly. Overall we got a good report, although there were some areas of deficiency to comment on. The QM Store cunningly forestalled unfavourable comment on the state of the two huts so recently used for sorting medical equipment. He had two lonely soldiers, each armed with a bucket and scrubbing brush, performing the Herculean task of cleaning the extensive wooden floors only minutes before the huts were visited by the inspecting teams. The ploy worked. The task was in hand – but whether it was ever completed is quite a different matter.

Another facet of our training involved a long march, starting from Bulford and taking us across Wiltshire and through North Somerset, to camp out for a few days on the hills just west of Combe Martin. A few miles inland from Ilfracombe we met American army parachutists camping in the same area and got on famously, so well in fact, that an off duty entertainment into nearby Ilfracombe was arranged. One night American paras were involved in an argument with local British army personnel. They resented the Yanks usurping their girl friends. So we joined in – on the side of our fellow paratroops!

My own part in the march from Bulford was a very mixed one. I was to march whenever I was free of other duties, but I also had to take an army truck to collect the rations that were needed for each camp site that we used during the week we were on the move.

On the second day out I felt far from well and reported sick, but the MO didn't diagnose anything and I believe he thought I was malingering, trying to dodge the marching part of this exercise. But when washing in a stream at the campsite a couple of nights before we were due to reach Combe Martin, I noticed I had a rash appearing. I showed it to the MO and he was quite apologetic that he hadn't diagnosed the symptoms, for of all things, I had measles. I was rushed off to the Camp Reception Station on the edge of the cliffs in Ilfracombe and there isolated in a small room that overlooked the sea. I had probably been through the worst of the illness before I got to hospital, but I was exhausted with all the marching while in the prodromal stages and was happy enough just to sleep for a couple of days. After that I began to feel quite fit and found the isolation and inaction extremely irksome.

The Matron of the hospital took pity on me and said that if I promised not to talk to anyone when I was out as I was still considered infectious, I could take walks along the lovely cliff-top and take her dog with me. (It seemed I was permitted to talk to the dog). He was an Airedale, a beautiful dog, but Matron did not divulge his less lovable characteristics and one was that he wanted to fight anything and everything on four legs. On our first morning out he tackled every dog we met, then took on cows and bullocks with reckless abandon and on one occasion tried to mix it with a mare and a foal. After vainly pursuing him right down into Ilfracombe town as he chased a small inoffensive dog miles from its home, I vowed not to take him again. Fortunately, more satisfying recreation was forthcoming. Some of the nurses were very good at smuggling a wet towel and swimming trunks back into the hospital after having had very unofficial bathes with me in a rock pool beneath the cliffs.

Initially I was amazed, but later amused, by the solicitude of a number of the officers of our Unit who turned up to visit me, particularly on the day before my discharge from hospital. It transpired that it was not entirely due to interest in my wellbeing, but rather that my presence in Ilfracombe was a good excuse for them to get into the town by means of the official transport laid on.

Our Unit had a remarkable CO and I firmly believe that every man respected him. Lt. Col. M.E. MacEwan was not a young man. He wore the wings of the Royal Flying Corps – the 1914-1918 predecessor to the RAF. For him to have done his jumps at Ringway with us when he must have been fifty, had already earned our admiration. He wore an impressive number of medal ribbons awarded to him by both British and Russian authorities. In fact he had been seconded to the Russians from the Royal Flying Corps and had finished up riding with a Cossack regiment when his 'plane was grounded for lack of spares.

It was said he had been a brigadier in a Territorial Artillery formation, a rank that he had voluntarily relinquished to command our Unit and I found he had a medal to prove it. He was assigned to us on his experience with air evacuation of casualties with the St. John's organisation. It is hard to imagine how he had found time, with all his other activities, to become a doctor.

As his name indicates, he was a Scot and rightly proud of the fact. When signing army orders for display on the notice board, he would sign just his surname without initials, telling me as he did so, that he was "The MacEwan of the MacEwans". He was the laird and so needed no initials. Be that as it may, we were all proud of our commanding officer and most of us suffered his little foibles gladly, in fact we secretly delighted in them.

One of these was his fondness for pipes, bagpipes of course and we had a really excellent piper in our ranks – S/Sgt. Anderson – 'Jock' Anderson as everyone knew him. Some of the Londoners, irrepressible Cockneys at heart, professed to hate the pipes and got up to a trick or two to get rid of them. But to be awakened by the sound of those pipes in Combe Martin on a misty summer morning in the lovely Somerset countryside was something very special.

Pipes were used in our Unit in place of the more usual bugle calls. "Cock o'the North" meant 10 minutes to parade time and that wonderful tune "Scotland the Brave" was our fall-in. Only once did I know those pipes fail to arouse the respect they deserved and that was on the morning we marched out of the camp above Ilfracombe. It so happened that S/Sgt. Anderson had had a hectic celebration in nearby Combe Martin the night before and didn't arrive back in our camp until about 10 minutes before parade. We had covered his overnight absence with some difficulty and he just made it on to parade in time. Parade was duly handed over to Col. MacEwan by our RSM and he gave the order for us to march off in column across the field and fairly sharply uphill to the gate that would bring us on to the road. As soon as the Field Ambulance was marching, Col. MacEwan called for 'The Pipes' and Jock Anderson, suffering from the excesses of the night before, inflated the bag and sounded the first few notes of some stirring Scottish march. It was at this moment that he started to march on the uphill section and it proved just too much for him. With a heartrending wail, the sound of the pipes died away. S/Sgt Anderson could pipe no more. Col. MacEwan said nothing but I'll bet he knew what was going on.

Soon after this episode we were placed under orders for overseas.

During my spell in hospital in Ilfracombe, my friend 'Dizzy' Davenport had done particularly well in the QM Stores and retained the job on our return to Bulford. This decision was further influenced by the fact that Sgt. Stevens who had been Chief Clerk for the Unit, was promoted to Staff Sergeant and put in charge of No. 3 Section. To replace him I was brought in as Chief Clerk and after I had consolidated in the position, it also brought promotion. I was made Sergeant, as opposed to the rather uncommon rank of Lance Sergeant that I had held in the stores. This odd in-between rank was now to be held by 'Dizzy' Davenport.

There was a heavy workload in the general office, made heavier by the order to prepare for overseas and I could well see why Sgt. Stevens had welcomed his promotion and opportunity to get into general field duties once more. At one stage I declined my TAB booster because we were so busy that I couldn't see how I could take the time off I knew I would need to recover. This was with the full cooperation of Major Wheatley, our second in command and we arranged that I should have my injections on home leave in a few days time. I was to do this at the Glen Parva Barracks in Leicester some 17 miles away and he gave me a letter to facilitate things. But there was a snag that I hadn't foreseen. When I had last seen this barracks about 18 months previously, it had been the depot of the Leicestershire regiment – 'The Tigers'. But when I fronted up there for the injection, to my absolute horror I found that it had become an ATS Training Depot.

I had to march from the main gate towards the Medical Inspection room right around two sides of the large square. It was a cardinal sin to walk diagonally across any drill square, particularly if there were squads being drilled thereon, which there were. To my horror, the squads and their instructors were all female!

Looking neither right nor left I moved around the periphery of that square as rapidly as I could. I think my face was almost as red as my beret as the catcalls and wolf whistles could be heard from all around the square and even the NCOs drilling the trainees appeared to be sharing in the fun. I hurried through the door of the Medical Inspection room but my embarrassment was to continue. Doors were hastily closed and curtains drawn across cubicles as the girls waiting for treatment were hastily spirited away.

After that experience, the injection itself was an anti-climax and I hurried back around the perimeter of the square, grateful that it was almost teatime and the drilling squads who had given me such a rousing reception were no longer there. About an hour later I was home and in bed and stayed there for almost 24 hours until the ill effects of the inoculation cleared away.

At the end of my leave it was back to Bulford where the heat was now really on and we struck more problems. One newly married man was determined not to go overseas and leave his wife so soon after the wedding. He was paraded, at his own request, in front of the Commanding Officer Col. MacEwan, vowing that he would refuse any order to jump – and after the seventh training jump this was a court-martial offence.

"Very well, that will be all right" said the wise and wily Col. MacEwan, "I shan't order you to jump!" He was confident, he told us privately in the office, that once overseas and away from his newlywed, the man would behave perfectly normally. He can't have been pleased at the sequel. The next Saturday afternoon, the soldier, still determined not to go overseas, picked up one of the large stones that marked the verge of a minor road to Amesbury and smashed it heavily onto his foot – and that was that!

Another problem was related to keeping up an accurate nominal roll of all personnel who were ready to go and had been warned for embarkation. It was unbelievable how many changes and variations there were to this list. In part this was due to the fact that one Section, No. 4, was to go by air, whereas the rest of the unit was to go by sea. As a man went sick, even for a couple of days, he was taken off the roll and a replacement drafted on. If he recovered in time, he was put back on the roll and his replacement removed. This meant keeping a full nominal roll of all ranks produced daily and on the final day before departure of the seaborne contingent, we actually had to prepare three separate rolls – the last of which was done at 2am on the morning of our departure.

There were other unexpected and unwanted complications. One medical officer and two senior NCOs of our unit were in Salisbury celebrating a couple of nights before our departure. They'd had a fair amount to drink and in a dispute that erupted in a fish and chip shop, they finished up by putting the cash register in the deep fat fryer! This might have been forgiven, for high spirits in the paratroops were often accepted as inevitable, but unfortunately the officer concerned was overheard (by an intelligence man) to say that their unit was going overseas. This happened around 10pm in Salisbury. Somehow or other those concerned made their way back to Bulford and slept it off. But things moved swiftly during the night. The breach of security must have been reported immediately and the War Office, often thought to be incapable of swift action, moved into top gear.

It had been my turn to be clerk on duty on that particular night and as usual, I slept in the office. Around 7am as I was packing up my blankets just before going off duty, I took an incoming telephone call.

"This is War Office, AMD6" said a cultured voice. "Captain ----- RAMC, is hereby posted to Fort Augustus and will today proceed by the 10.45am train from Salisbury. Rail Warrant to be issued. Motor transport to Salisbury station is authorised."

The voice then quoted the relevant authority for this and asked for my name, rank and serial number as indication that the message had been received, understood and would be acted upon. It was. Few in our Unit even witnessed the departure of the man concerned – a pity, for he was a good medical officer. The senior NCOs got off with a stiff reprimand and were required to reimburse the proprietor of the fish shop for damages to his cash register but it was not they who had breached security and they remained with our unit and duly went to North Africa with us.

≈≈≈≈≈≈≈≈≈≈≈

Chapter 9
North Africa

It was almost dark as our convoy neared the Straits of Gibraltar but we could see the distant outline of 'The Rock' dark against the northern sky. On our right, the starboard side, the lights of Tangiers blazed brilliantly by way of contrast. Next morning, well before dawn, Gibraltar lay far behind and when daylight came we could see that the convoy had already begun to split up on the open sea around us.

There were fewer ships with us now and most of those that remained were troop-carrying liners and Navy escorts and the quickened beat of our engines told us that we were making much faster progress. All that day and much of the night we sailed steadily eastward, heading for our landing place in Algiers. The excitement was tremendous and our energies overflowing after eleven days of virtual inactivity. We began making last minute preparations. The winches were uncovered, oiled and given trial runs, derricks were unshackled and swung to the 'ready' position for the rapid unloading of our stores in the morning. We packed our personal kits and complied with a thought provoking last minute order that instructed us to complete the Form of Will at the back of our pay-books, if we had not already done so. It seemed that it was true after all – the Army cared for you to the end!

Then just as the sun was climbing into the sky on that fine October morning, we entered the harbour at Algiers. There had been some action. The Navy had briefly engaged and silenced the shore batteries and had broken the boom across the harbour mouth. But for most of us the spectacular scene was in the water. There were huge jellyfish, many 4 or 5 feet across, some pale blue in colour some a reddish-brown. They floated aimlessly and probably lifelessly, past the ship. Presumably they had been concussed or killed by the under water explosions that had broken up the harbour boom, but I doubt if any of us had seen anything like that in our lives. We stared at them fascinated, as the liner slowly nosed its way alongside the wharf and moored. Then, looking up almost for the first time, we saw Algiers. A hotchpotch of ancient and modern buildings spread before us, all shining white in the early morning sun. Climbing up the hills behind the more modern central part of the city was the area known as the Casbah. This was the old Arab quarter of Algiers and even from the deck of our liner we could see how the buildings huddled and leaned together as though their upper storeys were embracing above the narrow twisted lanes that climbed among them. Close by this age old area of the city stood the very modern Corbusier designed hospital and it says a great deal for its style and design that it could stand there, in close proximity to buildings that had changed little in 2,000 years, yet not look out of place.

But now our interest switched to the unloading process that was in progress. The first surprise was the fact that the Royal Engineers were doing it, operating the winches and slings having already removed the hatch covers. The ship's crew stood by and watched. The reason for this unexpected behaviour was that the ship was now in a theatre of war and it was imperative that service personnel carry out the unloading. The work would certainly have been done more quickly and more efficiently by the crew who were familiar with the winches and derricks aboard the ship and we saw a number of loads swing hard against the ship's side and spill some of the precious stores into the water. Most of these were quickly recovered and eventually placed safely on the dock, but we saw three or four ready packed parachutes floating and once they were recovered we made a point of breaking them open to ensure that they would have to be re-packed. No one wanted to hear of some unfortunate para whose 'chute failed to open because it was damp.

Most of our medical stores were in panniers and these together with the non-medical stores, were stacked in a solid square, about 5 or 6 feet high, on the wharf. Local labour, Algerian wharfies, did much of the handling of these later in the day and it was fascinating to communicate with them. Some spoke French, but with such a heavy dialect that was difficult to follow, others spoke Arabic and some, coming as they did from Tangiers, spoke a form of Spanish. We quickly found that sign language was by far the most reliable means of communication. One of our Unit, Private Jimmy Pleasance, proved an expert, for he had lived with deaf and dumb people and found that much of the sign language he used was internationally understood.

No transport had materialised to remove these stores by the time darkness fell and between us we had to mount a guard to prevent the ever-present risk of pilfering. It was a warm, pleasant night and we patrolled in pairs round the two large square piles where our panniers and containers were stacked, enjoying the romance and the strangeness of this exotic place, when we were sharply brought back to reality. There was a thud and the sharp whine of a bullet ricocheting off the hull of the ship. Our first indication that not all the natives were friendly. We were almost immediately recalled to the ship to don our hard helmets in lieu of red berets and instructed to keep under cover as much as possible until one or two snipers had been dealt with. The ship's light above the gangway was switched off and we returned to the wharf and the stores in almost total darkness. From then on we confined our patrolling to the seaward side of the pile of stores. A few more ricochets whined and buzzed off adjacent ships, but we were not troubled again that night and it kept any would-be pilferers away as well.

Major Wheatley, our second in command, told Sgt Davenport and me to stay with the unit's equipment until two trucks arrived. We were to see them loaded and then accompany them to Maison Blanche airfield, just outside Algiers.

We waited all morning. No trucks arrived. Mid-afternoon came and still no transport to be seen. At one end of the wharf a painted Army sign read DDTS (Deputy Director of Transport Services) so I went along and expecting a Corporal or Sergeant to be manning the office, knocked loudly on the door and marched in. I threw a hurried salute when I saw it was the red-tabbed Deputy Director himself sitting there! I explained what the situation was and that all our equipment was wanted at Maison Blanche.

"Right," he said. "In the square behind this office are some trucks and drivers, take the first two you come to!"

I thanked him, saluted once more and Arthur Davenport and I went into the square expecting army vehicles to be lined up there. Instead we saw a motley collection of elderly lorries, all converted to be driven on 'producer gas' from the slow combustion of wood in converters trailed behind them, or mounted in front of their bonnets. We chose the two nearest. Their drivers spoke no English, one spoke French of sorts, the other came from Tangiers and his language was presumably Spanish. The first truck, with the French speaking driver, started fairly readily. About five or ten minutes after the driver stirred the fire in the converter the engine coughed into reluctant life, but the second truck just refused to start. Finally Lorry No. 1 towed Lorry No. 2 around the square and on to the wharf to load up our stores. By the time we reached the area where our stores were standing, Lorry No. 2 had begun to splutter into life and smiles wreathed the face of our Spanish-speaking driver. It took some time to load the couple of tons of stores on the two trucks, by which time of course, Lorry No. 2 had had plenty of time to cool down and it once again refused to fire. Lorry 1 driver took him in tow and now, with both trucks fully loaded, we started out for the Maison Blanche airfield.

Our progress was impossibly slow. All the roads from the waterfront at Algiers climb steadily through the city and 'steadily' was the right word to describe our progress. Pedestrians were walking almost as fast as we were driving. They tantalised us by offering gifts of fruit and wine. It was meant to be a joke and they were a little taken aback when we duly accepted some of these offerings by hopping out of the driver's cab, collecting the 'gift' and climbing back aboard the slowly moving vehicles.

As we neared the top of the long climb out of Algiers, the second truck's engine began to fire once more and shortly after the tow was released and we were able to proceed at around 20 miles an hour. It was soon after this that a small open Army Staff car came towards us and I recognised Major Wheatley and attracted his attention. He said not to proceed to the airfield as there had been a change of plan. We were to wait where we were for further orders. We did wait, long enough for the engine of No. 2 to cool down once more, so that when we were told to move on to Rouiba a few hours later, the towing procedure had to be repeated yet again. Meanwhile Arthur and I were remembering words of French that we had not used since our school days and were doing our best to communicate with our driver friend.

Before unloading these trucks and allowing the drivers to return to Algiers, we were destined to spend over 48 hours in their company and our French vocabularies improved every hour. Not once did they complain about not getting home. We shared food with them, slept rolled in camouflage nets and when the time came for them to leave us in Rouiba, we parted old friends.

It seemed that Rouiba was to be our base for some little time, but initially we were accommodated in considerable discomfort in the large sheds and barns of a vineyard. In a few days it became apparent that we were to remain here. The unit office was set up in an empty shop in the main street, close to the station and even closer to the Café de la Gare! Rapidly we made friends with the young proprietor of this establishment and soon were busily sampling his liqueurs as well as the more regular muscat. I thought this local muscat was excellent, as did a number of our soldiers, and with the rate of exchange that was operating it worked out at about the same price as beer in England and they chose to drink it in a similar manner – with devastating results! I watched a group of them down three or four large glasses each and walk out of the café with no apparent difficulty. They crossed the road on the way back to the vineyard buildings, a little unsteady on their feet perhaps, but heading across the open land in the right general direction. About halfway to their billets in the barns there were was a deep ditch, an irrigation channel, but now dry and grass covered. The little group stumbled, laughing, into a run as they descended the near side of the ditch. We waited in vain for them to reappear. When we went across to find out what had happened, we found that they had collapsed on the bottom of the ditch and were lying there, out to the world. It was a warm night, so we left them there. In the morning our sentry reported having seen a four-foot snake in that same ditch earlier in the evening.

There were dangers in Algiers we were blissfully unaware of. Large numbers of French and Colonial troops were stationed there, many of them in a huge barracks complex not far above the harbour. Admiral Darlan was the French commander and it was not known whether he would cut his ties with the Vichy French Government and side with us, or order his troops to resist our landings in Algeria and Morocco. Before our unit commanders had had time to warn us of the possible dangers of fraternisation with the local forces, members of the 1st Parachute Brigade had fanned out throughout Algiers. They bartered soap for wine, sweets for fruit and collected souvenirs from these colonial troops, making friends with them and even going into their barracks. I have always believed that this unofficial fraternisation must have influenced Admiral Darlan and his advisers as they turned a blind eye and after some days of indecision, the local French Forces decided in favour of the Allied cause. Actually, due to our ignorance of the possibility of danger I don't think we had ever had any worries on this score.

The German reaction to our entry into Morocco and Algeria was prompt. They landed in Tunisia in some strength. Our parachute landings at Bone, quite close to the Algerian/Tunisian border, were successful despite some hiccups at Gibraltar when the take-offs were in progress after refueling. The runway at Gibraltar was shorter than desirable for the heavily laden C47 aircraft and one of these aircraft failed to become airborne at the end of it and flopped into the sea. The paratroopers were quickly rescued, little the worse for wear, but were unable to take part in the landings.

It was reported that there was only one casualty on the drop at Bone. This was a paratroop Major, whose Sten gun, hanging on a long lanyard, struck the ground butt first, cocked itself and fired a burst of shots some of which struck the Major as he completed his drop. A very wasteful death, but the Sten gun was well known for its ability to cock itself if accidentally dropped.

We left Rouiba (to the sorrow of some who had made some good friends amongst the locals) and moved a little further away from Algiers to a town named Boufarik. Here, two of us had an amusing encounter with a member of the French Colonial forces. He was a very tall, thin Senegalese soldier and was one of the guard mounted on the Marie – the Town Hall and government centre in the middle of the town. The Marie was a fine building with beautiful gardens, surrounded by a high brick wall hung with branches laden with ripe tangerines. We loved these tangerines and were trying to knock them off the branches with our belts or anything else we could lay hands on, when round the corner came this 6 feet 6 inch Senegalese guard, with a rifle and bayonet of even greater length. We were caught red-handed trying to rob the Marie of its prized tangerines and were at a loss as to what to do. But the Senegalese gentleman had no doubts whatsoever. He advanced quickly towards us, bringing his rifle and bayonet smartly off his shoulder as he did so, and it looked as though we were to be the unfortunate principal players in a nasty international incident. A sharp upward thrust with his wickedly long bayonet – and a shower of ripe tangerines descended! A great white expanse of teeth appeared in this black face and with a murmured "Bon appetit!" he continued on his stately patrol around the Marie. Nevertheless, in future we purchased our tangerines. The next guard who caught us might not have been so understanding. In any case, we found we could purchase about 25 tangerines for 10 francs and at the rate of exchange of 400 francs to the £1, that was more than reasonable.

The war in Tunisia seemed remote from the small town of Boufarik in Algeria. We had a Surgical Team in Bone on the Tunisian border but no information for a long while as to how they were functioning. When we did hear it was to learn that one of our surgeons, Major GC Robb had done wonders, working non-stop for days with a badly injured knee. He had sustained this injury when a bomb had dropped outside his operating theatre and a fragment broke his tibia and kneecap.

Most of our Field Ambulance was then ordered to pack up and move by rail to the action in Tunisia. Our No. 2 Section and the 2nd Parachute Battalion did not accompany us as they were to fly in and land much nearer to Tunis itself, with the expectation of being rapidly reinforced by overland forces. The drop duly took place at Oudna, but the overland reinforcements never got through. This section of our Field Ambulance, including the medical officer, Captain JE McGavin and my close friend, Corporal Howard Jones were amongst those taken prisoner – the medics of course, staying to attend to the many wounded. It is surely an insight into the resourceful nature of the paratrooper that groups and individuals of the 2nd Battalion were turning up at Bone and other Allied bases for weeks after this action. They had fought and resisted capture while walking up to 250 miles through a very arid enemy-occupied territory to rejoin their mates.

Meanwhile we were boarding our train in Boufarik and our first introduction to the cattle trucks so well known to soldiers of World War I. A painted sign on each of these wagons stated in bold black paint: "Hommes 40. Chevaux 8." Well, we had no horses and only about 20 of us were allocated to each wagon. But the hard bare wooden floors, no seats or springing, iron-barred spaces of about a foot in depth that ran the length of both sides of the wagon just below the roof line, admitting both air and rain with equal impartiality, ensured anything but a luxurious first night.

However the ability to improvise soon showed up. A blanket and two webbing straps off our equipment was all that was needed to make a hammock and soon all of us were slung across the width of the cattle truck, swinging in unison as the slow train swayed along. It was just as well that we used our ingenuity, for the journey across Algeria to the Tunisian border was to last a week. We had been living off canned Field rations for some time – a box or carton that contained everything for 10 men for 24 hours – even thoughtfully including toilet paper. Tea was provided in the form of a powder, a mix of tea-sugar-milk that with the addition of hot water produced a pale brownish grey liquid. This was, in theory, tea. Obtaining boiling water when travelling in cattle trucks can be a bit of a problem, but initially we solved this by putting a wire handle onto one of the large tins of Army biscuits that came with the ration packs. With the tea-sugar-milk powder tipped into the tin, we would hurry along to the locomotive at one of the numerous halts that were continually occurring and say to the driver "De l'eau chaud, s'il vous plait, Monsieur!". The tin was then placed beneath the end of a pipe that protruded from below the locomotive just near the cab. There would be a mighty 'swoosh' and steam and boiling water would gush into the tin and we would return to our wagon triumphantly bearing our brew of tea.

This routine was continued happily for a couple of days, until one day we forgot to put the tea-sugar-milk powder in the tin and returned to the wagon with a tin full of hot water that looked much the same colour as our usual tea! The brown colour of the tea over the past few days had been due to rust rather than the tea, so other brewing methods had to be devised and they very quickly were. By cutting out the entire lid end of the biscuit tin and piercing a number of holes all round the base, we manufactured a small, crude but efficient brazier. From now on at any halt we would hastily grab bits of wood for fuel, perch another un-punctured biscuit tin of water on top of our new brazier and hey presto! In a few minutes rust-free boiling water for our cuppa. At times the train would move on again before our brew was ready. This was irritating and had to be circumvented. So long wire handles were attached to the brazier and someone would snatch it up when the locomotive whistled to herald our departure and continue the brewing on board. Further refinements included a few flat stones to prevent the base of the brazier burning the wooden floorboards of the wagon. We discovered that larger pieces of wood burned very slowly, but did not go out and could be quickly fanned to an intensive fire by the rush of air obtained by holding the brazier suspended on a stick out of the door of the moving wagon. A late night brew now became a real possibility and the sight of that long slow moving train, winding through the Atlas mountains with these fiercely glowing braziers sticking out from almost every wagon's open door was a sight that none of us will forget.

Winding our way through the foothills of the Atlas Mountains was very slow and a week was to pass before we came to the lovely sounding towns of Souk el Arba (the Fourth Market) and Souk el Khemis (the Fifth Market). We had arrived in Tunisia and at the end of our rail journey and we made our way by road to the outskirts of Beja, a small town built on the eastern slopes of a large hill. We were halted for some considerable time outside the town and the darkness was gathering as we fell-in on the road, just to the west of the town before marching in to the skirl of the pipes. It was strange to see German style writing in chalk on the doors of houses, indicating the number of soldiers they had proposed to billet there. It was a little unnerving to find the enemy so close and yet so completely unseen. Besides, the Arabs in Beja had no particular loyalties to either of the combatant armies and freely gave us information about the Germans – and equally freely presumably, told the Germans all they could about us.

So, knowing this, a little deception was enacted that evening. When we first arrived we had marched down the fairly steep main street of Beja and halted and fallen out near the bottom of the town by the railway level crossing. By this time it was dark and under orders to go quietly, we returned to the top of the hill by way of side streets. Here we fell in once more on the road, the pipes struck up once more and we proudly and loudly marched and whistled our way down the main street again. To the French speaking inhabitants who had greeted us before, we called out in decidedly phoney Scots accents: "We are the Gordon Highlanders!" The whole manoeuvre was repeated once more, with a different marching tune from the pipes. This time we claimed to be The Lovat Scouts! I doubt that the enemy was either confused or perturbed by this deception but it gave us all some much needed exercise and amusement after having been cooped up in rail wagons for a week. It also gave Jock Anderson's bagpipes a real airing.

In Beja most of us were accommodated in a school – the Infants' School – as we quickly realised when we found out how low the toilets were! Those toilets made me feel homesick for the first time since leaving England. No, not because they were anything like those in my own home, but because the porcelain ware of the toilets and the wash basins bore the brand name of a firm in Church Gresley. Church Gresley was just four or five miles from Ashby and I had been at school with the proprietor's son.

The officers of the Field Ambulance were accommodated in a house on the main road at the top of the hill. The school where the rest of us were housed was about a quarter of a mile lower down, well within the small town itself. As a Unit, we were still virtually inactive as far as medical work went. There was a lot of patrol activity by both sides, but little serious fighting and at that time very few casualties.

The Tunisian winter was surprisingly cold and wet and the Allied aircraft that were operating from unmade airfields tended to be grounded, whereas the German aircraft, flying from Bizerta and Tunis were regular visitors. While we were in Beja we witnessed the arrival of an American tank force, with fast, rather light 'Honey' tanks. They drove quickly through Beja heading east towards Tunis and two or three days later, rather depleted in number, they drove equally fast back west through Beja to Souk el Khemis. The poor devils had encountered German 'Tiger' tanks entering the North African campaign for the first time. A surprise weapon, their superiority provided a nasty shock for the inexperienced young American tank crews. A few days later these German tanks were halted at a spot in the hills known to us as Hall's Gap by an equally newly developed British anti-tank gun, the 17-pounder, kept closely 'under wraps'. The advantage between the two contenders went up and down like a see-saw in North Africa.

≈≈≈≈≈≈≈≈≈≈≈

Chapter 10
North African campaign – the End

For a week or two, leading up to Christmas, a few German aircraft, often including Stuka dive-bombers, would fly over Beja almost daily on their way to Souk el Khemis where the American units were refitting after their mauling. We would watch these small groups of aircraft go over, see the puffs of smoke appear in the sky around them as they neared their target and hear very faintly the distant rumble of their exploding bombs. One morning, I think it was a Sunday, Cpl Loveland and I were walking at the lower end of Beja by the railway crossing and were interested to see that there were trucks and a locomotive there. It seemed that the line was being brought back into use once more. We heard aircraft and high overhead saw the usual morning German aircraft patrol passing to the north of Beja on its daily run to harass the troops at Souk el Khemis. Watching them idly, I saw the leading aircraft swing in a gentle arc, descending rapidly toward Beja. "George," I said, "Its not Souk el Khemis today – it's sodding us!"

We sprinted off the level crossing into open land as we heard the spine-chilling scream of the diving Stukas and threw ourselves flat on the ground some 30 yards from the level crossing.

The bombs left the planes – we saw them – one was larger than the others – it might have been a 250-pounder – then we ducked our faces into the dusty grass. Almost immediately the ground heaved and shuddered under us and a cloud of earth and stones spattered down around the whole area and as quickly as they had come the planes were gone, their noise fading as they flew back to base. We quickly returned to the railway crossing and to our amazement there were no real casualties apart from the road, now showing a large smoking crater a few yards on the town side of the rails. Several smaller craters dotted the open country on the other side of the line. Some of the men working on the line would have been little more than 15 to 20 yards from the bombs but had the sense to lie flat and suffered only shock, deafness and the odd flying stone.

It was clear that the Allies were planning an assault and that we were to be very much involved, but as ground troops, as no aircraft were available for airborne operations. We were briefed on the details of this push toward Mateur on the road to Bizerta and Tunis. We knew what our task was to be and then, finally, the date and time of the operation – the early hours of Christmas morning. I am quite sure that only a few in our Unit had really strong religious convictions, but almost everyone felt that this was all wrong. Maybe, if there is one, the all-seeing Almighty thought so too, for early on the 22nd December it started to rain heavily. It kept up all of the 23rd and continued just as heavily for most of the morning of the 24th and the whole plan was aborted about 2pm that afternoon. It left us just enough time to plan and provide a memorable Christmas dinner, consisting of roast guinea fowl with lots of rather unusual local trimmings.

By Boxing Day lunchtime, most of the sore heads had cleared a little from the effects of the vin rosé obtained from the nearby monastery at Thibar. It was great stuff! The weather had also cleared and it was now pleasantly sunny once more. Just for fun, it was decided to hold a Donkey Derby up the main street of Beja. Volunteers were quickly forthcoming. The local population used donkeys for all transport purposes. There were plenty of them around. We tried to borrow them, but there was no way their owners would agree to this, so we had to purchase about 20 of them. A good donkey cost us about 100 francs – 5 shillings was the approximate English equivalent. After all the bargaining, great fun in its own right, there were a few trial rides – and falls – and the race started. The course was the full length of Beja's main street, from the bottom of the town to the finish outside the Officers' Mess at the top of the hill. Some of the animals must have been mules for they refused to go at all. But eventually about ten of them spread out across the road and started up at a steady trot with the rest of the unit shouting encouragement and running alongside. About two thirds of the way up the hill a few of the more sober riders were still mounted and strung neck and neck right across the road. At this moment a military convoy came over the brow of the hill and met the race head on. A jeep carrying a major of the

Provost Corps led the convoy and we could see the red caps of Military Police in almost every vehicle as they pulled up sharply behind the halted jeep. The major's face was like a ripe plum – the colour of his own hat – then praise be, he laughed!

Our CO, ever the diplomat, watching from the Mess, hastily sent a messenger to invite the major to join him in a Christmas drink. The convoy drew up at the side of the road while drivers and passengers took turns to sample our hospitality. But what of the Donkey Race? Well, it was never really finished and arguments were continuing months later as to who was leading when the convoy arrived. As for the planned push that should have taken place on Christmas Day, that seemed to be forgotten too. But after some keep-fit route marches in the Beja area, we were on the move once more, this time a little further south to the open country around El Aroussa and Bou Arada.

On these day-long marches we carried our own food and water and it was convenient when the good old Army stand-by of bully beef was part of the ration, to issue one tin to two men. The tins were the usual Fray Bentos shape, rectangular with slightly sloping sides, opened with a key that wound a thin strip of metal off all around the four sides. Quartermaster Sergeant Pruden and Staff Sergeant Anderson planned to share one tin, which the QMS carried on the march. Around midday, our party halted in an old quarry and some chose to seek the shade amongst the rocks, while others sat in the sun along the lip of the quarry face. QMS Pruden sat on the lip, opened the tin and ladled his half into a pannikin before tossing the half-empty tin to S/Sgt Anderson, who was seeking shade in the quarry below. Jock Anderson looked up to catch the tin straight into the sun, lost sight of it and the sharp freshly opened edge struck him on the nose immediately above his nostrils. It inflicted an awful cut and the end of his nose flopped down onto his upper lip. A first-aid dressing was immediately applied and the copious bleeding controlled. Meanwhile someone ran back to the main road and got a vehicle to come and take S/Sgt Anderson to a field ambulance that was operating quite close to us in Beja, only to find that they were packing and in the process of moving out. However they sutured the end of the nose back in place. But luck was still running against Jock Anderson. All the fine suture material had been packed and had gone on and his nose finished up re-attached by a row of twelve or more rather coarse stitches using something like carpet thread. When it healed it left an unsightly scar. Of course it silenced the pipes for a while – much to the delight of certain members of the unit, but the tale went round that QMS Pruden had launched the bully beef tin with an incredibly accurate aim so that he could become 'the most handsome man in the Unit'. For Jock Anderson, up to the time of his misfortune, could well have challenged him for that title.

It is truly an ill-wind that blows no one any good, for just over twelve months later Jock was back in his native Scotland being stood many a drink by his friends on account of his 'war wound'!

Our move to El Aroussa was without incident, although booby traps and landmines caused a small number of casualties in other troops. It was an area well away from any towns and each night the velvet darkness accentuated the magnificent clarity of the stars. Strangely, it seemed that the vehicles that went back to collect our rations and water from the Algerian border region were at greater risk than those at the front. Our water trucks in particular were sitting shots for patrols or aircraft. In fact the first fatality suffered by 16 PFA was the loss of Corporal Abercrombie on a rations and water collecting journey.

The small settlement of Bou Arada was just a few miles along the road to Tunis and there appeared to be rather an air of mystery about the place. Bou Arada was a sort of no-mans land. There had been fierce fighting in this area involving the parachute brigade and both German and British patrols seemed to enter it frequently. But there was little sign of either side attempting to occupy and hold it at this time. Near a crossroads in this area was a school, which for some reason had a number of showers attached to the main building. An Army Hygiene Unit quickly rigged up a system of heating this water and we were delighted to be able to go along for the occasional hot shower. There appeared to be some evidence that German forces also visited this place for the same purposes. But neither side ever damaged it or set booby-traps and rightly or wrongly, we came to the firm conclusion that the Allies used it

Mondays, Wednesdays and Fridays, while the Germans had it on Tuesdays, Thursdays and Saturdays!

Amongst our office stores and responsibilities were the Tunisian maps, flat unfolded sheets that measured about 3 feet by 4 feet. These were in such large numbers that they made a stack well over a foot in depth. Many of them were of limited use as maps for they would show a small area of Tunisia accurately mapped in detail, with large areas of the rest of the sheet being simply white paper, overprinted with the grid and the words: 'Insufficient Information'. But if they were not used as maps, they were handy as insulation. We would spread our groundsheets out, arrange a four or five inch layer of maps between the rubber sheet and our sleeping bags and sleep much warmer as a result. The days were warm, even hot at times and the ground dusty. But every night the intense cold produced a ground sweat that made the surface treacherously slippery and the 'stand-to' at first light each morning was an icy agony, not relieved until the sun warmed and dried the chilly ground.

Winter is the wet season in Tunisia and the January we spent there was no exception. One rather wet showery day, enemy activity had greatly increased in our immediate area and a withdrawal was in progress. We had virtually no transport and it was a case of marching out and this we did about mid afternoon. As darkness overtook us it began to rain much more heavily and for the next four hours or so it rained incessantly and we were soaked through. Around 10 or 11pm, the CO informed us that it was now felt safe to rest for the night, tents would be issued (these were 'pup' tents, accommodating two men in each) and we would camp on the hillside adjacent to the road. No lights were to be used and we were urged to be as quiet as possible. Everything and everybody was soaking wet and no one bothered to erect a tent as far as I know. In groups of four, we spread one tent flat on the ground, laid another over the top of it and all four of us got in between the wet canvas in all our soaking clothing. The Quartermaster, at the CO's request, issued a rum ration, brought round to us as we lay in little colonies of four under our horizontal tents! In the morning the rain had passed, the hillside steamed in sunshine and we fell in once more to march off to a more permanent camp, awaiting the colds and pneumonia that seemed almost inevitable. Only one man reported sick – something had stung him in the night. The question is – was it our fitness that protected us? Or was it that timely issue of rum?

Shortly after this we were withdrawn from the forward area and conveyed by road transport to Souk el Arba, where, after a lengthy wait, we were to be reunited once more with our "8 Horses, 40 men" cattle trucks for the return journey to our base near Algiers. Our wait in Souk el Arba, lying stretched out in the early spring sunshine, was enlivened by the entertainment provided by a stork. There were three or four untidy piles of sticks on the high points of a number of buildings around the station yard. On each of these stork nests sat a stork, presumably the female of the species. There was definitely one male stork and I am sure that I have read somewhere that the stork mates for life. I am even more certain that this particular stork had not read that book. He was certainly mating for life – dear life! – flying at intervals to each of the three nests, where, apparently revelling in the cheers and ribald encouragement from the troops watching avidly from below, he did his best to ensure the future of the entire stork species.

Our return railway journey was decidedly quicker than our outward one. This time we had British Royal Engineers as drivers and firemen on the locomotive, for it seemed that there had been strong feeling amongst some of the Algerian rail drivers who were dead set against the Allied cause. They had not only been driving the trains slower than necessary, but had also rather neatly created hold-ups by lengthy and unnecessary shunting operations across level crossings on important roads. A number of Allied convoys had been delayed in this manner before the ploy was discovered. Now the locomotives looked better maintained and we made good time back to our main base in Boufarik. However there was no improvement in the comfort of the wagons with their 'square wheels'.

Once back in Boufarik, we were barely given time to wash and press our uniforms ready for a day or a night out in Algiers before being told that we were needed back at the front in Tunisia. But this time we were not to travel by rail for the urgency was real and the Navy was standing by in Algiers to convey us to the port of Bone by destroyer.

Taken in trucks to the dockside in Algiers, we boarded our waiting destroyers. Some of us were on HMS Wheaton, others on HMS Wilton and we were amazed at our first sight of these vessels, for they were old-fashioned four-funnelled ex-American ships that had been 'traded' for one of the British West Indies islands. After about 48 hours on the Wheaton I can say with absolute certainty that Britain was robbed!

Of course, they were not intended as troop transports and our grossly overcrowded conditions could not be helped. But the small round hatches and vertical steel ladders between decks were extremely testing for the army boots of obvious landlubbers, particularly if you happened to be in a hurry to get up on deck. I know, because immediately after the main course of quite a good meal served to us in the Petty Officers' Mess, I had to make a very hurried ascent of such a ladder to get to the ship's side on a matter of extreme urgency. There was a lot of laughter in the mess as I left, but I was not the only one to have to exit hurriedly – just the first! Nevertheless, to the surprise of the sailors and my mates, I returned and ate the sweet course – and kept it down – well, until next morning anyway.

The following afternoon I was to get very wet in circumstances that were quite a shock to me. The two destroyers were heading east along the North Africa coast in what I thought was a medium swell, but which the Navy men aboard spoke of as a 'calm'. Feeling decidedly fragile, I was dozing in the afternoon sun on the aft deck – the very low part of the destroyer at the stern end for other landlubbers – when the look-outs on both boats spotted something shining in the water about a mile away on our port bow. Immediately they accelerated and swung towards the sighting. As they did so the surge of acceleration pushed the stern of the vessel about a couple of feet lower than her normal cruising depth. A wall of water came rushing up at me where I sat. It looked huge, but I suppose it was less than a foot deep, even so it was quite sufficient to wet the lower part of my body very thoroughly as I scrambled for higher 'ground'. Everyone laughed at my partial dunking, but at that moment we were all more concerned with the object that had been sighted. It turned out to be a barrage balloon that had probably broken loose and deflated before coming down in the sea. A pocket of trapped air was keeping it partially afloat and a portion of the silver fabric made a low gleaming dome in the water. A couple of rifle shots quickly put paid to its buoyancy and it slowly sank as we resumed our journey.

Before reaching Bone that evening we had another burst of excitement when an enemy aircraft dived at us from a great height. If I had ever had any doubts previously, that diving aircraft completely convinced me I would much rather be in the army on dry land at such times, rather than all at sea with the Navy in a glorified sardine tin. The apparent utter loneliness of a ship at sea when being attacked from the air, was to me, quite terrifying. On land the attack might be on the camp next door – not necessarily on yours – but at sea there was no next door. YOU and only you were the chosen target. As it happened the aircraft didn't drop anything. It probably had nothing to drop, but if its aim was meant to worry us it did so very well. My relief as I stepped ashore in Bone late that evening was not only because I am a poor sailor.

It was dark as we came ashore and climbed aboard waiting army trucks, but even in the darkness we could appreciate something of the steep nature of the terrain as the trucks whined and wound their way in low gear through the hills. I well remember the cold of that wet winter night in those hills and how at every opportunity we jumped out, stamping our feet and swinging our arms to restore some warmth to our limbs. Our destination, although we did not know it at the time, was the Tamera Valley east of Tabarqa and near Sejenane, some miles north of Beja. The British division already fighting in this area was under very heavy German pressure and was being pushed back and suffering considerable casualties. The 1st Parachute Brigade was sent in to stiffen resistance and halt the withdrawal. In all we were to remain in that role for something like 10 consecutive weeks and during that time we, in the field ambulance, were to deal with an alarming number of casualties. I have often thought that this period was perhaps the 16 PFA's finest hour.

Many of the young soldiers (and some of them were very young indeed) making up this division were from the Lincolnshire and Leicestershire regiments. The last named, 'The Tigers' were my home county regiment. We were horrified to learn from some of their casualties that they did not even know the name of their platoon sergeants. They had been 'collected' from depots after other units had been broken up and had been brought quickly into action without time to get to know and learn to trust their officers and NCO's. Many of these young men were on the verge of cracking up under the strain of a battle that was going badly. Some came through our forward dressing station diagnosed as NYDN ('Not Yet Diagnosed Neurosis').

Our CO devised an unusual plan to deal with these cases and it appeared to work extremely well. In a little valley to the rear of the battle area we established a Rest Camp. It consisted of a single large marquee for our 'patients' and a tent or two for staff. The men, given better food and plenty of rest, wrote letters and read books that we scrounged for them. Their morale improved miraculously, but the smartest move of all was bringing in parachute battalion NCO's just for 24 hours so that they could get to know each other. When they returned to the battle area they acquitted themselves well under the care and guidance of these NCO's. It was all very unofficial of course, but it worked.

Our field ambulance set-up in the Tamera Valley proper was extremely close to the fighting and many of the minor wounded paratroops joked that our forward orderlies and stretcher bearers had been so near that, as they put it "They caught me as I fell!" Casualties were quickly brought down the steep wooded sides of the valley to where our Advanced Dressing Station tents hid beneath the cork oak trees close to the riverbed. Here they received immediate attention from one of our surgical teams before being evacuated quickly to the full size field ambulance that was serving the division. It worked out better for the Parachute Field Ambulance to operate totally as a 'forward unit', providing stretcher-bearers and urgent treatment while the much larger non-parachute field ambulance remained a few miles further back. They provided on-going care and more involved surgery needed before evacuation could be arranged back to a Casualty Clearing Station or a General Hospital. In a way, they became a forward Casualty Clearing Station, able to concentrate all their efforts and manpower in one large tented locality, while we picked up and patched up the wounded for both our Brigade and the Infantry Division.

At times our Dressing Station came under fire, although the German aircraft usually respected the Red Crosses displayed on the ambulances. On one occasion when German mortar fire was harrying some of the troops, mortar bombs landed almost in our midst. Colonel MacEwan ordered us to move the wounded to the shelter offered by the banks of the dry gravelly riverbed some 30 yards away. Typical of the man he was, he set an example by immediately seizing one handle of a stretcher and some of us grabbed hold too and set off, crouching and involuntarily ducking at the crump, crump of exploding mortar shells on the roadside by the Dressing Station.

"It's all right! It's all right! No danger. Nothing to worry about!" our gallant Colonel encouraged us and then stood spellbound like the rest of us, when a large mortar fragment scythed its way between the three or four stretcher parties, its path clearly visible as it sliced off the huge onion-like plants in its deadly journey. The Colonel did have the grace to say, quite quietly, "H'm, not so all right after all! Let's get this man down into the riverbed at the double!"

At quieter times we would conceal an ambulance under one of the nearby trees and as minor wounded came in, treat them and dispatch the ambulance when it had a load. One day, a patient had waited in the ambulance for quite some time. He wasn't urgently in need of further treatment so we delayed departure until further casualties justified the ambulance trip. Strangely none were forthcoming. It was a very quiet afternoon and Sergeant Wetherby went to see if this patient would like a cup of tea. As the sergeant walked towards the tent that served as cookhouse, he gave a cough and fell to the ground. A bullet lodged in the muscles of his chest. We could see it through his open necked shirt and it suddenly popped out! We assumed he had been hit by a spent bullet from the fighting on the hill-side above, slapped a dressing on the wound, gave him a sedative and packed him off in the ambulance alongside the man who was about to get his cup of tea. When Weberly's shirt was removed at the main dressing station, it was obvious that the bullet had not been spent at all, but had struck him in the back and passed through his chest. Afterwards he told me he remembered nothing about that journey but when he came to the man in the next bed was saying: "Hey! Where's my cup of tea?"

Statistics showed that wounds of comparable severity responded better the earlier they were assessed by surgeons (even if eventual treatment was not carried out immediately). In our six weeks or so in the Tamera Valley, we had been working in a situation which almost exactly met these requirements, which was very fortunate for the 600 or so wounded we handled during this time. Our stretcher-bearers had only a short, largely down hill carry to the valley floor. Here our surgical teams could provide immediate highly skilled treatment, and sometimes within minutes of the trauma occurring the patients were evacuated to receive advanced surgical care.

Even with all the hard work and the sadness of burials there were some moments of light relief. Some German prisoners with minor wounds were brought in for treatment. They were surly and barely spoke apart from giving their name, rank and serial number. Then one of them caught sight of the parachute insignia on my arm and said, "Was ist das?"

"Fallschirmjäger (parachutist)," I replied.

"Ja?" His face lit up and he told us he belonged to the Herman Goering Parachute Regiment and having discovered something in common we parted the best of friends. These German parachutists carried a concealed knife in a pocket on the leg, much sought after as a souvenir. One wounded German on a stretcher looked piercingly at my red beret and beckoned me across. As I went up to him to find out what he wanted, he fumbled somewhere down by his knee and I jumped back hurriedly. But his actions were well intentioned. He offered me his knife – handle first! I accepted it as gracefully as I could, for in a strange way I could understand that

116

there was a tenuous link between us. We were both parachutists, both doing the same sort of job. In some ways the only difference was the fact that we served different masters.

The German pressure along this front had broken up the 2nd Battalion at Oudna and the two parachute battalions that made up the bulk of our brigade were badly reduced in number and strength as their weeks in action continued. Unlike a normal infantry force they were not equipped with the heavy machine guns and mortars that were needed in this near-static engagement. They were much better equipped for a quick 'in and out' attack than for a long holding operation. Their heroism in battles around Tamera Valley was at times close to madness. On one occasion a small force of the 1st Battalion were holding the head of the valley where the road from Tunis and Bizerta entered it. They had been reduced in number to little more than 10 men and were being strongly pressed by a force of 20 or 30 German infantry. Unable to hold back the enemy by fire from their foxholes and suffering under pretty accurate mortar fire, they leapt from their cover and charged a force two or three times their size. The sheer surprise and ferocity of their charge pushed the enemy back, but a few days later German tanks penetrated the valley and we were forced into a withdrawal.

At the time of this small fierce engagement at the head of the valley, our dressing station was barely half a mile away from the action and we were well aware of the threat it posed. Always a man of action, Colonel MacEwan mustered the Royal Army Service Corps drivers of our unit (the only men who had rifles) and told them to take up positions amongst the trees "Engage any enemy who comes down the road," were his orders.

Since the bulk of our transport and its personnel were several miles back our 'MacEwan Token Force' mustered only 6 men – and one of them would have to be recalled if we wanted to use the second ambulance. Colonel MacEwan then addressed us and said: "Medical Corps personnel – er – er – put your Red Cross armbands on!"

But it was obvious we had to move and within a couple of days we had withdrawn to the site where our unofficial Rest Camp was established. But even here, a mile or so up a side road that had no exit other than the main Tamera valley road, we were not secure. Soon orders came to pack up and move out as it was very probable that the German force would shortly be in control of the main road.

The office lorry was quickly loaded and we were the first vehicle to start down toward the junction. In heavy rain, on a bend just 100 yards from our camp, we met the Colonel in a Jeep. He told us to pull off the road a little and he would lead us out when the other vehicles were ready. We pulled over and waited for 20 minutes or so by which time the last of the daylight was fading. The Colonel returned with the other few lorries behind his jeep and shouted to us to pull over a little further off the track and then to tack on the back of the convoy. Our driver started his motor, moved over a little and waited as the three or four other trucks followed the jeep down the hill and then he let his clutch in to follow. Nothing happened. The wheels spun slowly, but without grip. He accelerated a little, the wheels spun more rapidly and our back end swung gently sideways off the wet and muddy track and deeper into the ditch. No one spoke but I think all three of us realised instantly that we were in real trouble, for we were well and truly stuck. Another vehicle could easily have towed us out but all the vehicles had gone by now and we were very much on our own.

We made futile attempts to move, but the mud was so soft that we were simply digging deeper trenches for the back wheels. We checked our ration packs and a quick calculation showed that we could live for 60 days before feeling hungry but we fervently hoped our absence from the convoy would be quickly noted and that someone would return and tow us out.

They did not return. Uneasily we took it in turns to try and get some rest while one stood guard – a very alert guard I might add, for we had no real idea of how close the Germans were. At first light a mule squadron of French Colonial troops wound slowly up the track. Even before we asked they told us that the mules were too exhausted to try and pull the truck out of the ditch. No help would be forthcoming from that quarter. However they did tell us that the Germans were on the main road at the junction with the track we were on, so that we couldn't get out that way. We had unloaded stores in an effort to lighten the lorry and I invited the muleteers to help themselves to the rations and they needed no second invitation.

We knew this track petered out at the brow of the hill behind us, but I thought there was a chance that we could drive across what looked like fairly open country, if only we could reach the brow of the hill. With the mud drying rapidly in the sunshine, camouflage netting dug in under the wheels and everything unloaded, there was a chance of getting clear. We were trying to do this when an officer of a Commando unit covering the withdrawal came along and suggested we get a move on as the Germans were near and we could already hear small arms fire. And then our driver disappeared!

George Loveland and I calculated what we could carry and what would have to be left. Long-awaited mail had arrived for the unit the previous day, but there had been no chance to sort or distribute it. That mail, we felt, just had to be carried out with us. Most importantly the Security Box had been left with us; a strong green enamelled box, about 18 inches long, 10" wide and 6" deep. It contained important unit papers, some cash, but of greatest concern was the fact that it contained the Slidex Code and its key, the cypher system then in use by the whole 1st Army. I couldn't know at the time of course, but Army Headquarters had reason to believe that Slidex One had already been compromised and had already swung over to the use of the reserve alternative, Slidex Two, which was also in this box. If that fell into enemy hands, the 1st Army would have no option but to suspend the use of the Slidex code entirely, without any readily available alternative.

So I took the Security Box, George took the sack of incoming mail and very regretfully we had to leave behind many letters written by the lads of the Unit awaiting censorship before dispatch home. We took chocolate bars from ration packs and anything else we thought would sustain us on our journey for we had no idea how far we had to go.

We filled our water bottles and when we were ready to start, I opened the cap of the petrol tank of the lorry, put paper and rubbish around it and pulled the tab on one of the small incendiary devices kept in the Security Box for just such a crisis. The delay incorporated in this device enabled us to be near the brow of the hill before black smoke rose from the vehicle. "We have ignition!" said George quietly.

Shortly after there was a muffled explosion as the petrol tank went up and we set out, knowing there would be little left of value to the Germans. After an hour or so, we halted for a breather and were amused and secretly delighted to see one of our small folding office tables, thrown out when lightening the lorry, sail past – carried on the head of an Arab!

We aimed north and west, for where we were most likely to find other British Army units. Although it was still officially winter, the sun was hot. About three in the afternoon we came to a reasonably wide but shallow river and holding our packs well above the water, waded in. At first, our boots, trousers and webbing anklets kept the water out and for the first three or four steps there was a cool sensation without any feeling of wetness. Then the water penetrated and was cold and delightfully refreshing so that we revelled in this waist deep paddle to the far bank. Once out of the river, we climbed gently and steadily for quite a while before coming over the brow of a low hill.

We could see a railway line in the distance and what appeared to be a small station. There was life and movement around it and hoping that it was friendly life, we aimed for it. About half a mile further on we had to climb a fence to cross an expanse of bare ground. We were being closely watched for we saw the occasional glint of binoculars. I thought I could see the odd red beret, but admitted it was probably wishful thinking. As we neared the station we could see quite clearly that there were paratroops there as well as other army personnel. But to my great surprise we were greeted by Colonel MacEwan himself, delighted to see us of course, but even more delighted to learn that I had the Security Box and contents safely in my possession. He told us of the tremendous worry there had been over Slidex Two. If the code had fallen into enemy hands it would have caused a colossal problem for the Allies.

We casually asked why everyone had watched our progress with such close interest over the last stretch of bare ground.

"Oh" said the Colonel, "it was rumoured that the area had been mined, but we thought it wouldn't help much if we tried to shout and warn you!"

≈≈≈≈≈≈≈≈≈≈≈

Chapter 11
Out from battle

Colonel MacEwan took George and me back to where our unit was now based in his car and I believe he had quite a celebration that night. We also enjoyed our reunion with our mates and they were delighted that we had brought their mail from home. But their joy was short lived when we had to tell them that all those laboriously written letters they had submitted for censorship had gone up in smoke. Our popularity vanished almost as quickly as their letters had!

About this time we were moved back to an area nearer Tabarqa and the coast. This was a rest camp for after ten weeks of continuous fighting, the remnants of the Brigade were exceedingly weary to say the least. The site was in a locality where tortoises were common and people adopted them as pets. It was not uncommon to see painted tortoises; white, with a Red Cross on top and in tiny letters round the rim: 'Protected under the Geneva Convention'. Others had neatly executed number plates with War Department numbers thereon – and 'Please Pass. Running In!'

During this rest period we spent much of our free time on one of the beaches near Tabarqa. Swimming in March was exhilarating and a run on the silver-white sands in the spring sunshine compensated for the winter 'nip' that was still present in the sea.

The Allied forces were now growing considerably in strength. Better weather was making more airfields available and the 8th Army had swept around the Gulf of Gabes and was pushing the German forces back on Tunis and Bizerta. We were to be involved in the push through Sejanane to Bizerta and one section of the Field Ambulance would provide medical services for a unit of the French Colonial forces known as the Goums. They were beautifully black, shorter and thicker-set than the tall Senegalese and they were pleased and proud to have our medical unit serving with them. The various units moved quietly into position for launching their attack. Our medical tent was set up as an Advanced Dressing Station, with the Goums helping us in every possible way. The attack was to start before dawn and we were surprised when around midnight,

Goum soldiers came to our tent, removed their army issue boots and socks and lined them up neatly by the tent door. They left silently, grinning and excited, to mount a surprise attack under cover of darkness. There were few casualties among them, but they were glad we were there. We were equally grateful that they did not offer us any battle souvenirs – for it was rumoured that one of their fascinating but less endearing habits was collecting the ears of their enemies!

The battles for Bizerta and Tunis were soon over with the Germans evacuating as best they could, but our side took numerous prisoners. After the battle we drove very briefly into Bizerta, passing a local airfield where an absolute graveyard of bombed, crashed and sabotaged aircraft had been bulldozed into a mound hundreds of yards in length. In Bizerta, wrecked areas in the dock yards still smoking were evidence of the German withdrawal, but at this time we saw nothing of Tunis, being almost immediately on our way back to Boufarik, our base near Algiers. Our stay there was short, whisked away again to a tented camp close to the Moroccan/Algerian border. This was to be our home for some hot dusty weeks before returning to Tunisia once more.

The return to base near Algiers was uneventful, but you couldn't have said the same of the first few days and nights. Everyone was anxious to celebrate the victory in Tunisia and our return to the fleshpots of Algiers. We were all eager to get into the café-bars and make up for the weeks when the NAAFI ration of one bottle of beer per man had failed to materialise. In fact there had been a number of times when neither beer nor cigarettes were forthcoming. So the headlong rush to the bar counter could be easily understood and it was our small unit that was largely responsible for producing more casualties in the first 48 hours back in civilisation than months of battle had managed to do.

In action, we had been very fortunate, only two killed and a small number wounded and of these, some were relatively minor cases. But on the debit side, the whole of No. 2 Section had been lost at Oudna or Depienne in the battle of Pont du Fahs. Most of them were taken prisoner but we had no information as to their fate.

The first night of leave resulted in a host of injuries, some minor, some serious. There were black eyes, cut hands, sprains and broken fingers, all probably resulting from bar room fights. More seriously, one of our drivers had a broken jaw and worst of all, Corporal Paddy Dwyer lost a leg in a motorcycle accident. His injury was a real tragedy, for he had been engaged in a good Samaritan deed, taking the man with an injured jaw to hospital. Paddy was a delightful fellow with a fine physique. He had been the Northern Ireland services middleweight boxing champion and we would miss him badly. Another poor unfortunate was shot through the scrotum by a bullet ricocheting from a cobblestone pavement. Friendly fire, as a soldier of our own Brigade fired the ricocheting shot from a pistol. He had been celebrating rather too well and fancied himself as a cowboy!

When we left to move westwards and set up under canvas again, it was on the bare slopes of a hillside just south of the town of Mascara. Conditions were rough. It was very hot, very dusty and aircraft taking off from the airstrip at the base of the hill produced willie-willies, fiercely spinning columns of wind and dust that swept through our tents, picking up anything that was not firmly held down and whisking it away. Water was in short supply. Two of us were forced to share a 50-cigarette tin full of hot water for shaving and the number of mugs of tea available each day was severely curtailed.

There was one mild blessing. The nearby airstrip was an American base and we were living on American Army rations that included large tins of fruit juice. We loved the orange juice and pineapple, but found the apple juice sweet and rather tasteless. We didn't get a juice issue every day, but welcomed it in no uncertain terms when it was on offer. Imagine how we felt a few weeks later when we were required to make a hurried move and found that our cook had buried dozens of large tins of tomato juice and passion fruit juice under the sand of the cook-tent floor. His explanation, which barely saved him from a lynching, "I didn't fancy either of those juices!" So he didn't issue them.

To give the men a break from the discomfort, a Rest and Recreation Camp was created on the Mediterranean coast near

124

Mostaganem. It was extremely simple. A pup-tent, your bed roll and mosquito net and a cook (fortunately not the juice secretor) were just about the total amenities. But compensation in the form of a beautiful little cove, with a diving raft anchored about 20 yards offshore and the incredible clarity of the warm water, made the camp an absolute heaven. A few days there, with no parades, no duties, swimming whenever we felt like it, enjoying local grapes and watermelons and the occasional trip into the lively town of Mostaganem, were just what the doctor ordered. To top it off, the weather was superb. We went there in small groups, taking it in turn to be released from duties in the main camp and we all loved every moment of it.

Mascara was not far away from Sidi bel Abbes, one of the most famous bases of the French Foreign Legion. Our Regimental Sergeant Major got permission to organise a trip for us, in conjunction with members of the 3rd Parachute Battalion. The place was fascinating. Dazzling white barrack buildings dominated the small town with its innumerable cafés and bars serving drinks at outdoor tables. On one occasion we found ourselves sharing a table with French Foreign legionnaires and conversing as best we could with them. Over muscat, or whatever else they fancied, we talked to men from France, Finland, Spain and Germany. At first it felt a little strange to be buying a drink for a German soldier, but anything was possible in that bizarre spot. It was very hot indeed and to escape the worst of it, a few of us went to a local cinema. The film – in French – was beyond most of us, but the delightfully clean, cool interior more than made up for that. Refreshed, we re-emerged into the harsh sunlight, found somewhere to have a meal and continued to enjoy the exotic atmosphere.

Just at sunset, a nasty incident threatened to ruin the day and severely strain relationships between the 1st Parachute Brigade and the American 1st Cavalry Regiment. These Americans were stationed in the town and obviously from the 'bull and whitewash' surrounding their headquarters they were very much a spit and polish unit. Their military band played in the square during the afternoon and just before the flag lowering ceremony of Retreat at sunset, they played the National Anthems of the Allies. A rather inebriated paratrooper stood at wobbly attention for the Marseillaise and for God Save the King – but staggered off when the Stars and Stripes was played. He probably didn't recognise it. He had not gone far when a white helmeted, white gaitered American MP shouted at him: "Stand still!" and hit him with his truncheon. In no time at all, three other paratroopers were wiping their boots on this military policeman, by then horizontal in the gutter.

American reinforcements rushed in and jeep loads of military policemen struggled to restrain the milling paratroops, three of whom were eventually seized and taken to the local guardroom in the gaol. Within moments, thirty or so angry red beret soldiers were threatening to storm the building to recover their mates, but the American military police responded by placing a line of guards, guns at the ready, across the front of the guard room.

"Back to the trucks! Get your weapons!" a hot headed paratrooper shouted and a few ran off to do just that. But at that moment our RSM came on the scene and tried to restore order. He told the American lieutenant that if he would keep his men out of the way, he would enlist some of us (who were completely sober) to get the angry paratroopers back in their trucks and out of town. The plan was for the three men held in the guardroom to be released immediately and we would take them straight back to the trucks. While the RSM was busy placating the American officer, a lonely GI, completely unaware of all the trouble and tension, came strolling out of a side street and tagged on to the back of the mob besieging the guardroom. Before he had time to ask what was happening, he was knocked out cold by a paratrooper from the rear. Whereupon our RSM apologised profusely, the American lieutenant tactfully looked the other way and we got everyone back on the trucks and drove rapidly out of the town. The upshot was that there were no more trips to Sidi bel Abbes for any of us. Next day it was officially placed out of bounds to all Airborne forces personnel.

A few weeks later we were once more on the move, back to Tunisia. This time we were to fly in the Dakota C47 aircraft that were regularly using the airstrip immediately below our tents. It was a fascinating flight. We took off early in the morning, before the sun had time to heat everything up. It remained cool for the whole flight largely because our aircraft had no door – or at least, if it had originally had one, it had been removed. We flew virtually the length of Algeria and Tunisia at very little over 5,000 feet, just high enough to clear the tops of the foothills of the Atlas Mountains. We had a Michelin guide to North Africa, complete with town plans and with the pilot's assistance were easily able to identify several of the towns, including Kairouan, before landing on the airstrip at Sfax. Jumping out of the plane the heat hit us, like stepping into an oven.

Soon lorries arrived to convey us north to the town of Sousse and near there we were deposited in a tented camp in one corner of a huge olive grove. This was to be our home for some considerable time and when most of us finally left it, it was to carry out the airborne assault on the Ponte Primosole Bridge north of Syracuse in Sicily.

The time spent in that camp passed slowly. It lacked amenities, it was hot, very dry and little worthwhile lighting was available to brighten the long hours of darkness. There was no electricity and only a limited number of pressure paraffin (Tilley) lamps to share. I was rather fortunate. I 'lived' in the office tent ('living', in this sense meant unrolling my sleeping bag on the sand of the office floor at bedtime) and most nights could enjoy the luxury of a Tilley lamp. Not every night by any means. Some nights we had to manage with hurricane lamps or our homemade night-lights; a string wick immersed in whatever oil or grease we could scrounge.

Leave was permitted in small groups on the outskirts of Tunis. The recreation camp was rather like the Mostaganem one; a simple pup-tent, mosquito net, sleeping bag and a duty cook (a man we hardly ever troubled, electing to eat out whenever possible). This camp was right on the beachfront, close to the Sultan of Tunis's palace, with a name sounding something like 'Hammenet Sousse'. We spent our days exploring Tunis or the nearby ruins of the ancient city of Carthage, famous for its associations with Hannibal and his elephants and his attempt to capture Rome. Not to mention the romance of Antony and Cleopatra. We quite often spent the evenings swimming in starlit darkness in warm water that produced the most incredible phosphorescence as we dived. All too soon we were back in those stifling hot tents in the olive grove, preparing for the Sicily invasion.

Leading up to this event, Colonel MacEwan spent much of his time at Brigade and Divisional Headquarters and it fell to Major Wheatley, who was our acting CO, to prepare the Operation Order for our unit in the forthcoming action. He dictated the details to me and I typed the orders out on stencils and read them to him as we checked them. For security reasons no one else was involved or aware of the forthcoming events. The actual date had not yet been decided upon and all dates were in the form of 'D-day', 'D+1' etc. For further security, Major Wheatley told me not to run the copies of the stencils off until he said so and in the meantime, lock them in the security box, chain this to the very solid tent pole – and move my bed in alongside it! All of which I duly did and it was 8 days later that he told me to roll off exactly 20 copies and carefully burn any sheets spoiled in the process. I unlocked the security box to remove the stencils, made on old-fashioned wax impregnated sheets. To my horror I found that the heat in the tent had melted them into a solid block! They were useless and we had no spares available!

For the rest of that day I typed furiously, 3 carbon copies at a time, until the required 20 copies were completed. Major Wheatley signed each batch as I finished it and the first copies off the rank went off by dispatch rider to Brigade HQ and the battalions taking part. Our own medical officers were the last to receive theirs and they got them barely 24 hours before we took off. But take off we did and the Sicily Operation was under way.

≈≈≈≈≈≈≈≈≈≈≈

Chapter 12
Ponte Primosole

About 4pm the wind had dropped, but the Tunisian sun on this July afternoon was still scorching the arid countryside. The steel sides of the Army lorry were unbearably hot to the touch and we were grateful when it bumped to a halt beside our plane and we could hop out into the shade of the huge wing. Number 91. That was us. Gone were all the flashy signs and names that had distinguished these planes a few days ago. Now the sun glared down upon clean, trim planes, dull grey in their camouflage paint, the bold white numeral toward the rear of each fuselage their only relieving feature. Obviously this was a business trip we were embarking upon.

We sweated profusely as we struggled to fit our parachutes over the seemingly endless equipment we had to wear and carry. Windproof smocks, small packs that didn't seem so small now, Bren pouches packed with bandages and drugs, entrenching tool, water bottles and inflatable life jacket – and if you please, the over-smock to top the lot. Then having got so far, there remained only the task of worming one's way into the parachute harness, adjusting the straps here and there, until a happy medium of security and near-comfort was obtained. At last when all this was on our jumpmaster, Captain Lipmann-Kessel, passed along the line of laden men, checking this, checking that, content only when he had hit the quick-release box a sharp blow – just to check it wouldn't open when it shouldn't!

This done and the jumpmaster satisfied, we stripped off our kit and left it in large heaps close by the silent aircraft. Then, lighter by many pounds, we jumped back on our lorry to be taken to a place where our cooks had prepared a meal for us. It was a little cooler now and soon we were getting stuck into bully beef, potatoes, cabbage and carrots, to be followed pretty rapidly by a good pudding (one that Mother might or might not have been proud of). Then tea – lashings of it, replacing the perspiration lost in our exertions and stocking up on liquid in anticipation that there might well be little to drink – over there. Although most men carried two water bottles, one was earmarked 'For Wounded Only'. It was wise to drink plentifully while it was still possible.

We wandered back to Aircraft 91, lazing around the plane while the containers of our major equipment were fixed, like bombs, beneath the wings. Our crew chief knew his stuff. Containers were fixed and release mechanisms tested in what seemed little more than minutes.

Hidden in a miniature dust storm a bouncing jeep delivered our pilot, co-pilot and navigator and with their arrival the tempo quickened. "Take off at 21.30 hours!" Half an hour earlier than expected. "Come on! Get a move on!" Bag and baggage, we climbed aboard.

"Enough stuff for an Army!" murmured someone.

"Thank heavens we don't have to wear all our gear for the first hour of flight." Another muffled comment......

All aboard and closed up. A whirr and a roar as the starter stirs the silent engines into life. A pulsing throb as first the port and then the starboard motor roars and the whole plane quivers with unleashed power. Dry lips are furtively licked, for tonight will be the first time for some of us to be dropped into enemy territory.

Comparative quiet follows as the pilot throttles back and allows the engines to warm up gently. Then almost imperceptibly, brakes off, we roll slowly forward, bumping a little over the rough ground to the side of the runway, there to await our turn in line with many, many other aircraft. We're turning and excitement mounts as the nose points up wind and the roar of the motors increases dramatically. We're off!

Are we – hell! A vicious bumping from the tail that was slewing sharply from side to side signals that all is not well with No. 91. The motors are cut and we roll off the runway and come to a stop. Even as we do so, a lorry at the head of a plume of dust races towards us and pulls up alongside the plane. Some mechanics tumble out, dropping a spare rear wheel out of their truck as they do so and disappear under the tail. So that was it. The rear tyre burst. But that wasn't going to stop us. As the last man jumps out of the doorway, a powerful jack raises the tail and mechanics rapidly unbolt the damaged wheel and replace it. Less than 10 minutes later, we are back on board with 91 roaring her war song and this time we are airborne.

Airborne, only a few hundred feet up, roads, huts, a few houses are laid out below, a land of long shadows in the last minutes of the setting sun. There, to our right, is the Roman amphitheatre of El Djem, losing none of its grandeur through lack of stature as we look down upon it.

Soon the sea is below us, an incredibly flat calm sea. We watch our shadows chase over it, ever further and further to the east, until the sinking sun robs us of light. Sunset and the rapid onset of darkness is the signal for lowering the blinds over the neat little windows.

Then all too soon it is once again into all our gear – no mean feat to don it all in the limited space – and once more jumpmaster Captain Lipmann-Kessel passes along the crowded plane to check each man's harness. From then on we sit, getting hotter and hotter, watching an opposite number in the dim light of the small blue globes as he sits, tense, jaws working hard on consoling chewing gum.

"Hook-up!" Here it comes – but what's another jump anyway? It's what's waiting down below that matters….

The crew chief brushes past us down the aircraft, turns out even the blue lights and in the sudden darkness fumbles with the catches of the door. Door off – and some of us catch a glitter of the sea. Much closer than I had thought – we are very low – the water silvered by the light of a low moon.

"Stand up!" We hang on straps as in a crowded bus, swaying as we stand – and wait.

Five minutes, ten, fifteen? A lifetime? Through the now empty doorway I glimpse an edge of land and moonlit water. A finger of searchlight gropes for us and touches our tail. Even as it does so, tracers flash along its path and sputter through the floor of our aircraft. Vainly in the wildly yawing plane, we try to stand to attention, hoping that our boot soles will protect our vital parts should more bullets come our way.

More searchlights, more flak, it can be felt as well as heard as it bangs and slaps above us. Funny how detached it all seems. Just as though it isn't really happening at all, a disturbingly realistic dream.

It's Green! "Go! Go! Go! 1, 2, 3, 4, 5, 6, …7…" and as my turn comes, I console myself that 7 really is my lucky number. Down, down and then the reassuring tug on the shoulders as the canopy fills its silken lungs. Alone, completely alone, in a suddenly silent world – and too high – much too high for comfort with searchlights and machine guns looking for us!

There is a way of getting down a little quicker. Pull the rigging lines in a bit. That's better – near enough now perhaps – let go of the lines! A sudden flop as the canopy expands once more; a slight jerk as my descent is slowed. Here comes the ground – I think. It's hard to be certain in the darkness, but I release my harness and hold on hard to the lift webs by my shoulders, my knees pressed tight together, and elbows in of course! Down! A smothered ouch! as my buttock brushes hard against something a few feet from the ground. But I am down – safely down – and must stay right down, till I know the score – and for God's sake drag your chute off that anti-glider wire! Do you want everyone to see it?

Someone coming? Should be one of us – SHOULD be – take no chances. Challenge – hoarse whisper, "Desert Rats!" and the soft reply, "Kill Italians!" It is some of the others. Swiftly we link up to search the darkness for our containers of surgical equipment.

Then for the first time since "Stand-up!" had echoed down the plane, thoughts become words, whispered words for the enemy may be very close, as orders are passed around. "Take this -" "Give me a lift -" "Bring the trolley over here -" as we gather together near a small stack of straw.

Minutes pass slowly as we wait for our surgeon. Sounds flood in, the persistent whine of mosquitoes, the distant thrump of bombs on Catania airfield, the sharp crack of a rifle, the vicious chatter of automatic weapons, as somewhere nearby in the darkness, our 2nd Battalion moves toward their objective, the bridge over the River Simeto – the Ponte Primosole.

Out of the darkness, RSM Brock joins us. He tells us something that we had already guessed – not all of us had made it down. Our surgeon, Captain Kessel and three operating room assistants are unaccounted for. We have already found all the containers of our surgical equipment. RSM Brock then informed us that we had been dropped some four or five miles from our objective and that it lay due east......

We moved off in that direction, very heavily laden with equipment and three men short in the carrying teams. Silently cursing every one of the legions of irrigation ditches that crossed our path, we tried desperately to refrain from slapping at the infuriating mosquitoes that plagued us. At times our route had to be slightly north or south to avoid hazards, but we were always aiming for the east.

Sweating and straining in that sweltering night, we kept on. We skirted fires burning in the long stubble and gave suspiciously quiet farms a wide berth and gratefully snatched a few moments rest whenever a flare split the darkness around us and made us dive for shelter. On and on we plodded, oblivious of the odd scratch from barbed wire and the prickle of thorns, yet strangely conscious of the haunting smell of the wild sage that lay withering in the stubble. The vicious mosquitoes seemed the most immediate threat. They were pestilential! We had been provided with anti-mosquito cream, but soon decided that you had to apply it directly to the pests as they flew past for it to have any real effect.

Each time we fell flat for a bursting flare, we were a little slower to rise, slower to shoulder the packs, slower to cross the obstacles. About 4 am we reached the road leading past the farm we were making for. Captain Ridler and RSM Brock went ahead to check that it was safe to approach, leaving me in charge of our small party. We were moving much more quickly and easily now on a surfaced road.

Just before reaching the lane that wound its way to the farmhouse according to our map, we heard a vehicle approaching from the north. The distinctive clatter told us it was a tracked vehicle – and we knew that we hadn't brought any of those by glider! Hurriedly dragging our trolleys into the ditch, we lay by them, very still and silent in the deep shadow of a hedge. A German halftrack lorry rumbled by. In it, facing each other sat a number of soldiers holding their weapons silhouetted against the eastern sky. A small infantry support gun was towed behind their vehicle. They passed by and minutes later, well before we reached the turnoff for the farmhouse, there was an explosion and a short burst of fire. This told us that the lorry had been seen and dealt with, well before it could reach the bridge.

The farm looked deserted, but it was not. It came as a bit of a shock that it was the temporary headquarters of an Italian detachment, but, equally, how were they to know that our total armament consisted of a Sten gun and a few pistols? Fortunately, they took no chances and surrendered quickly; seemingly glad to be out of a war for which they now had little enthusiasm. Three of them slipped down off the roof in response to a shouted "Venite qui!"

Soon before the sun rose and they were hard at work with us, cleaning out the stables and cowsheds ready to receive the wounded. The smell of the carbolic solution we sloshed around was almost overpowering.

Around 6am the first casualties arrived. The earliest had not sustained serious life threatening wounds and they were soon dressed and settled as comfortably as they could be on the straw covered floors. Some of the Battalion men made their way back to the bridge as soon as their wounds were dressed, for they were well aware how very few of them there were to hold it. But now, in full daylight, the tempo of the battle was increasing as attacker and defender sorted their positions out.

By 8am our operating theatre, the kitchen and scullery of the farmhouse, was really busy, the numbers of patients growing as stretcher bearers from the RAPs and our sections, brought in the more severely wounded. We missed the surgeon, Captain Kessel, who we had not seen since we left the aircraft, but our stick had retrieved all our Surgical Team equipment. The other surgical team, under Major Longland, jumping from another aircraft, had lost much of theirs, so that the equipment we had so laboriously brought to the farm was to prove invaluable. Major Longland quickly became grossly overworked. We did our best to assess the urgency of the new cases as they arrived. But often we had to rely on a rubber-aproned surgeon coming out of the kitchen (sorry – operating theatre) in between patients, to confirm or alter our selections of the most urgent cases to be next for surgery.

Our small staff was desperately busy cleaning, dressing and giving pain killing injections and sulphanilamide tablets. We were almost in a flap – and it was slowly getting worse. Quite early that morning a dispatch rider from Brigade HQ came in with a request for information on the number of casualties we had received. I took the opportunity of asking him to pass on a message to Major Wheatley, our Officer Commanding at this time, should he see him at Brigade HQ. I knew that Major Wheatley had jumped with the Brigade staff. That dispatch rider did wonderfully well. He must have gone to a lot of trouble to find Major Wheatley and pass on my message which was that the Field Ambulance MDS was set up in the farmhouse and that we had most of two surgical teams present, but only one surgeon. Major Wheatley at once realised the problems we would be experiencing and made his way to the farm.

It was not long before he arrived and we were rushing about a bit, no panic, but not as calm and efficient as we should have been. I will never forget his arrival. He walked in quite unexpectedly, took off his battle dress blouse and hung it over the back of the folding wooden chair by the farm door. Then quite quietly, he said: "All right! All right! Settle down – I'm in charge now!" As if by magic things did calm down. Of course the presence of another experienced surgeon, able to assess a patient's needs immediately on arrival, made all the difference, as did his ability to relieve Major Longland in the theatre about half an hour later. But I still believe his calm unruffled leadership had as much to do with the orderly running of that dressing station as did his undoubted medical and surgical skills.

Work continued unabated. Already we had nearly one hundred casualties on our hands and many of them required continued care throughout the afternoon. There was one man I'll never forget – a glider pilot with shocking abrasions of both legs. We had immobilised him in two Thomas splints to try and give him some relief from the pain he experienced on any movement. These were the days before antibiotics and every few hours one of us would have to raise his head and shoulders slightly to administer four sulphanilamide tablets and a drink of water. Throughout the day, lying in straw on that hard stone floor, there was no hint of complaint from him. Unfortunately with the lapse of time, I have forgotten his name. But I remembered it long enough to ensure that before leaving Sicily I made inquiries as to how he had fared and was given encouraging news. He had stood up to the rough journey back to base hospital very well indeed.

By about 5pm or was it later? the sound of small arms fire had virtually ceased. Away to the south we could hear the rumble of heavy guns as the advancing 8th Army punched its way up the east coast of Sicily. Now that it had gone quiet around us, we assumed that the 1st Para Brigade must have succeeded in their task of seizing the Ponte Primosole bridge and that it would be more or less intact when the tanks and transport of the main army rolled north.

The sun had just gone off the crudely walled little garden as I walked into it from the farmhouse. The garden lay behind and a little below the farm buildings. Inside, our weary surgical teams were cleaning up after the last of the patients. They were lying in the cowsheds and outbuildings that still reeked of carbolic. We had made them as comfortable as possible on what little straw we could find around the place. The German and Italian wounded outnumbered the British patients, partly due to the fact that many of our Paras insisted on returning to their units after having their wounds dressed. A wisp of smoke curled up from the small fire in the garden and a large pan 'borrowed' from the farmhouse steamed gently above it. Geordie Hodgson, his torn trouser leg revealing a bandage just below his right knee, stooped over the fire, thrusting a dry stick into the glowing embers to speed the boiling of the freshly refilled pan. Our plane had been hit several times as we were standing waiting to jump and Geordie had received a flesh wound in the leg. He bore it well on our hard five mile slog from the dropping zone to the farm, pulling his weight in spite of it.

"Tea, Serg?" Geordie offered me a mess tin three parts full of the strange grey liquid that always resulted from the army issue.

"Thanks, Geordie," I replied, tactfully choosing to ignore the smoke grimed hands that held out the mess tin beneath the equally smoke grimed face. "How are your friends?" This last inquiry related to the one German and the thirty odd Italian soldiers also occupying the garden. They were prisoners and since our fighting men could not be spared to guard them, they had been passed over to us, the medics, to keep an eye on. Some of them had been with us nearly all the long hot day. The German made his way up to the farmhouse from the garden and asked if he could help with the German wounded and for a while he did that. Then, when no more of his countrymen were arriving, he had attached himself to Geordie and the fire in the garden and helped produce boiling water for the rest of the day. He was a short, sturdy man, showing little reaction when mortar bombs landed nearby. Now, he glanced up from where he was squatting by the fire, as I sipped the scalding tea from the edge of the mess tin and with a nod and half a smile he acknowledged my presence. I had little doubt that he found rather more in common with his British enemies than he did with his Italian fellow prisoners.

Drinking the tea I suddenly realised how tired I was and then remembered that it was now 36 hours since I crawled out of my tent beneath the olive groves in Tunisia. In those 36 hours, we had flown across the Mediterranean, parachuted onto the plains of Catania in eastern Sicily and trudged hard for some hours in the hot humid darkness carrying the surgical team equipment to this farmhouse. We had swept and dug out the litter in the cowsheds, scrubbed them as well as we could with carbolic and then waited for the wounded to arrive. Once they started coming in, in the early morning, we had helped receive and treat well over 100 men. It had been a long day – and for some of us it was not yet over.

≈≈≈≈≈≈≈≈≈≈≈

Chapter 13

Sicilian exit

A few minutes before I had gone down into the garden for my tea break, Major Wheatley told me to take half an hour's break and rest as much as I could. I had thought that this was to be a short break before I was required for night shift and I was a little surprised to find that George Loveland had received the same instructions. But a much bigger surprise was in store.

The OC called eight of us together and an oddly assorted bunch we were. CSM Rowe and Corporal Power, both of the Service Corps; the United Board (Methodist) Padre, RSM Brock, myself, Corporal Loveland and three other RAMC personnel. He told us to get our kit, for we were moving out. By next morning, he had heard from the brigade commander that the main German forces retreating from the south would pass through our area. While the Brigadier believed that the Paras could defend and hold the bridge itself, their handful of men could not protect our farm location as well. Major Wheatley, Major Longland and Captain Ridler, the dental officer who acted as anaesthetist, would remain with the orderlies and operating room assistants, attending to the wounded in the dressing station. The CO then divulged that he had selected us to form the nucleus of a new Parachute Field Ambulance should the rest of them be taken prisoner! Our task was to thread our way through the retiring German and Italian lines under cover of darkness and join up with the advancing forces of the 8th Army. On quiet contemplation we all reckoned that the night shift might have been preferable!

The way Major Wheatley phrased it, it sounded almost an honour to have been chosen to try and make a break for it. But when you came to examine the trades and skills of our party, we were in fact of least value when it came to care of the wounded. In plain English they could well do without us for the time being.

As the Mediterranean darkness fell, we set out at once in silent, single file and climbed into the surrounding hills. Officially we were armed. CSM Rowe as the senior RASC member present was supposed to be carrying the one Sten gun. He led the way up the hill with his pistol in his holster, happy in the knowledge that Corporal Power, bringing up the rear of the tiny column, was carrying the Sten gun. At the same time Corporal Power was slightly less than happy that CSM Rowe had the Sten gun as he felt he could have made better use of it should the need arise. But there was no Sten gun! So unless the Padre possessed a secret weapon, our total armament consisted of two Colt 45 pistols amongst eight men.

Once our eyes adjusted well to the darkness, we could see the outline of trees and rocks silhouetted against the sky. Over and over we halted in response to the silently raised hand of the man in front and listened intently. Was that a whispered Italian command? Could that be the outline of a feathered Bersaglieri cap against the night sky? We estimated that we passed through a small company of Bersaglieri troops and that they may have seen us, but not knowing our strength (or lack of it) had chosen not to attack us.

Around 2am, we had reached the southern limit of the hills and the strain of creeping through noiselessly was beginning to tell. Extreme fatigue was taking its toll and stumbles, dislodged stones and muttered oaths threatened to reveal us. It was then that we found the drain.

An open, dry, concrete drain, about 4 feet in depth, contouring the hill and going roughly in the direction that we were aiming for. It may have been a leat designed to collect whatever small quantity of rain fell on those arid hills. Grateful for its presence, we walked along in it, confident that with a slight stoop we were well below the skyline and would not be seen.

After a period of good progress, CSM Rowe and RSM Brock halted us and went forward on their own to agree on our future route when we left the drain. On their return they found six slumped bodies in the bottom of it – sound asleep! It was agreed that one guard must stay awake, but the rest were allowed to flake out. The guard would do only a half-hour duty – no one could be trusted to remain awake for longer than that.

When we moved from the cover of that excellent drain there was the faintest hint of light in the sky to the east and we knew that daylight was on its way. Making better time now, we pushed on downhill and soon came to a large orange grove and under cover of the trees headed south for another hour. Daylight caught up with us and still we didn't know whether we were in German held territory or had succeeded in reaching the advancing 8th Army. There was a small brick built barn that had a little loft above it. We approached cautiously and climbed a ladder to the loft above, pulling it up behind us before settling down in the hay for some real sleep. No guard was maintained – we had all had it – and we slept as peacefully as if we had been in our own beds at home.

Rudely awakened and brought back to reality by the sound of low flying aircraft and gunfire, we tried desperately to see the markings on the aircraft and locate where the anti-aircraft fire had come from, hoping that would tell us whether we had got back within 8th Army lines. Craning our heads out of the small unglazed window that ventilated the loft, we failed to see what we needed, but, to our surprise, spotted a startled Sicilian farm worker almost immediately below. His shocked appearance at seeing us, with our blackened faces and unkempt hair after sleeping in the hay was hilarious, and he legged it along one of the groves of orange trees as hard as he could go. Perhaps it was our laughter that convinced him we were not all that dangerous, for when we came out of the barn a few minutes later, he slowly and cautiously approached us and we coaxed some information out of him in halting Italian.

Rightly or wrongly he gave us the impression that the German forces had withdrawn from the area and that the Allies were nearby. Of almost greater immediate interest was that he was carefully feeling a number of the hard green oranges hanging on the trees and selecting one here and there for us. To our amazement they were sweet, with plenty of juice and quite delicious – but we failed to discover the secret of how to tell which green oranges were edible, for all the ones we picked were green throughout and very bitter.

Confidence grew as it seemed unlikely now to be picked up by retiring German forces and we walked down a lane that conveniently headed south. A little way along this lane we saw a man about a quarter of a mile ahead, standing by a small bridge over a deep ditch. A track led from this bridge to some farm buildings.

The man stared at us as we approached, then as we advanced, leapt into the ditch and crouched in the culvert under the bridge. RSM Brock told me to try my Italian and ask the way to Syracuse. I did my best. Leaning over I started: "Per favore, Signor…..quale est la strada …"

There was no time for more. With a yell, the man dashed along the ditch, scrambled up the bank and bolted for the farm buildings – and we still didn't know if we were heading for Syracuse or not.

About an hour later, while resting in warm sunshine at the top of a narrow track that wound down a short steep hill, we were delighted to see some troops approaching who were clearly British. They seemed pleased to see us too and announced with pride that they were the "DLIs, mon." But their strong Welsh accents were quite wrong for the Durham Light Infantry of the Tyne and Tees Division, even though they bore that divisional insignia. We discovered then that they had belonged not so long ago to the Monmouth Light Infantry – which of course explained their lilting accents. They told us the quickest way to Syracuse and said we could probably get some food from a tank squadron that was harboured up in the trees not far ahead.

Even more important than food, as far as I was concerned, was to find one of these tanks using one of our camouflaged silk parachutes as its personal camouflage. On the assumption that we had a much greater right to it than the Tank Corps, I removed it and conveyed it safely back to our unit in North Africa, using it as bedding for a number of nights on the way there. And dare I confess it? I managed to smuggle it home on our return to England some months later. In my defence I must add that it had been ruined as an operational 'chute because most of the shroud lines had been hacked off.

I suppose it would be wrong to suggest that the rest of our journey into Syracuse was uneventful, for part of it involved travelling in a captured Italian Army vehicle that we 'liberated'. Another notable event was to meet a jeep, and out stepped the famous General Montgomery – who personally thanked us for our efforts. That evening we met our own divisional director of Medical Services, Colonel Eagger, clad in a large white seaman's pullover, nondescript blue trousers and gumboots. It transpired he had been in a glider that had ditched half a mile off shore and had swum to the beach in his underpants!

All this was after passing through Lentini. As we reached this little town on its hill, British tanks with huge flail arms mounted across their fronts to deal with land mines, were negotiating the narrow streets with great difficulty. Most of the houses had four or five steps up to their front doors, four was all right, but five was not. The flail arm could only be elevated to clear objects about three feet above ground level and the fifth step was slightly more than this. Bewildered and angry residents shook their fists at the tanks as they crawled slowly up between the houses – taking every step higher than the fourth with them – and any handrails too.

Syracuse was alive with Allied soldiers and seamen of every sort and size. Provided with food and told to go and rest somewhere out of the way, we did just that and during the day our numbers steadily grew as more and more members of our unit found their way in. The officers and lads that we had left at the farmhouse dressing station the night before had quite a story to tell. Some of the withdrawing German forces had come through the farm. A major in charge of them had inspected the farmhouse and the wounded. He thanked our CO for the care we had taken and asked if he would like the British wounded to be evacuated to Catania. Major Wheatley politely declined this offer, saying that he thought the 8th Army would soon be there. The German major agreed and departed, taking his wounded fellow countrymen with him. It all seemed remarkably civil.

Another night sleeping under the stars in Syracuse followed and the next afternoon we learned we were to return to Tunisia on a large LCT. The Landing Craft Tank resembled a giant metallic shoe box, with huge outward opening doors at the front and a ramp that let down when the doors opened. Our vessel was moored about 400 yards off shore and there were small assault craft running a ferry service out to it and we had only to walk down the ramp of the assault landing craft and up the ramp of the larger vessel to get aboard. But – and it was a very big but – we had acquired transport that we dearly wanted to take back to Tunisia. The vehicles were

Fiats; about the size and shape of the electric milk delivery vans that ran around English cities in the early mornings. They were powered by small petrol engines and would be ideal for taking small parties of men down to the beaches from that hot, dusty olive grove camp. At first, the naval officer in charge of loading operations completely forbade us to try to load them, then in the face of our obstinacy, he told us that we would never get them safely up the wave washed ramps from one vessel to the other. Finally he turned his back on us and muttered something like "Someone's sure to get drowned."

However we got them out to the LCT and by sheer muscle power manhandled them up that awkward ramp. Once back at our North African camp, cleaned and serviced, they proved an absolute godsend for our recreational transport needs. But before that we were in for a lively night.

It was a warm evening and most of us, medics and Battalion men alike, stayed on deck, watching the late light fading on the activities ashore and in the harbour. In any case there was nothing to attract the men to go below. Below were vast empty, featureless metal decks designed for people moving in numbers rather than comfort. About midnight, ship's personnel were under orders to get us below decks. Everyone moved very reluctantly. A few of us had tucked ourselves into a pile of tarpaulins under the open metal structure at the base of the bridge. We found we could remain quietly hidden there. The reason for clearing the decks was that a German air raid was expected on Syracuse in a short while. The Oerlikon guns on the ship were manned and a few Parachute Gunners were stationed at No. 1 Gun at the bow to make up for some crew deficiencies.

Right on cue the air raid materialised. Much of the blast seemed to be aimed for the port and shipping and the Oerlikons were soon throwing up a vigorous barrage. At the same time, large smoke producing candles were ignited at several points around the vessel to provide a smoke screen. Unfortunately these were not well sited in the circumstances. Several were close to the ventilator intakes for below deck and as the smoke gushed forth, the nearby ventilators sucked a lot of it in and pumped it down below. Almost immediately the coughing of unfortunates down there could be heard throughout the ship. We kept stumm and out of sight in our relatively comfortable spot and congratulated ourselves on having found it.

After a particularly lively few minutes of action, with a lot of gunfire and bombs dropping on or near the shore, there was a lull. A voice over the Tannoy system boomed out "No. 1 Gun. No. 1 Gun. Have you opened fire yet?"

The response was "No."

The Tannoy crackled again. "No. 1 Gun. No. 1 Gun. Why not?"

The reply was clearly heard as an exasperated "Haven't seen anything to fire at yet – sir!" Obviously the Army men wanted a visible target, whereas the Navy gunners threw up a barrage.

The night passed without further excitement and around dawn, everyone still below decks was rounded up to join the majority now on deck. We were about to leave the harbour and just before getting under way, we were all required to stand to the ship's rails. It appeared that our vessel was not de-Gaussed – that is, it was still likely to set off any magnetic mines that might have been dropped in the night's air raid. It was presumed that we would have a better chance of survival if we were on deck, should we be unfortunate enough to pass near such a mine. It was reassuring to know that the authorities took an interest in our safety!

The sea was calm and it was a lovely sunny day. The only unpleasant feature was the way the flat front of those giant doors repeatedly slapped against quite small waves. An intermittent but irritating jar could be felt throughout the ship. A Battalion man approached me as I lay in the sun. He asked if I could get a dressing for a minor wound on his arm – and then I recognised him. He was an acquaintance from Ashby, here, in the middle of the Mediterranean. He had a superficial but rather messy wound on the right forearm and I promptly got one of the surgical team orderlies to clean it up and dress it properly. A month or so later in Italy, because of something I knew about his background, I was able, indirectly, to help this man get out of a serious military charge arising from a nasty incident in the little town of Altamura – but that is between the two of us.

Once we docked in Bizerta, army transport soon spirited us back to base and for the clerks of the unit there followed an amazingly active 72 hours. It was obvious that many things had gone wrong with the Ponte Primosole action, although equally some innovations had been extremely successful. Lt. Col MacEwan had returned to us and immediately began to write a very full report on all aspects of the Medical Corps role in the battle. Much of this he dictated either to S/Sgt Eric Stevens, Corporal Loveland or to me. The three of us worked around the clock, taking it in turn to rest, while one or other of us set out and typed this remarkable document. Col. MacEwan didn't seem to need rest – plenty of coffee and the odd glass of whisky kept him going during those hectic three days. Later we were to learn that much of the information we produced was to greatly influence the planning for the medical dispositions of the airborne forces in the Normandy landings.

≈≈≈≈≈≈≈≈≈≈≈

Chapter 14
Back to Blighty

After our return from Sicily we endured a few boiling hot weeks under canvas in those olive groves near Sousse, a boring location some distance from any life form other than the inevitable military presence. The trips down to the beach on our 'liberated' Italian army vehicles were an absolute life saver. The acquisition of these vehicles from Syracuse had not gone unnoticed by the authorities and there had been a strongly worded Army Council Instruction published to the effect that: 'In future, NO vehicle of any type will be removed from a theatre of war!'

While the unit remained under canvas in eastern Tunisia, L/Cpl Chris Jelley decided he wanted to change his religious persuasion to that of Atheist. Our newly promoted commanding officer, Lieut. Colonel Wheatley, whose father had been a minister of religion, was rather reluctant to permit this change but could not see how, under King's Regulations, he could legitimately refuse the request. He procrastinated for a couple of days, during which he studied the Army Act and King's Regulations closely. Then one morning, he called me into his office tent and in obvious good humour, said, "Sergeant, bring L/Cpl Jelley in please." As Jelley was also a clerk in the Headquarters section, it took me only a moment or two to get him into the CO's tent.

"Ah, Lance Corporal Jelley —" said the Colonel, "concerning your application to change your religious persuasion. That will be quite in order, but you do have to follow the provisions of King's Regulations and for a probationary period you must see the minister of your newly chosen religion once a week. Is that understood? Right... that will be all."

Exit a crestfallen Jelley, leaving a smiling CO and an astonished and admiring orderly sergeant!

However, the last laugh was to belong to Chris Jelley. When the bulk of the Field Ambulance moved to Italy a few weeks later, Chris was left behind as clerk to the small detachment in charge of an officer with limited experience in army administration. Seizing his opportunity, Jelley again presented his request, citing the appropriate King's Regulation – but omitting the proviso regarding interviews with the minister of the chosen religion. The request was duly granted and the appropriate Part II Order signed by the unsuspecting officer was published by the detachment. When a copy of this order reached us, the parent unit in Italy, Colonel Wheatley was obviously disappointed, but had the grace to smile wryly and murmur, "Well perhaps the Lance Corporal won that round!"

Within weeks of returning from Sicily we were busy preparing for another move and another landing, but this would be different, for we were to go by sea. We embarked from Bizerta, this time in a much smarter craft than the previous LCT. The Princess Beatrix was a Commando mother ship with an interesting history. When the German panzers streamed into Holland and Belgium she was already launched but incomplete, being fitted out at the time. Unable to proceed under her own steam, she was towed to Britain and her fitting out completed there. Intended for the cross Channel and North Sea ferry services, she was much faster and considerably more comfortable than the LCT and she was about to take us back to Italy, a run from Bizerta to Taranto.

En route, somewhere near the island of Panteleria, we saw a number of warships approaching. They were ships of the surrendered Italian Navy, cruiser type vessels, closely shepherded by three or four fussy little British destroyers and in the late afternoon sunshine they made a magnificent picture as they sailed past us on their way to Malta.

We pressed steadily on and in darkness entered Taranto harbour and proceeded to disembark without any sign of enemy activity. We boarded railway trucks in the adjacent sidings and waited to move north. I was responsible for ten men and at 11pm three of them disappeared. We saw nothing of them for an anxious three hours. It was around 2am when they returned, in obvious good spirits, and told us they had been enjoying quantities of chips and brandy. They were very lucky the train had not moved off, for it did so shortly afterwards.

During the night there was an air raid on Taranto Harbour. Among the bombs were some naval mines strung on a cable at a depth where they were a menace to shipping. In the dark early hours of the morning, one of these mines detonated under HMS Abdiel, a minelayer that had also been pressed into service as a troop transporter. There were airborne soldiers on board, including some of our sister Air Landing Field Ambulance, the 181st In the darkness there was no indication of where the land lay and men who were known to be good swimmers were lost. It is presumed they swam in the wrong direction when their ship went down.

The train only went a short distance out of Taranto before halting to deposit us. Our HQ was set up in a rather lovely house close on the edge of the upper reaches of the harbour. But three days later we were bemoaning our position for we were engaged in the grisly task of recovering the blackened swollen bodies of our comrades as they floated ashore. The bodies were quickly taken elsewhere, but we retained their AB64's (a soldier's identity and pay document) for identification and casualty report purposes. Understandably the bodies had a very strong smell, but we had not reckoned on the pay-books themselves being so strongly impregnated. They remained in the office overnight and next morning the whole room reeked of this dreadfully distinctive smell. We hastily put the offending books out on the verandah, but even with all the doors and windows open it was 48 hours before the office ceased to be very much on the nose.

From Taranto we went almost due north to the small hill town of Altamura, where we took over an Italian hospital that until recently had held Allied POWs. After a hurried evacuation they had left the mail behind and we found most of the letters were addressed to New Zealanders. As the names of the senders were on the backs of the envelopes, some of us took on the job of writing to them to say that their letters were being forwarded through Red Cross in Switzerland. Some months later and back in Algeria once more, replies arrived from New Zealand homes saying how much they appreciated hearing what had happened – and that a fruitcake had been dispatched to us by way of a 'thank-you'. To our amazement it arrived not many days later, sealed in a tin and in perfect condition. It was absolutely marvellous! Some forty years later, I actually met the lady who had sent it, in Auckland, and we still exchange Christmas cards.

After cleaning up the horrific mess in the Altamura Hospital (the toilets had continued to be used although the water supply had been cut off for about a week) we opened up a Dressing Station and began dealing with the wounded once more. However we soon found ourselves operating more like a small hospital, as our brigade was hit by an outbreak of Epidemic Catarrhal Jaundice and our patients were as yellow as dandelions – rather unhappy dandelions. The treatment, basically a fat free diet, was not at all popular!

The Allied advance up Southern Italy continued and in due course, we too moved forward, going northeast to the coastal town of Barletta, as the push towards the airfield centre of Foggia continued. Our unit moved into Barletta about 48 hours after the enemy had withdrawn. There was no street fighting and little obvious damage to the place, but German engineers had been determined to make life difficult. The town water supply had been very effectively cut, but of longer lasting nuisance value was the concrete poured into the sewage system at strategic points. It was highly effective and the city was totally constipated – but we were not! And that is why an imposing 12 seater trench latrine was dug just to the west of some screening bushes about fifty yards from our new headquarters.

This latrine was a structure of clean well-smoothed white wooden seats; two rows of six suitably shaped holes back to back and even a wooden back rest for those intending a longer stay. Placed behind the shrubs, privacy should have been assured because an embankment of a disused light railway ran along about 10 yards away further to the west and blocked the view from that direction. But because of a damaged bridge on another line, this line was unexpectedly brought back into use. Morning and evening, several crowded tram-like carriages would go past – and the passengers would wave and cheer like mad, shouting witty Italian comments that were quite lost on us, but obviously appreciated by their fellow passengers.

Apart from the trains – and the ladies who approached us regularly when we were, so to speak, anchored to the spot, to ask if we had any laundry we wanted doing – there was one other big problem – flies. Thousands of large and medium size black flies infested the trench beneath the woodwork and an orderly was given the daily task of disposing of them.

He did this by pouring petrol liberally through a number of the seat holes, dropping a match inside and stepping smartly back as the flames whooshed up inside the trench. It worked well, but had to be repeated daily to keep the fly population under control. One morning, around 8am, he had splashed his petrol about, only to find that he had used his last match in igniting the office refuse. He returned to the office to ask for a match and met a dispatch rider on the way out. The dispatch brought messages from Brigade HQ a few miles up the Adriatic Coast and on leaving the office went straight across to the latrines to commune with nature. Settling down, he idly lit a cigarette and discarded the match into the adjacent seat hole. With an almighty whoosh – thrump, the heavy wooden construction jumped several inches, but despite the handicap of his breeches scrunched round his ankles, the man leapt at least three feet in the air! For once, the passengers in the passing train were stunned into silence.

Badly shaken, the rider was brought over to our Field Ambulance office where he loudly declined the offer of a chair, and even more vociferously our offer to get a doctor to examine him. After a cup of hot sweet tea he appeared to recover his composure and prepare to leave. But as he circled the yard on his motor cycle we noticed that he remained standing on the footrests. His parting words were: "After the North African campaign I reckoned I was battle hardened – but not at that end!"

From the military angle, life was relatively quiet in Barletta. Hostilities to the north of us were confined largely to patrol activity and we were not inundated with casualties. Unfortunately one casualty was one of our own unit. During action in a small town or village, Pte Fred Kitchen, a popular young fellow from Nottingham, suffered a broken jaw from a flying mortar fragment. He was treated and evacuated to a general hospital in Bari, where several of us visited him. He seemed cheerful enough, although he had to converse by pad and pencil as his jaw was externally pinned and immobilised. From there he was evacuated to a general hospital in Sicily and subsequently to a base hospital in North Africa. We were shocked to receive notification that he had been first placed on the 'seriously ill' list and then on the 'dangerously ill'. Eventually he died. It was hard to believe this news and even harder to accept it.

Life went on in Barletta and one of our more enjoyable recreational activities was to swim in the Adriatic Sea – despite the fact that it was now late autumn. But nothing stood still in Italy and we were about to move yet again. We were not told our destination, indeed there was a lot of mystery surrounding it and had we known what it was, how excited we all would have been. For we were going home – back to Dear Old Blighty!

The first intimation was accompanied by some mysterious instructions. We were told to remove all parachute wings, all Airborne divisional flashes and worst of all, our beloved red berets had to be packed away and we were issued with the regulation army cheese-cutters. Shortly after, disguised and disgusted, we boarded a train one evening in Barletta that took us overnight to Taranto. The carriages must have been alive with fleas as we had a horribly irritating and scratchy night.

In Taranto our spirits lifted. Alongside the wharf a delightful little French 'liner' awaited us. We were told she was a one sixth scale replica of the Normandie and she looked it, but perhaps it was as well that the height between decks was normal. For most of us it was the first time we had used hammocks for sea travel – a strange experience that took a little time to become accustomed to. To lie awake at night in the faint blue light and see rows of loaded hammocks swinging from side to side in slow but perfect unison was quite eerie. Snug in one's own hammock, the ship's movement was barely perceptible and this had one major blessing – no one was seasick on that fast trip to Algiers.

As the vessel pulled into Algiers harbour on a morning of vivid blue sky, it was hard to recall that it was almost exactly a year since we had landed there at the start of the Algerian and Tunisian campaign. The wharves were quiet, just a few ladies of the oldest profession from the nearby brothels enjoying the early winter sunshine. But they were to disturb things considerably. One of the

Battalion men shouted a greeting to a young woman he obviously recognised. A cry of delight went up from the shore. "Les paras sont revenus!" So much for the concealment of our paratroop identity!

We had indeed come back, but not for long. Within a few days we were re-embarking on the SS Samaria, this time bound for England.

For obvious reasons the Airborne personnel were split up and dispersed aboard a number of ships. A large convoy was being assembled to convey many units of the victorious 1st and 8th Armies back to Britain to prepare for the inevitable assault on Europe. The convoy sailed slowly, boringly slowly. The Samaria didn't roll – she pitched gently fore and aft. As she was carrying no cargo, for no Army units were taking any of their heavy equipment back with them, she was floating high in the water. On most of her forward pitches the stern would rise sufficiently for the screw to come partly out of the water. It thumped violently as it did so and the whole ship shuddered. As luck would have it, our allotted area of triple bunks was right aft and we got the worst of it. Sleep was hard to come by, but our spirits remained high. We were going home.

A bit of excitement occurred just as we were leaving Gibraltar. The convoy was sailing placidly along, making comparatively good speed. Suddenly, one of the liners of the Empress class sounded its siren repeatedly and swung hard to starboard in a wide circular course that, fortunately, did not involve her in a collision with any other vessel. The convoy sailed on its course and the Empress ship fell well behind. Later we were to learn that she had experienced a total steering breakdown and she was towed into Gibraltar for repairs. As a result, some of the troops on board, including Airborne personnel, didn't reach Britain in time to be home for Christmas, but at least they all completed their journey safely.

We rounded Northern Ireland and headed into the Mersey to berth at Liverpool. Light-heartedly we expressed acute dismay on meeting another troopship setting out, loaded with ATS girls and WAAFs. Just our luck! We get home and they ship the girls out!

As we came alongside the dock and sailors threw the mooring lines ashore, a band struck up. It greeted us with a selection of lively tunes, all of which seemed to be of Boer War vintage, as also perhaps, were members of the band. Suddenly, a hugely powerful voice from a soldier aboard rang out: "You've got the wrong bloody war!"

By late afternoon, in rapidly approaching darkness, we were aboard familiar maroon coloured LMS coaches and about to set off … but where? I couldn't believe my ears when the CO told us that we were going to Melton Mowbray! Not only was Melton in my county, but it was barely 20 miles from home. I was almost home! Almost but not quite, for after two nights in bitterly cold below zero weather, in huge unheated temporary quarters, approximately half the unit was sent on Christmas leave.

Getting them away with leave passes, railway warrants and ration cards meant a lot of hard work for the three of us in the office. The conditions there were far from ideal; cold as charity, not properly set up and not well lighted; but everyone was cheerful – even the Scottish lads amongst us for they had been promised they would be home for Hogmanay.

And that was how it worked out. I was home in Ashby a few days before Christmas and while George Loveland held the fort in Melton Mowbray I was spending a wonderful Christmas with family and what friends were still around. So many men in the services were not so lucky, but one special friend of mine was coming home for a short break. This was Eddie, now in the Land Army in Lincolnshire. I went to see her parents and they told me she would be on the late bus from Nottingham. I literally met her in the darkness of the winter blackout in the walkway through the Lamb Inn yard – a short cut to her home –

"Eddie?" I startled her.

"Who's that?"

"It's Jack."

She gasped with surprise, hugged me and we walked blissfully to her home. I hoped Eddie was happy to see me and while I knew that all over Britain this Christmas and New Year there would be many families regaled with tales of North Africa or Italy, all that was

153

in the past. We had come home – not to stay for long perhaps – but what a super feeling it was! Perhaps only returning servicemen and women can know that particular feeling.

≈≈≈≈≈≈≈≈≈≈≈

Chapter 15
Culverthorpe Hall

The early days of January 1944 were bitterly cold. After fourteen months in the warmer climates of North Africa and Italy we really felt it. There were night temperatures of 4° or 5° of frost several nights in succession. The turf outside was iron hard and even indoors it was bitterly cold. For the duration of the war in Europe there were no weather forecasts broadcast in Britain and this seemed to make the hardships intensely personal.

I had returned to Melton Mowbray in time to release the Scots of our unit, now impatient to get home and celebrate. One advantage was that as only a few of us were holding the fort in temporary charge of the stores, each of us could have 5 or 6 new Army blankets on our beds – and we needed them. My stay in Melton was shorter than I would have wished, for I was so near home. Just a few weeks there and we learned we were on the move again, this time to Culverthorpe Hall, near Sleaford in the adjacent county of Lincoln. Sleaford was a little outside the radius of the country I knew well through my cycling trips, but I was familiar with the place names, having been in the general area a few times on the way to holidays in Skegness.

Culverthorpe Hall was a handsome building, facing south onto a wide expanse of grass that stretched down to a rather reedy lake. Its large windows benefited from almost all the sun there was, though during that early spring this was not very much. The men were billeted either in the stables or in Nissan huts set up just to the west of the house. A number of senior NCOs had rooms in the house. These rooms had been the servants' quarters and were reached by narrow staircases. The one I shared with Sgt. Price of our trasport section had only a minute skylight, but it was very conveniently connected to the unit office by a small narrow stairway.

Our first task was to get back to full strength once again. We had lost the whole of No. 2 Section in North Africa and although we had received some replacements while still overseas, more were needed. For a while we had a surplus of medical officers, all of whom had volunteered for parachute duties and on completion of training jumps, were posted to our unit for field training. We were already qualified, due to our experience in action in the previous year, but the training courses involved all of us and were often great fun.

Culverthorpe was some 4 or 5 miles from the town of Sleaford, well embedded in the Lincolnshire countryside with little more than hamlets in the vicinity. There was a NAAFI in a large Nissan hut in the grounds for the other ranks, but officers and senior NCO's had to make do in their own respective messes, or somehow get to Sleaford, Grantham or Rauceby.

Sleaford and the larger town of Grantham appear on any decent map, but you might have to look very hard for Rauceby. In peacetime Rauceby was tiny, merely a County Hospital for the mentally handicapped. In wartime it had been enlarged, upgraded by the RAF and turned into a hospital specialising in burns cases. When an aircraft caught fire, pilot and crew could suffer horrific burn injuries – quite frequently involving the face. Very soon our surgical teams were working alongside the RAF surgical teams, keeping their hand in and gaining invaluable experience. Some of us were to be involved in the rehabilitation of these men who had varying degrees of disfigurement. We admired their pluck and responded with alacrity. One less altruistic reason for our eagerness to help was that their hospital had good recreation facilities and ran excellent dances at least once a week. And there were some very attractive WAAFs and Nurses among the staff.

We were encouraged to take burns patients out as much as possible and we often took them into Sleaford to pubs or cafés, helping them to readjust to contact with the public. Initially they were very conscious of the shock on people's faces, but the Sleaford people soon learned not to show their dismay and most men forgave the odd outsider startled into betraying emotion. In fact we had a lot of success and of course we needed no encouragement to take out a nurse or a WAAF!

An illustration of this positive result was an Australian flight sergeant, who must have been frightfully disfigured initially, because when we began taking him 'out on the town' he had already had five restoration operations on his face and it still looked ghastly. One night, as we returned him to Rauceby Hospital, with "See you next week Harry! Same time?" he said, "No, sorry lads, I'm booked for operation number 6 next week. Give me ten days and I'll be with you again – if the bloody bandages aren't covering both eyes!"

Ashby was still only about fifty miles to the west – slightly less as the crow flies but country roads were never direct. I had begun to think that my bicycle would be a great idea. The local roads were remarkably free of hills, quite well surfaced and like most of wartime Britain, unusually free of traffic. So the first time I had the opportunity of a weekend pass, I went home and found it very difficult by public transport. Cross-country travel in England had never been easy – all roads and rails lead to London. It seemed that the quickest way home for me was to go by rail from Sleaford to Peterborough, Peterborough to Leicester and Leicester to Ashby. Alternatively I could hitchhike or use the infrequent bus into Grantham, take another infrequent bus to Nottingham and there hope to catch the X99 bus to Ashby (notoriously overfilled and stranded passengers unable to get aboard were left at the depot in Nottingham). So I used the rail route, missed the last train from Leicester to Ashby, spent the night in a services emergency sleep centre on the station and caught the 6.15am train next morning.

When I eventually got home, the first thing I did after breakfast was to check my bicycle and its lamps – I was quite determined to cycle back to Culverthorpe. I had a pleasant Sunday at home and quite late, around 11pm I think, I set off on the fifty mile ride back to return to duty. It went wonderfully well. The night was dry and clear and once my eyes adjusted to the darkness, I found I could see the road, hedgerows and the outline of buildings. I couldn't see the signposts of course, for they had all been removed in 1940. But I had a good map of the area and knew my route across the North Leicestershire lanes reasonably well. I had a little difficulty around Grantham, but by then I was within ten miles or so of Culverthorpe and very confident of arriving safely and in good time.

I was back and checking into our guardroom by around 2am, turned in for a few hours and woke to start the new week very pleased with myself. I now had personal transport at hand and it was easy to pop over to Rauceby whenever I wanted to. Sleaford no longer remained a problem involving catching buses at inconvenient hours. Anyway some buses didn't return to Culverthorpe but left you with at least a mile and a half of country lanes to walk to the Hall.

We knew that D-day was going to happen soon and we were training hard and living furiously. Some of us got interested in running medley relay races and competing at RAF sports meetings at local RAF stations. The medley distances were two runners of 220 yards, one 440 yards and one half miler. Our best performance was to come second at RAF Spalding and although we were about 8 or 10 yards behind the winner we didn't feel at all disgraced. The winning team had J.W. Alford in it, a South African Olympic runner who ran the final half-mile leg.

In late May, after several army exercises, some involving parachute drops both in Lincolnshire and the Cotswolds, we began to realise that D-day must now be imminent. But I think it still came as a surprise on the morning of June 6th to hear that it had already happened – and that we had not been involved. In some ways it was a bit of a let down. We had quite thought we were indispensable!

Forty-eight hours later we were briefed for a drop near Everecy in Normandy just inland of the British landing zone. We were advised that there were a few German tanks from an armoured formation there – not very comforting news. Twenty-four hours later, the briefing was revised – there was now a full German armoured formation there and elements of a second. Another day went by – the operation was called off. We breathed again.

So time slipped by and still we waited. In early September there was a stirring and a hint that something might be happening and it was. 'Operation Comet' was launched. It involved the 1st Airborne Division and the Polish Parachute Brigade in seizing bridges across the Rhine and other rivers right up to and including Arnhem. We prepared, stood-by, even a sea-borne section with our transport and spare clothing was alerted – and then it too was called off. We were told to forget all about it and not to talk about it. To keep our minds off it, our unit went on a cross-country march to Skegness.

For once I was able to join in the marching rather than be confined to the office. I thoroughly enjoyed it except for the usual blistered feet. We used makeshift accommodation each night – a school in Spilsby, a windmill in Billinghay and a sports pavilion on our arrival in Skegness.

Then back to Culverthorpe and routine once more and general preparation exercises for an operational landing in Europe, still without any specific target being named. And then, almost immediately, a specific operation was in the wind. 'Operation Market' was in essence a much stronger version of the cancelled 'Comet'. This time the 1st Airborne Division was to take and hold the bridge over the Rhine at Arnhem. This battle was to become a legend.

So much has already been written about the battle of Arnhem and there are so many facets to the errors that may or may not have been made, that I do not intend to dwell on this side of the subject. Our part in the action was never in doubt. It was succour for the wounded. For the short time that the 16th Para Field Ambulance were permitted to do this, I believe we did the job remarkably well.

The 17th September 1944 is a date written across the hearts and minds of all of us who were at Arnhem. Each would have a story to tell, different from the one his companion told. My memories include lighter moments in the final days in England. One of these was the exchange of our English currency for Dutch guilders. These were officially 'Allied Military Authority Dutch Guilders'. We had used their counterpart in the form of 'Allied Military Authority Franks' in North Africa. But we referred to these Dutch guilders as "phoney guilders".

Having taken all our English money away from us (there was a ban on our taking English currency with us) a unit trip to the cinema was planned for the Saturday night. This was to be to the near famous 'Cinema in the Woods' at Woodhall Spa. The outing when it eventuated was hilarious. For a start the cinema was small by normal standards and while the senior officers had decreed we could go, we must be segregated from the general public by two rows of empty seats. If anything could have drawn attention to us, that most certainly did. Added to this indignity, we had to pay the price of admission. How? We had only Dutch guilders! So we solemnly paid Major Gordon the calculated fee in guilders and he in turn somehow squared it with the cinema manager. I have no idea how. I can't remember what the film was and it didn't matter, but it was fun and that was really important as come the morning we would be dicing with death at Arnhem.

Our flight in from England started at RAF Barkston Heath, near Grantham, just a short drive from our base at Culverthorpe. That Sunday morning was superb; calm, sunny, just a hint of autumn in the air. Everything appeared so peaceful there in the English countryside it was hard to think of battle. From the airfield we could see the odd farm tractor chugging along a lane to a farm a mile away, while a few people wound their way up the little hill to Barkston Church for the morning service. I thought of Rupert Brooke's 'Grantchester':

"Stands the church clock at ten to three?

And is there honey still for tea?"

There was the usual struggle to get all our kit on and the parachutes on top, but the air of calm efficiency about the ground staff and aircrews who went about their business around us settled our nerves. Food and drink were provided shortly before it was time to board the plane and we struggled up the little aluminium steps draped with all our gear and relying on the helping hands of ground staff.

As we climbed aboard we noticed that RAF staff lined the front of their office blocks and hangars. On an elevated deck of one administration building we could see a gathering of bigwigs, both Army and RAF; gold braid in plenty and surprisingly, some American uniforms too. There were WAAFs gathered in front of their offices too and it felt rather nice to have such a send off. We had flown on operations before of course, but having the odd Arab standing idly by was a pale comparison.

Engines began to cough and splutter into life and soon even inside our aircraft the sound was ear-splitting. The airstrip's tarry surface glistened in the sun as we taxied toward the Barkston Church end of the runway. Slowly we turned and the roar increased in strength as the planes rushed down the runway for take off.

A hazy sky limited our view of Lincolnshire's flat countryside as we settled into formation and judging by the position of the sun, we were heading south-east. As we crossed Lincolnshire and Norfolk other planes joined us. To the south, well away from us and flying their own route, were the gliders and their tugs, probably from runways in Oxfordshire. They would proceed at their slower speed and arrive a little behind us.

Below was the edge of England and the waters of the North Sea. We passed over a small coastal town. Someone knew that town – Aldeburgh in Suffolk. Perhaps those people down there were wishing us luck and we were going to need all the luck we could get......

The flight over the sea is smoothly uneventful. Why anyone should be airsick on such a smooth flight is hard to imagine – but they are. Better to look out of the little window and be reassured by the fighter escort high above and to our south, while below we pass over ships spaced out at intervals of a few miles along the line of our flight. Someone at hand if we were to go down in the drink.

Is this Holland or Belgium? We don't know and we are not going to have time to find out. There's a windmill on fire down there – someone says a German anti-aircraft gun has been put out of action by our fighter escort and it is strangely comforting. Our chutes have been on for some little time and tension is rising as the moment for the jump approaches.

"Stand up!" "Stand to the Door!"

The customary commands are automatically obeyed. We are lower now, the flat land of Holland racing along underneath us looking wet – floods everywhere.

The red light goes on. Any moment now.

"Green light!" and Number 1 goes out the door. We shuffle forward to follow him. The plane yaws a little, keeping its formation and I am momentarily pressed back by the rush of the slip stream, then the folding stretcher and blanket I am carrying gets caught in the air rush and I am plucked from the plane like a cork from a bottle. The tug on my shoulders tells me my 'chute has opened and I look down at the flat land beneath my feet and my companions' 'chutes just a few feet lower than I am. There is no

161

obvious sign of enemy activity and I breathe a sigh of relief. Odd thoughts flash through my mind. Major Gordon has jumped just behind me. I've been told he is carrying the 'comforts' funds for the unit – might be a good idea to see he comes to no harm!

Down! A gentle bump and as my chute collapses to the ground one of the early gliders sweeps in to land, narrowly missing it. As Major Gordon and I were the last two to jump, we are close to the far end of our allotted DZ (Dropping Zone) and almost in to the LZ of the Gliders – which is the reason for their proximity. No time to worry about that. Leave the 'chute, collect your gear and rendezvous by the containers, then head quickly for the cover of the trees at the edge of this wide stretch of heathland.

A short halt at the trees, a count is taken, we are all present and correct and safely down. Orders come to move off and we follow the line the fighting men are taking just ahead of us. Our route takes us through some light woodland, past a shot-up German staff car. There are two officers still in it, both dead. No time is wasted on them as we press on toward the city of Arnhem and the bridge. We are in single file and keeping close to the hedgerows at the edge of the lane, but had rather expected more urgency such as double marching to speed up our advance.

There is a sudden sound of firing ahead. We are halted and press into the hedges and bushes and wait. The first of several irksome halts and waits. We are nearing the small town of Heelsum…..

It was there that some of us decided to eat our haversack rations and while we huddled, half hidden, in the hedges of the gardens fronting the road, we took out our generously thick sandwiches of the standard wartime 'grey' bread, politely called 'white'. Almost immediately small children appeared out of the houses and gardens as if by magic and stared hungry-eyed and fascinated at the sandwiches. They thought it was cake! Their present meagre rations meant that they were not old enough to remember white bread and certainly not cake – so what did we do? The obvious. It is fair to say that we may have regretted our generosity about 48 hours later, but I don't think any one of us could have eaten those sandwiches in front of them.

There were two main thrust routes into Arnhem, one code-named "Tiger" and the other, "Lion", taking the more southerly road, nearer the River Rhine. I think we were intended to proceed initially on "Tiger" route to our intended destination of the St. Elizabeth Hospital, but enemy resistance made it necessary to be switched to "Lion" and follow the 2nd Para Battalion along this road. The afternoon was now well advanced and the light was fading and we were held up yet again at the railway line. Men of the 2nd Battalion cleared a short length of the railway embankment of Germans and the rest of their force pushed through under the railway arch, closely followed by the Field Ambulance. Seemingly, the Germans mounted a counter attack, retook the railway line area and we, the Field Ambulance and 2nd Battalion were virtually the only units that got into Arnhem city centre in any strength. After that our journey to St. Elizabeth Hospital was hurried but successfully carried out.

Once there we expected to be involved in the collection and treatment of casualties, but we were surprised to find that the wonderful and courageous Dutch people had already begun to bring them in. Our operating teams went into action and the warmth of the reception by the Dutch hospital staff was so inspiring that we went flat out to keep up with their energy and courage.

The leading battalion, including us, was relatively close to the Rhine Bridge. There we were to remain, more than a little isolated from the rest of our division. The following morning found us in the thick of battle. At one stage we had airborne troops at the western end of the Hospital and German troops at the eastern!

Shells fired from south of the river hit the hospital in the basement area. It was probably German guns engaging small armoured vehicles on the slope between the river and us. Two of us were just passing the glazed entrance to the basement corridor when the shells struck. The glass in the doors shattered and dust and flock from mattresses filled the air. Hesitating as to whether to go in to try and help anyone who had been injured by the shell burst, our minds were speedily made up by a blonde Dutch nurse who dived fearlessly into the mess in search of casualties. We followed and did what we could, before continuing on our way to the lower basement entrance. We were now bringing all casualties in through this entrance, as it was well protected by the raised ramp to the main door on the floor above.

The German troops entered the hospital in mid afternoon. For a short while they permitted us to continue our work with little interference. Then an altercation between our CO, Lt. Col. Townsend and German officers over whether treatment priority should be given to German wounded was brought to a head when a German came in and alleged that a bomb had been thrown at his troops from the hospital. It was exceedingly unlikely, as few of the British soldiers there were in any state to throw anything, but the accusation was enough. All but the operating surgical teams were at once taken to a basement area and held under armed guard.

We were kept there for some time and two of us, guided by one of the Dutch nurses, tried to sneak away by a small back staircase. Unfortunately we met a German guard with rifle and bayonet coming down the stairs and were smartly returned to the basement. As the afternoon wore on and the light began to fail, the German guards brought us up from the basement to a room at the eastern end of the hospital. They had opened a small door about two feet above the garden. We were told to jump down with hands above our heads and were doubled quickly away past a strong detachment of German infantry deployed along the road. We were marched past the Arnhem Station and on to what I think was the Zutphen road and taken to some cold, dark concrete air-raid shelters. Here we spent the night in mental and physical discomfort, for the beautiful sunny Sunday morning had degenerated into cold, heavy rain that was to continue for many hours. It suited the general mood. But we still hoped that the second lift of airborne troops would solve our problems and that we would soon be freed. This bad weather was also affecting England and that second lift was grounded.

Next morning we were ejected from the air-raid shelters and marched out of Arnhem under strong guard. It continued wet and miserable and I don't know if we were pleased or sorry when a rather decrepit lorry was produced from somewhere and we were loaded aboard to be driven, just slightly faster than our marching pace, toward the town of Zutphen and the German border.

One of my fellow prisoners was an old friend, Corporal Howard Jones. We had been companions since the days of the 10th Light Field Ambulance advance party to Sussex when the unit left Market Warsop. Taken prisoner with the rest of the section at Oudna in Tunisia, Howard had been held in Italy and when the Italian forces withdrew from the War, had escaped in company with a few others. Eventually they managed to get through to the Allied Forces in Southern Italy – and here he was, a prisoner again! But his previous experience gave him the ability to advise and encourage as the idea of captivity became distressingly clearer every minute.

Our journey in the decrepit motor wagon terminated after an uncomfortable hour or so at a large warehouse, somewhere on the outskirts of Zutphen. We were hurried out of the vehicle and into the dim interior where there were already other prisoners. The rest of the day was spent in this warehouse, forbidden to stand up and moving around was done at the crouch or on hands and knees. More prisoners arrived from time to time, among them RAF crews who had been shot down in their valiant attempts to bring aid to our beleaguered division. We gave them a cheer of encouragement as they stumbled into the near darkness from the watery sunshine of late afternoon.

Another small group of RAF crew came in amid stunned silence for there was a British Navy lieutenant with them. Immediately our imaginations began to work overtime. Had the Navy been called in to try and force its way up the Rhine to help? Was the situation now so totally desperate? Our anxiety for news and an explanation was all-consuming, but had to be satisfied slowly and surreptitiously by whispered word of mouth. As the story progressed, subdued chuckles – something we had not heard for many hours – spread around as we saw the funny side.

The Navy lieutenant had been home on leave. He had heard what was going on in Holland from an RAF friend who was flying in supplies on the Monday and he had persuaded this pilot friend to give him an unauthorised lift. He had travelled as an unofficial 'dispatcher', one of the aircrew who pushes out the loads of supplies at the right time. The rest we could guess. The plane had been shot down.

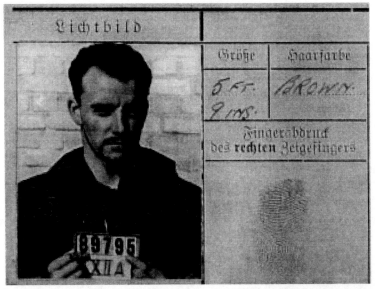

This naval officer was now a prisoner of war – and at the same time officially on leave in England! We laughed, but it had serious complications when you thought about it. Technically he was probably guilty of desertion. Service personnel on leave were forbidden to leave the country and he would have quite a lot of explaining to do when he returned home at the end of the war!

≈≈≈≈≈≈≈≈≈≈≈

Chapter 16

Prisoners of war

That warehouse was a nightmare. There were no toilet facilities and one of the MOs suggested we make use of one corner of the building as a makeshift latrine – and refrain as much as possible! Few of us managed to get much sleep despite our exhaustion after about 72 hours without real rest.

In the morning we were herded into some railway trucks standing near the warehouse and stuffed in, still under close guard. The train eventually moved off and made a short journey to what, I believe, was the town of Enschede, on the Dutch/German border.

They let us out for a brief stop and some Dutch people were allowed to feed us in a building that appeared to be a sports pavilion set centrally in a large playing field area. They gave us boiled potatoes and cooked apple and it was truly appreciated. Another highlight was that we were allowed to use the toilet facilities.

From Enschede, the train conveyed us south by a devious route through the Ruhr. Looking through the bars of the cattle trucks we could see bomb damage both to the railway lines and to nearby buildings. The most memorable sight was a view of Cologne Cathedral, standing tall and apparently undamaged, but completely isolated in a sea of the rubble of bombed buildings. Our train stopped at a small station whose name I did not see and we de-trained and were marched to a Luftwaffe interrogation centre. Here some German Intelligence Corps officers addressed us, speaking perfect English without any trace of accent. They told us we would be spending the night there and that we would be interviewed, either individually or in small groups. The camp was not too uncomfortable, though no food or drink other than water was provided and in the morning it was clear that they had lost interest in us, having decided that we were Army personnel and not RAF. The German airborne forces came under the command of the Luftwaffe unlike their British counterparts.

This turned out to be a POW staging camp at Limburg on the Lahn near Frankfurt. The Senior British Officer present had given his parole on our behalf not to attempt escape before arriving at our next destination. The giving of parole meant that we could travel in comparative comfort in passenger coaches as far as the station nearest the camp. Here we de-trained again and marched to Stalag XIIA and while passing through some of the suburbs of Frankfurt on the way there we were verbally abused and angry civilians threw stones at us. Perhaps it was understandable that they should act in this way, for heavy daylight raids by US Flying Fortresses and night raids by the RAF were making their lives a misery.

When we arrived, Stalag XIIA was a mad crowded jumble. There seemed to be thousands of Allied troops of several nationalities from many corps and units, all crowded into huge marquees that were pitched close to one another. It was here that we were registered and photographed and as my friend Howard had explained to me earlier on the march out of Arnhem, it was now relatively safe to try and escape! Until you are registered as an official POW and are 'on the books' so to speak, you have no real protection under the Geneva Convention. If you should attempt to escape unregistered and are shot while doing so, there would be no inquiry as to the circumstances. You would in all probability be put down as 'Killed in Action'.

While waiting our turn for registration, I was startled to be greeted by none other than Corporal George Loveland and Sergeant Arthur Davenport, both from our unit and both of whom I had last seen back in Lincolnshire. They had travelled to Europe by sea with our heavy equipment. Now to our amazement, here they were, prisoners like us! They explained how their vehicles were following behind an armoured column somewhere near Nijmegen, not far from Arnhem, when there had been a sudden German counterattack from the east flank that had split and disrupted the convoy. They had been taken prisoner and now awaited registration and dispatch to a POW camp somewhere in Germany. To my great disappointment, they were regarded as separate from us because they had not been captured at Arnhem although they were clearly of our unit. As a result they were sent to quite a different camp and we were fated not to meet up again.

For us, the Battle of Arnhem was truly over and the battle for existence in a prisoner of war camp was just about to begin. It began almost immediately with a far from pleasant journey.

After a few days in Stalag XIIA, about 150 of us were marched out to nearby railway sidings and loaded into cattle trucks. Twenty of us were incarcerated in one third of each truck, wired off with barbed wire from the remaining two thirds, which was occupied by two German guards. With a little straw strewn on the floor, we travelled in this fashion for nearly 6 days. The train moved slowly, often halting for long periods while damage to the track from air raids was repaired. We were often diverted on to infrequently used side lines, but seemed to be travelling in a generally north easterly direction, albeit by a very roundabout route. We did pass through Kassel and I think Magdeburg, and we skirted the eastern fringe of Berlin and saw commuters waiting on suburban stations.

Once we were let out at some unnamed sidings and given a little food and the use of toilets. While cooped up in the truck, two buckets were passed round. One was full of water for drinking, the other was empty – at least it was when it was passed in through the wire.

Early one morning, we arrived at Neubrandenburg station.

I still wonder whether an error was made. A larger number of our Airborne Division prisoners were sent to Brandenburg. Were we sent to Neubrandenburg by mistake? I liked to think so. It consoled me to believe that the Germans could also make silly little mistakes. Confirming my suspicions that our arrival was unexpected, it seemed they didn't want to let us in. Of course this had its funny side; but we were weary and after what we had been through, all we wanted was to lie down. Even a POW camp has its attractions in such circumstances.

Kept standing forever outside the main gates, we were counted and re-counted, both by our guards of the train and those of the camp. Finally the gates were opened and we were admitted and the counting procedures were repeated yet again. And then we were signed for, just like a registered parcel!

Further confirmation came that an error had been made. I discovered that we were the first British prisoners ever to come to

Neubrandenburg. There were French, Polish, Italian, Serbian and Russian prisoners here, but no British. I was sure the intention was to send us to Brandenburg.

Our first night was spent in miserable discomfort, quite as bad as on the train. After a kit search, in which I was robbed of my airborne smock and a tablet of soap by a light-fingered searcher, we were herded in near darkness into a large unlighted concrete floored room. Part of the floor was occupied by fixed steel pipes and machinery and without bedding of any sort, we settled down to sleep on a cold hard unyielding floor. Of course we were all awake very early next morning – hunger had a lot to do with that. But it must have been nearly midday before it was announced that our 'rooms' were ready.

'Home' was to be a drab weatherboard hut, felt-roofed and set on a sloping open space amongst many identical huts and all surrounded by high barbwire fences. Elevated watchtowers stood at each corner of the compound and at intervals along the two longer dimensions of the rectangular camp. Only the "High Street" (our nickname for the central road) was sealed, the rest was rough and dusty. We found out later that there was a continuation of the camp to the south, separated from us by a No Man's Land of more wire and guard towers. This was a camp for Dutch Army officers.

A few weeks after we moved in, a considerable number of American prisoners arrived. Virtually all of them had been taken at Bastogne in the last German major offensive through the Ardennes. Over the ensuing weeks their number continued to grow until they far outnumbered the British contingent.

Our barrack room accommodation was about 75 feet long by 30 odd feet wide and it was divided into 'stalls' by 7-foot high wooden partitions. These partitions didn't reach the rafters that were about 10 feet above the floor. Each stall was roughly 12 x 15 feet and had a window set in the outer wall. There was an entrance porch (with urinal for night use) at the eastern end and at the opposite end, a couple of steps led down to ablution troughs in a lean-to style addition to the barrack room. In the ablutions room plenty of cold water was available but there was no provision for hot. There were no toilets in the hut apart from the night use urinal at the entrance. The proper toilets were close to the periphery wire, about 40 yards uphill to the east.

Originally each of the stall spaces held four triple bunk beds and the nine stalls each accommodated 12 of us. Between November 1944 and March '45, our numbers rose steadily until each stall had 6 triple bunk beds and finally it reached 8. At this stage, 24 men were living, eating and sleeping in an area of 12 ft x 15 ft. and this situation was repeated in every 'stall'.

Immediately to the left of the entrance, the walls of the first 'stall' extended right to the ceiling. This 'luxury apartment', provided some privacy for the four men who usually occupied it. In charge was the Senior Warrant Officer Class I, RSM Ted Brock, who was our appointed 'Confidence Man'. His duties mostly involved dealings on our behalf with Hauptmann Klingraf, the Camp Commandant. To assist him in this role he had a Deputy Confidence Man, another Warrant Officer and our fluent German speaking interpreter from one of the Para Battalions. We sympathised with them in the multifarious difficulties they encountered in representing our complaints and presenting our requests.

There were two round 'pot-belly' type stoves (for which there was no fuel) and two long tables and benches set up down the length of the middle of the room. When we moved in we were allowed a small quantity of straw for stuffing a hessian palliasse and two paper thin blankets. This proved completely inadequate when a Baltic winter set in. We would go to bed wearing all the clothing we had, the thin blankets carefully wrapped around our bodies and our feet, complete with socks, thrust into army webbing packs. Even so, the nights could be bitterly cold and seemingly endless. Our windows were tightly closed and our breath condensed on the cold glass and froze. By December the ice on the inside of the windows did not thaw sufficiently during the day to melt away and so the icy thickness steadily built up. By the end of January there would have been an inch thick layer of ice on each window on the north side of the hut and it is possible that this added thickness actually helped insulate us a little against the extreme night temperatures.

The 'proper' toilet deserves special mention. It was a brick built structure and it stood on the high side of our huts where the ground sloped up more sharply to the perimeter fence. Its floor stood about 7 feet above the ground level and you entered up brick steps and the facilities inside were very basic indeed. They consisted of six 'stations', four seats set at right angles to each other separated by wooden wings. A large metal ventilation shaft provided the backrest to each seat. They were not water closets. All faecal matter dropped into the brick chamber below and the method of removal of this material was quite fantastic.

The camp authorities made use of what we called their "Secret Weapon". They brought in a wooden cart, about 10 feet in overall length, with four large spoked iron wheels that supported a cylindrical tank, oval in section. A central steel dome, about a foot in diameter surmounted the tank and sat, perched on a compression spring, just above a metal tray of comparable size. It looked a little like a smaller version of the old style railway fuel tankers that bore 'BP', 'National Benzole' and other familiar names. A 6-inch diameter pipe, wire-reinforced, was attached to the upper rear of the tank and its length was coiled along its side. A small iron ladder was bolted on so that the German orderly, who of course we had dubbed "Dan the Sanitary Man", could reach the dome and tray easily.

The method was simple and ingenious. "Dan" drove the horse and cart to the lower side of the brick toilets. The free end of the 6-inch pipe was clamped to a pipe that led into the depths of the base of the toilet building. Next came the clever bit. Methylated spirit was poured into the tray just below the rim of the dome and Dan would waggle the dome up and down on its spring, splashing some of the meths into the dome and inside the tank. He then climbed down the ladder, waited a moment or two for some evaporation to occur, then climbed up again and applied a match to the meths left in the tray. The flame warmed the outside of the dome, vapourising any meths inside and when the meths burned down to below the rim of the dome it ignited the vapour inside with a hell of a wumph! The rapid consumption of the oxygen inside dome and tank caused a vacuum, the dome clanged down hard on its surrounding tray, acting effectively as a valve, so that the tank continued to suck furiously on the pipe in the depths of the cesspit. Once the latrine contents were on the move, normal syphoning took over, because the cart was on a lower level and this continued until the tank was full.

Dan and the long-suffering horse would then walk off, through the camp and out of the main gates. The stench was awful. Nevertheless, some brave souls actually considered the possibility of clinging on underneath the cart for an escape route. Freedom at a price? Most of us decided it just wasn't worth it unless you were totally devoid of a sense of smell!

Apart from talking about Food and Escape there were few activities within the camp. We were all Warrant Officers or Senior NCOs and therefore not required to work unless we chose to do so. Boredom was our greatest enemy – after hunger. There were very few books available in English. We had access to the English language section of the Polish prisoners' library, but there were few books of real interest in that section. I read only three during the 8 months of incarceration. They were The Robe by Lloyd C. Douglas and Country Cured by Homer Croy and I enjoyed both to the full. The third book? Well that was a massive treatise on poultry farming! How desperate can you get?

Food and talking about it, even if this was a form of self torture, occupied most of our time. When we first arrived at Neubrandenburg at the end of September the food provided was meagre and of poor quality. By March/April it was almost non-existent. The daily bread ration progressively decreased from a 2-kilogram loaf of dark rye bread (we suspected that it was adulterated with sawdust) divided among six prisoners when we first arrived, until the same loaf was being shared between 18 or even 20 men in April of 1945. There was little sustenance in the remainder of the diet. Soups were painfully thin and often unpalatable. One was basically made out of sugar beet and was particularly inedible. The carrot soup was the most acceptable and the cooked potatoes were sometimes good but all too frequently they had been poorly prepared and they were cooked with rotten potatoes included. Of course the taste was terrible. By early December many of the

Arnhem prisoners had lost as much as 35-lbs. I was 10 stone 8 pounds when leaving England in September and was down to 8 stone 2 pounds at the end of November.

In mid-November we received our first Red Cross parcels, one between two men. These came almost literally as lifesavers, particularly for those poor unfortunate men who suffered acute gastric reactions with the issued diet, for it quite often had a highly irritant sand content. One of my particular friends developed a gastric ulcer and was in pretty poor condition by the end of the year. We used to give him much of the milk and butter contents of our parcels in exchange for the foods he couldn't tolerate and I believe this helped him survive until our release. Fortunately Red Cross parcels came through more frequently after mid-November. On the 7th December we actually received one standard parcel between 2 men, the same on the 21st December and a 'special' Christmas parcel on the 23rd. Bliss!

We noticed that the types of food in the Red Cross parcels were very American in character and we were soon quite knowledgeable about the different brands of American instant coffee. Nescafé and Maxwell House brands became household words, but Barrington Hall and Tiffany did not make it onto the British scene after the war. Spam was routinely included and oleo-margarine was the substitute for butter, both much less familiar then to English tastes than bully beef and Stork margarine. The Christmas parcel was, by contrast, quite British in character – not as well boxed up and more variable in contents from parcel to parcel, but much more to English style and tastes. Years after the war I was told by one of the Warrant Officers who had been our leaders that no Red Cross parcels had come through British channels throughout our stay in the camp. All the parcels we had received were 'gifts' from the Americans in the camp who had received parcels within 10 days of their being admitted. He rather toned down my admiration for them by telling me that whenever we got one parcel between two men, the GIs got a parcel each!

It is widely believed that talk amongst men-only groups is 99.9% on the subject of women. I can categorically state that in the absence of a normal food ration, this is definitely not the case.

Until just before Christmas when two Red Cross parcels arrived over a space of three days, I can't recall any talk or discussion of women. The eternal, dominant subject was Food – to the virtual exclusion of all other topics. Then, over the two or three days of Christmas, rejoicing in the feeling of being relatively well fed for the first time for a long while, the conversation relapsed – or rose – to normal barrack room standards!

Our daily routine changed a little for the better after we managed to 'tame' our Gefreiter (corporal) Lightfoot. He was so called because of his stealthy approach on rubber soled boots. When we first arrived in the camp he would have us outside at 6am for an early morning counting parade. But we played up on these parades. We would move in the ranks when he was looking elsewhere, or create a 'blank file' and generally confuse his counting so that he usually had more prisoners than he should have had. He took the hint. At a few minutes to 6am he would go around our barrack room and count us in our beds. But strangely he would never do the same for the adjacent huts of American prisoners next door to us!

There was another odd 'preferential treatment' bestowed on the British prisoners. At very rare intervals, officially of 4 weeks, but more often 6 or 8 weeks, we, the favoured British, received an issue of very dilute beer. The semi-official reason for this was because the British (like the Germans) were recognised as a beer drinking nation – so we got this issue and none of the other nationalities in the camp ever did! Was it a genuine gesture on the part of the German authorities – or a subtle way of causing a little bit of jealousy and strife among us? However the beer was so weak and insipid that there was no danger whatsoever of it stirring up anything.

Christmas in the camp was oddly relaxed. Lights were left on throughout the night – although perhaps the RAF and American Airforces knew where the camps were anyway for they didn't trouble us. The German guards who patrolled each night within the wire and around the immediate vicinity of the huts were withdrawn. We were 'free' to come and go as we wished between the various national compounds and I visited my friends in the French huts and also in the Serbian section and discovered that we all have different ways of celebrating Christmas.

We arranged a challenge soccer match for Boxing Day between the French and British. During 'practice' the ball was accidentally put through a window of the large central kitchen. The window was shattered and the Germans were pretty annoyed about it and confiscated the ball. As far as the French were concerned, that was it – they shrugged their shoulders, pulled a face and said "Pas de balle, pas de jeu!"

The stubborn British saw it differently. The game went ahead. Complete with referee and two linesmen, the players lined up and ran and puffed their way around the Küche Platz and even had a penalty awarded and taken – but without any semblance of a ball! It was a laugh – and a way of keeping warm on a very cold afternoon.

The months of January through to March were increasingly hard. The basic issue of food was further reduced and we literally survived on the contents of the Red Cross parcels. It was a cold, dry winter and we had only a little snow early in the winter months. The dry winds preserved the powdering of snow but mixed it with the dust of the hard red soil and for some weeks we lived in a slightly pink world.

News slowly came through that the Allies were pressing on. We heard of the crossing of the Rhine at Remagen Bridge quite soon after it had occurred but other news was often delayed. However we knew the war was ending – and so did the Germans. Discipline that had been tight began to waver in many small ways. An example of this was that four of us 'worked' or shirked each weekday in the Camp office looking after Prisoner of War record cards. To get to the office we needed a pass, an Ausweis, to let us pass the sentries on guard at the gate out of the British and American compound on to the "High Street". (Internal barbed wire fences between the various nationalities had been erected just before Christmas). One morning when we produced our Ausweis for the sentry at the gate, he pushed it away.

"Nix Ausweiss!" he said loudly and added, showing us a cigarette, "Dies ist Ausweiss!"

The Commandant, Hauptmann Klingraf had a dog, a dachshund of course. In those days I could do a very creditable imitation of a dog growling and barking and at odd times after von Klingraf had arrived with his dog and was at work in his office, I would bark and the little dachshund would go mad. He charged around the office complex, barking furiously with Klingraf shouting at him to be quiet while we were doing our best not to laugh. There were two German soldiers who worked with us and officially kept us under observation – they both egged me on to do a 'barking' performance.

Those two German soldiers were very different in character. The smaller one's name was Pohl – an inoffensive little man, who worked quietly and unobtrusively around the place. One Sunday we had given our parole and were allowed out to collect wood for our stoves in the barrack rooms. Pohl was escort for four or five of us and around midday he rather diffidently invited us into his nearby home. We were introduced to his wife and given a drink of acorn coffee. In a strange sort of way I felt that Pohl was pleased and quite proud to be able to introduce us to his wife. I was always convinced that if we could have given him a pair of striped trousers, a black coat, a bowler hat and a tightly rolled umbrella, he would never have been picked out in a crowd of London city businessmen in the morning rush.

The other guard, Eric, was the classic 'old soldier' who knew the ropes very well indeed and could be relied upon to secure the best for himself out of any possible situation. He openly said he was a Hitler supporter – until things began to go wrong for the German forces and now he hadn't a good word for him. He had seen plenty of action and had been wounded and that was why he was at present a clerk in a POW camp. It was difficult not to like the man for most of us knew British soldiers who were the spitting image.

In March we heard news that things were going badly for the Germans on the Russian front. Some Russian prisoners were brought in, but we also heard that German wounded were passing through and literally thousands of prisoners and displaced persons were moving westwards. Many of these were Allied prisoners and those that were sick or badly frost-bitten were often dropped off in our camp and added to our critically crowded barrack rooms. One night several of us were called out of bed to go to the main gate, where two or three horse-drawn carts stood piled with what seemed like khaki clad sacks of potatoes. They were British soldiers, terribly emaciated by weeks of walking back from the east. Suffering horribly from frostbite, they could walk no longer. We were detailed to carry them back to our barrack rooms. Our first reaction was 'We can't!' Our own lack of food had weakened us so much that we feared we couldn't physically carry these poor devils. But we had to try. I moved towards one side of the cart and one of them put his arms around my neck and I carried him in my arms towards our hut. There was so little of him, that it was almost impossible to believe that these inanimate bundles were living people.

News came that German reinforcements were urgently needed on the Russian front. Any camp guards who were fit enough were advised that they were about to be sent off to the eastern front. Eric was one of those to go. He asked almost timidly if we would shake hands with him before he left. I had no difficulty with that at all and we all wished him good luck and commiserated with him on being sent off on a pretty horrible job. He made light of it and joked that he would soon be back. Predictably, about 10 days later, a few Russian prisoners were brought in. And who should prove to be in charge of them? Eric, of course! He truly was an old soldier who knew all the dodges.

During the last days of March and early April, food issues became even more erratic. Some days no bread came and steadily the number of men who had to share the 2-kilogram loaf increased from 6 to 10 and even up to 12 at times. Russian aircraft were now making almost daily appearances overhead and if the wind was easterly we convinced ourselves that we could hear the sound of heavy guns.

By mid April, there was no doubt about it. We were hearing distant gunfire and rather pitiful little cameo convoys of horse-drawn carts with wounded lying on straw were passing down the lane at the top end of the camp. Equally pitiful reserves were making their way to the front. Elderly German soldiers and young boys not yet out of their teens were on the way to try and stem the Russian onslaught. It was hopeless and was quite futile.

It must have been about the 25th or 26th April that the Camp Commandant told our Confidence Man that we were about to be moved out. We knew all too well what that meant for we had seen the physical state the poor wretches were in who had been in these other evacuation marches from the east. We took a vote on it and just about 100% agreed. So we said, "We'll stay put!"

Our Confidence Man (RSM Brock) said he didn't know how the Camp Commandant would react. Hauptmann von Klingraf listened to what Ted Brock had to say and then, through the interpreter he took on a sobering tone, saying quietly, "I do not have enough troops to force you to do anything. You can stay for the time being."

He added, however, that the troops retiring through the area were an SS Division and he would have to inform their Commanding Officer of our refusal to move and he gave us a friendly warning that the SS might take a different view of the situation. Ted Brock returned to us and relayed the message. He told us he thought we should remain in the camp – but he also suggested that we get our running shoes on and have our small kits packed ready to make an exit at the double if we were forced to do so. A few hours later we knew the SS Commander's return comment on the matter. It amounted to his saying that that he personally did not bloody care what we did, just so long as we didn't get in the bloody way of his troops!

The next couple of days were full of rumour and excitement. We could hear the rumble of guns to the east and south. We made tentative preparations to stay put in the camp and let the battle go over or round us. We dug trenches in the open areas and prepared doors removed from barrack rooms to lay across these trenches to provide some cover if the battle literally came over the top of us. There was little more we could do and so we waited and did nothing – and doing nothing was perhaps the most difficult task of all.

Those two days dragged by. Some of our companions planned to leave the instant the German guards left their posts. They believed we should have left the camp when the Commandant had informed us that we were to be moved. Quite quietly and unofficially, they continued to plan to slip away the moment the guards relaxed their control. Their idea was to move west towards the advancing British and American forces. Indeed it was in that direction that the German forces were moving, for they had no intention of surrendering to the Russians if there was any possible alternative.

In the tremendous confusion that ensued after the arrival of the Russian forces and their devastating assault on the town of Neubrandenburg, some of our fellow POWs did set off heading west. Some weeks later, back in England, they told us that they had soon been picked up by German soldiers, taken to their local commander who asked them where they thought they were going.

"Wisssmar." they replied, and he asked "Warum Wissmar?"

"There are British troops in Wissmar."

"Stimmt," he said, "wir gehen nach Wissmar," and they did!

180

But for those of us who stayed on in the Camp and were there when the Russians arrived there was a night of excitement and some dramatic days ahead.

≈≈≈≈≈≈≈≈≈≈≈

Chapter 17
Two on the road and Barbara

In the late afternoon of April 28th, 1945, the rumble of gunfire to the south and east of our camp heralded the advancing Russian army. As dusk fell, a few rounds, probably mortar shells, exploded at the edge of the woods fringing the wide clearing beyond the perimeter of our camp. At once, our German guards were seen hurriedly descending the ladders from the towers commanding the corners and strategic points along the wire. They were quite obviously obeying previously issued orders, but we gave them an ironic cheer to speed them on their way. Earlier that day we had piled the sandy earth on doors removed from our barracks over our hastily dug trenches. They would afford little protection in the event of severe fighting through the camp, but the making of these trenches had been an outlet for our nervous tension. Now we stood around outside, our few belongings packed in small packs and watched, expectant and excited, ready to dive into the cover of the trenches if things hotted up.

Around midnight, in the first minutes of April 29th, Uncle Joe's Army came past and in places even through the barbwire of our Stalag. The German forces withdrew hurriedly into Neubrandenburg, except for a courageous anti-tank gun crew that dug in about 500 metres down the road, where it fought stubbornly until silenced by superior firepower. After that, all seemed so quiet that we returned to our bunks and tried, mostly unsuccessfully, to get some sleep. But who could sleep at such an exciting time?

The store containing the Red Cross food parcels was broken into, not by Russians, but by all the different nationalities of prisoners trying to grab and defend their own brand of parcel. We rushed to do just that and a bit of good teamwork resulted in our own syndicate of four doing pretty well for itself.

By sunrise most of us were up and walking around OUTSIDE the perimeter wire in a state of euphoria. We looked on in amazement at the activities of the Russians. Down in the town of Neubrandenburg some 3 kilometres away, they had deployed tanks overnight and self-propelled guns and rocket launchers along this edge; all ominously threatening the town. Close behind these guns were support vehicles, even mobile kitchens where huge pots of soup or stew were simmering. They looked like whaling pots complete with blubber, but the smell was rather better. Militarily all was quiet. The soldiers were eating, resting, or maintaining their vehicles. We learned the Russians had given the Germans until 8am to leave the town, but they had chosen to hold on, particularly in the area around the railway station. Precisely at 8am the barrage started and the town was shelled remorselessly.

About mid-morning Russian tanks rolled down the hill and with the help of the infantry soon took the town. Some of us walked down there about 36 hours later. It was not a pretty sight. Civilians fleeing the conflict had been caught in the gunfire and fallen in the roads. I remember seeing a man and a donkey he must have been leading. They had been caught in gunfire, fallen in the roadway and then rolled almost flat by the advancing tanks. Neubrandenburg is a historic town with some beautiful medieval half-timbered buildings. A few of these seemed to have escaped major damage, but many had not. But what I remember most – and probably my companions would say the same – was that flattened man and his donkey in their futile bid to escape.

But we were still elated to be free once more and very eager to be on our way. Perhaps to-morrow. Impatiently, we awaited events that just did not happen. Some of our lads had left the moment the German guards hurried away, but more of us had remained. Now those who had stayed began to wish that they, too, had made a dash for it.

After Russian officers had made the initial contact with our representatives and removed their own emaciated POWs, we were left entirely to our own devices. No camp administration, nothing. After some days, contact was re-established with local Russian Commanders and we pointed out that we had had no bread or in fact any food other than Red Cross parcels for almost a week. They delivered a huge truckload of bread and an almost equivalent amount of meat – whole un-butchered carcasses. Electricity had not been restored and in addition the cesspit toilets had not been emptied for some days before the Russians' arrival and now seven days later you could say that things were humming.

So four of us decided to take to the road and make our own way west. Brian, Roy, Howard and myself were to be the four-must-get-theres. First we looked around for a suitable handcart to carry our gear and spare food. There were a number of these four-wheeled 'dog carts' round the camp and we found a good one. Then first Brian and then Roy decided they would stay on and wait for official transport home. That meant the chosen cart was much too big for just Howard and me. So that is how we came to take the smaller, older, "Barbara" on our travels. We set out with Barbara very early on Sunday May 6th.

Saying au revoir on the Saturday had been difficult. Auguste Lepoitevin, my good friend from Southern France was strongly against our going. On the other hand, Captain Helmer, our Dutch officer friend, wished he could come with us, but being a Regular Army officer he regretfully decided he had to stay put and so he wished us bon voyage.

Rightly or wrongly the pair of us set off at dawn. That May Sunday morning was crisp and beautiful and no one else was awake. Our cart was heavily laden with Red Cross food, blankets, ground sheets, Howard's portable typewriter 'rescued' and 'liberated' from the now deserted Stalag office, a spare pair of jackboots, cooking pans and two German metal respirator cases as water containers – not to mention pliers, an axe and a spanner. No wonder the little cart groaned and wobbled its way past the pond below the Dutch Offlag. Here we filled our water cans and joyfully took what we hoped was the road for Bargensdorf. But who called it a road? Lorries had been along it, horses and cyclists had been along it and we went along it – but it still wasn't a road. Quickly we realised that the map we had purloined from the wall of the camp office had its deficiencies. Our present road was quite clearly marked as a road to Bargensdorf, but this soft, sandy track hid large loose stones to trip our feet and our overladen unstable handcart tipped up on end. Two hundred metres of this and we were shedding all the clothing we could – four hundred metres and we had a real sweat on despite the chill of the early morning. Soon we were wearing our shorts.

We made these specially for the trip, cutting down two camouflaged denim suits worn by SS troops. Later on these shorts were the cause of our having a worrying hour or two.

When we turned off this awful track at Bargensdorf, conditions improved a little. We found quite a firm footpath so that the narrow iron bound wheels didn't bog down and the little cart began to move more easily, for the first time allowing us to walk side by side, pulling the handle. Until this time we had been forced to have one at the front pulling and the other at the back, bent double, alternately pushing and lifting Barbara's wheels out of the soft sand. Our choice of these minor roads was deliberate. We had learned that the Russians were collecting up any POWs making their way along main roads and installing them in camps, to be returned to their respective countries as soon as was convenient. For the time being we had had more than enough of 'camps' and preferred to remain at large on the minor roads.

Just before we came to the village of Rowa, Barbara was christened; fairly literally too, for one of our water cans had sprung a leak. Howard suggested the name. He had once known a WAAF called Barbara, alleged to be just as contrary and self-opinionated as our vehicle appeared to be. We never formerly agreed on this but the name stuck to our dogcart just the same.

In Rowa we had a long drink at the village pump and tried hard to communicate with two charming young ladies with no success, we couldn't even decide on their nationalities. However, the fact that they didn't run away from us was encouraging and it seemed that non-fraternisation only applied to west of the River Elbe – and we were still well to the east of that obstacle.

From here we travelled on reasonably hard footpaths until we reached a deserted airstrip and on the hard level surface of this, Barbara rolled merrily along. The trouble was, she was far from tractable and it seemed she would go where she wanted and not quite where we wanted her to go.

When we reached Ballwitz, Howard tried his German on a Pole (a two-legged one naturally) and he directed us through the village. Again we filled up with water at the village pump and I tried conversing with some French POWs who were standing around rather forlornly. We pressed on, through some more very loose dust that slowed us up severely. There followed a hard, hot pull up a slope through ein Busch (a small wood) where hidden pine roots in the soft sand promptly tipped up Barbara yet again. Wearily we replaced everything and headed for Zachow. I pulled, Howard pushed and within sight of Zachow the erratic front wheel disappeared in loose sand and so did most of our kit. More adjustments had to be made before we reached the village and it was here that we met our first kindness.

The night before, thanks to a Scotsman rendered very noisy by illicit Schnapps, no one had managed to sleep in our barrack room until 3 am and we had set out at 5 am. We were very far from our usual fitness and in addition we were just so tired. In Zachov we asked for water and a barn to sleep in. We were given milk and an offer of blankets. The blankets we declined because of our very dusty legs. Stretched out wearily on the clean straw in the cool barn we slept for about 2 hours. Around 5 pm we drank more milk and set off for Usadel. But someone said the town was 'kaput' and a little short of Usadel, some civilians went through Howard's army trouser pockets. He wasn't wearing them at the time and they had dropped off our cart unnoticed. They might have left them on the road instead of throwing them away over the ditch. Fortunately his copy of "Vanity Fair" was left lying on the road nearby, otherwise we might still be looking for his trousers. By the way we were wearing shorts.

Hereabouts we reached 'Anticipated Obstacle No. 1'. In the days before we left the POW camp we had pored over our only map and identified particular spots where we were most likely to encounter Russians – and opposition to further travel. Anticipated Obstacle No. 1 was the main road from Neubrandenburg to Berlin. We needed to go along this road for about 500 metres before we could turn into minor lanes once more to reach Prillwitz. We knew it was forbidden for a vehicle like Barbara to be on a main road. These were reserved for Russian convoys. At the junction where we had to enter the road we could see two Russian guards – though subsequently one turned out to be a female Pole. She had a rifle slung on her back and two flags in her hands. Both guards were in uniform. A cigarette for the man and some smiles for the lady OK'd our entry to this forbidden territory and back we went for Barbara where she was cooling her axles under a tree.

When we returned to the main road again, we found to our chagrin that the guards had been changed. There was now just a single Russian Military Police girl on duty. She had an automatic weapon slung on her back and it was with great trepidation that we advanced on to the road with a dobra den and wide smiles – and we stepped out in our chosen direction as briskly as we possibly could. 500 metres further on we found the minor road to Prillwitz, much to our relief.

For the next few kilometres we suffered sweltering heat and were fiercely attacked by mosquitoes. We were hot and bothered as we neared Prillwitz and a little ashamed of Barbara's very wobbly undercarriage, so we abandoned her under a tree on the village outskirts while we went on to look for a spot to spend the night.

The village was crowded. Its normal population of about 150 was nearly doubled by the presence of about a dozen large horse drawn wagons, each carrying a big family of displaced persons making their way home. One and all took us for Americans. We sorted that out and indicated our homemade Union Jack arm bands and asked for the nightly barn. Discussion broke out immediately as to whom we would honour with our presence. A strong voiced woman of 35 to 40 won the day by saying she had ein Mann in her house who spoke English and as she was wearing the red and white armband of Poland, we followed her. We ate, we drank both coffee and schnapps and we slept in quilts on real beds. At least, Howard slept. My stomach, enfeebled by eight months 'light duty' as a prisoner, rebelled over bread spread with pork fat and coffee and schnapps – particularly the schnapps. About 3 am I had to grope in the gloom for a bucket. To sounds of ill-smothered mirth from Howard's bed, I found it.

Despite the long hard day that we had spent getting as far away from Neubrandenburg Camp as possible, we were the first to wake next morning. After quietly filling all the household buckets with water from the pump, we inspected the now silent village. A heavy scent of lilac blossom wafted up from the numerous bushes that adorned the little gardens of this village by the lake.

Breakfast was good. Pancakes – more than we could eat – and they soothed my upset stomach nicely. About 10.30 am, we were ready to be shown round the village by our hostess's daughter, Anna – who we fondly imagined, must be the village belle. On further reflection I am prepared to admit that eight and a half months in a POW camp can badly affect one's judgement.

She brought us back by way of the churchyard to see the effects that billeted soldiers can have in such places. Some prankster had removed about half the organ pipes and strewed them among the pews. We managed to return some of them to their rightful places, but others we just returned. The results, to say the least, were remarkable. As I crawled into the organ loft with an armful of spare pipes looking for their correct places, notes floated up or failed to float, as Howard made a spirited effort to play 'Onward Christian Soldiers'.

Dinner came and apparently the menfolk were to dine alone. Howard and I were two-thirds of the menfolk and we sat down determined to follow our host meticulously in everything he did. However, I promptly revoked when our host began knocking back a glass of schnapps. My troubles last night and our tour of his private still where he brewed this lethal stuff from potatoes had made me determined to avoid any further contact with it. A little put out by this, our host equally obviously decided to follow our every movement from then on. Stalemate! On the table was a dish of meat, rather fatty and definitely part of a pig. There were boiled potatoes and a bowl of hot golden fat – the 'gravy'. Three soup plates held what I took to be milk soup. Howard (maliciously) urged me as 'senior rank present' to make a start, so finally I took the plunge on the milk soup, closely followed by Howard in support and, after a slightly surprised pause, by our host. The 'soup' proved to be of finely grated rhubarb and some rye meal stewed in milk. Had we done right or wrong? Was it soup or afters? We shall never know.

Safely through dinner, in came the family, then brother-in-law and sister from over the road, the doctor and his wife who both spoke some English and were provided as interpreters. The brother spoke French, but quite the strangest French I had ever heard. He was a Pole and he had worked in France for three years, then twelve more in Germany – and his French frequently seemed a mixture of all three. However it was an evening of good cheer and these folk had little cause for smiles. But on this occasion they were determined to enjoy themselves. Someone played a mouth organ and there was singing and laughter until a sudden silence fell on the room and all conviviality was restrained. Two Russian soldiers had come to the door and had to be strategically talked out of the house.

Whit-Monday in Britain was a holiday so we three took a day off. Tuesday saw us starting out at 10 am with Anna and her infant accompanying us for about a kilometer. Soon we were on our own, trudging uphill to Hohen Zieritz, passing through without incident apart from the whole population turning out to gape at us. On a bend, just out of this village, we came on two cowherds tending their charges with the able assistance of the most beautiful Alsatian dog (a German cowherd). Howard, who spoke a little German, chatted to the men and I talked to the dog. The men were greatly relieved to learn that the war was over, our Polish friends having told us this the previous evening. The dog however was concentrating on my pocket. It contained a rich Canadian biscuit. We parted good friends – he had the biscuit!

Moving on over the hill we were climbing, we soon came in sight of Peckatel on the main Neustrelitz road. We followed this road for some kilometres before turning right into an avenue of trees that led to Klein Vielen. Here we stopped to brew up some coffee, having ascended quite a steep hill puffing a bit. While we were drinking our coffee, a shepherd joined us and although conversation was difficult, we asked him the way to Lippen. He directed us DOWN the hill we had just laboriously climbed. Lunch finished, we returned down the hill to the village and again asked the way to Lippen. We were told to return UP the hill once more and follow the route we had first thought to be the correct one. So we went up with thoughts full of that shepherd, wishing him many things in many unpleasant places, although I must say that the Russians painting over German signs in Cyrillic didn't help.

189

Through the woods we went to Lippen where we were greeted by Russians – with very ready arms – hand grenades to be precise, fortunately poorly thrown. It seemed that they had not been close enough to see our Union Jack armbands and thought we were Germans. It was those darned SS shorts! The magic word Angelenski squared matters – or maybe it was the American cigarettes that did the trick – either way, we left without further delay for Kratzburg.

This part of the journey was perhaps the loveliest from a scenic point of view. Pleasant tracks through thick pinewoods, numerous small lakes reflecting the brilliance of sun and blue sky on a glorious afternoon; surprise views when our path wound along a hog's back ridge between two incredibly blue tree-ringed lakes. Finally we looked down on Kratzburg and beyond, where yet another lake sparkled in the late afternoon sun. We skirted this lake about an hour later on the last kilometres of our journey into Granzin, where a lady evacuated from Berlin went to immense trouble to find us a suitable barn for a night's rest. This was not easy to do for many barns had been blown up or burnt when German munitions stored in them were destroyed. It was strangely moving to see milk herds returning off the open heath to stand, quietly waiting to be milked, in barns where little more than the foundation walls remained. When we did find our barn it too was partially destroyed and we had to prepare and eat our meal closely watched by a small group of people, marvelling at our Red Cross food. We would obviously be a topic of conversation for the next few days.

Barbara had not withstood the day's journey at all well. Her undercarriage now showed distinct tendencies to be bow-legged, so she went to the local blacksmith for a face-lift. This cost us a 1-lb tin of margarine, but it was well worth it for she moved far more easily when we started out next morning for Boek.

Just outside Boek, as we came out of the trees and approached the first houses, we saw a small group away to our right – four young Germans under guard of two Russians on foot and one on horseback.

The horseman was suddenly heading for us, flat out, with an automatic weapon, something like a Tommy gun, laid across his saddle. He was holding this steady with his right hand as he galloped up. About 10 metres away he shouted fiercely, "Deutsch?"

We shook our heads furiously and bleated "Nein! Englisch!"

I don't think he really believed us, but we were allowed to continue separately from the Germans, but under escort just the same.

The Russians had their control post in a large house in Boek. An officer in charge, who spoke a few words of German, questioned us. They made a rather perfunctory search of our handcart and we thought this was the moment to say goodbye to Howard's 'liberated' portable typewriter. Luckily we had two identical German army issue backpacks; mine packed with food and Howard's containing his typewriter. They went through mine first and we kept them interested in some 'Swift' American cheese while we swapped packs. They searched my pack again – as they thought – and marvelled at how much food we had. But they made it very clear that they were looking for weapons and actually asked did we have any. Again, we shook our heads vigorously and then I had an attack of honesty and said "Ah, except...." Instantly their grips tightened on their weapons as I burrowed within the folds of our blankets and produced the little axe for chopping firewood.

They seemed to think this was the best joke for a long time, slapped us on the back and finally gave us (and the handcart) a lift on a lorry for a few kilometres along the way. They dropped us at a road that went to Recklin, a concrete road, excellent for Barbara. But we hadn't been told there was an airfield at Recklin and a very important one at that. Its great size came as a nasty surprise and looked like becoming 'Anticipated Obstacle no. 2'. Huge hangars and administration buildings confronted us and we were stopped every few minutes by sentries who demanded documenti or papiri. All we had was a scrap of rather scruffy paper with something written in Russian to say that we were English, trying to make our way home. We had to talk hard (and hand out numerous American cigarettes) and we were mighty glad to see the last of Recklin and head for Vietzin and the bridge at Vipporow.

Now this bridge was one of the places that we anticipated might prove difficult. The bridge crosses a broad canal at the southern extremity of the Muritz See, the second largest lake in Germany. The lake stretches far to the north but we could clearly see the guards standing at the other end of the bridge. So we decided to procrastinate. We sat on the edge of the Muritz See and bathed our sore feet. And we ate some of our choicest Red Cross delicacies – just in case we were forcibly parted from them when we tried to cross the bridge.

While we sat there, we saw what proved to be virtually the entire population of Vipporow over 12 years of age, marched out along the road we had just travelled on from Recklin. Later we learned that they were made to fill in craters and clear bomb damage on the airfield. Rested, much cleaner and now well fed, we approached the bridge. Incredibly, there were no guards at all and we tramped unchallenged over the temporary wooden structure into the town.

Almost immediately we met a man in uniform who took charge of us. We thought he was a Spaniard and he certainly seemed to speak Spanish fluently, but he also spoke Russian, Polish and some German. He said he had fought in Spain in the Civil War, but that more recently he had been with the Russian 'Blue' Army. Whoever he was he went out of his way to help us. He found us an empty cottage and then spent an hour looking for a Russian soldier friend to write a note for us, saying who we were – two English soldiers making for Witttenberge and would any Russians please assist us and show us the route. The Russian soldier who wrote this couldn't find his officer to get it signed – so he signed it himself! This pencil written document helped us get safely through to Wittenberge (as distinct from Wittenberg – no final 'e' – where Martin Luther burned the Papal bull issued against him and his teachings). It is one of the best testimonials that can be given to an army apparently unhampered by red tape and rubber stamps.

There was an amusing incident at Vipporow, which was otherwise a rather miserable place. Howard had an admirer! A young lady, nameless and almost shapeless, appeared to take a great fancy to him. Around 10 o'clock that evening, he helped her replace a wheel on a small pony cart. Between 5 and 6am next morning she came to greet us, saying "Allo" to Howard, who slept

192

blissfully, stretched on his couch. At 8 am there she was again and once more he was obliged to go and change another wheel – at least that's what he said he did.

By 9 o'clock we were striding out of Vipporow along the Robel road, fortunately shaded by some large trees, for the morning sun was already really hot. All too soon we had to leave the ease of the metalled road and take once more to sandy tracks as we made across country for Karbow and Kambs. Mistakenly taking an unnecessary left turn cost us four hot weary kilometres and in exchange gave a chance meeting with a German who had been a POW in England and had been repatriated. He spoke of Goot Essen, Goot cigarettes, Goot tabac – a thought provoking comparison.

From Kambs to Wredenhagen our route was along the main Wittstock road, but at Wredenhagen we took to the lanes for Zachow. By now the sun was scorching and we did little more than 400 – 500 metres at a stretch, usually resting in the shade of trees along the sun-baked lane. Howard's legs began to look an angry red colour. He was badly sunburnt. At Zechow we halted for a bit of lunch and a rest in the shade and asked a farmer and his wife for water and a barn to sleep in. We were offered milk and the best bedroom! We accepted the first, but politely declined the second. While dozing in the barn after our lunch, a heavy thunderstorm made us decide to stay put for the night and so we had supper with the family. Fried potatoes, two eggs and creamy milk – oh such luxury after prison camp food!

After the meal Howard excelled with his German conversation, but we soon returned to the barn for a pleasant night's sleep, lulled by the drumming rain on the iron roof.

It was now the 11th May and we were washed, breakfasted and pushing out along a little used track for Massow and Freyenstein. On the edge of a wood some 2 kilometres from Zechow we found unexpected company. A young German lady, small, stoutly built, auburn hair plaited and coiled round a lightly freckled face, she was carrying a small bundle tied in a coloured shawl. We asked the way and she told us without hesitation. She told us more. "I know you are English. You have spent the night in a farm at Zechow and you are trying to get to Wittenberge." And could she please come with us?

This poured out practically in one breath. She told us she had been in a concentration camp for 2 years for refusing to be sent to a munitions factory. She had been evacuated from an eastern camp by the German authorities when the Russians threatened the area. The column she had been in was closely followed and harried by the Russians, until there was a big battle at Recklin airfield. The Germans completely lost control and the column, their virtual prisoners, and it dispersed. She (her name was Soni) had found her way to Zechow and had rested there two weeks. Now she wanted to come with us to Wittenberge and then make for Hamburg where she hoped her sister was still living. We hadn't the heart to tell her how heavily Hamburg had been bombed. Anyway, she was strong and helpful, pushing Barbara along without even being asked to do so.

Her presence livened our days considerably. Another person to talk to – for Howard and I had begun to run out of conversation. But Barbara obviously resented the new arrival and began her tipping up tricks again.

There was about 6 kilometres of rather pleasant pinewoods before reaching Freyenstein. We passed through the town with some trepidation for it was quite large and rather full of Russian soldiers. Then we turned off for Halenbeck and 3 kilometres before reaching this village, we stopped for a biscuit and jam lunch and a roadside brew of coffee, resting until the cooler evening hours arrived. Once again the day had been so very hot that the sun scorched Howard's sunburnt legs and they quickly become inflamed.

In Brugge we pulled up for the night in a standard barn-hotel. The farmer's whole family came to see us, including two young daughters. They didn't come empty handed either and supper was extra good – potatoes cooked in milk and butter, washed down with lots of fresh creamy buttermilk. We were living well, for of course these dairy farmers had little or no outlet for their milk as there was no transport available. Later, after a wash in the dairy, we turned in on the straw. Soni was still with us and insisted on remaining close by us, so we gave her a blanket and Howard and I shared the other.

The 12th May brought a pleasant awakening with an elderly farm hand bringing us a great bowl of milk still warm from the cow. It was Saturday, so we decided to have a rest day to see if Howard's legs would improve. The farmer said we were very welcome to stay there all day and we did, resting and reading in the nice, though neglected garden. A lazy day came gently to an end and we bedded down in the straw once more, ready for an early start next morning.

Up at 7 am and ready to move off by 8.30 am, but (not for the first time) taking our leave delayed our start until 9 o'clock. Then it was off to Grabow, to swing south for Preddol after some 4 kilometres. Skilful directional work, or maybe a lucky guess for I had lost my compass in the straw at Brugge, found us at Triglitz without touching Mertensdorf as expected. There were large numbers of Russians there and I was worried about trying to take Soni through with us, for I didn't think they would welcome anyone trying to take a German across the River Elbe to the American sector. Rightly or wrongly, to the Russians, any German is a bad German! However we stepped briskly through Triglitz with nothing more than questioning looks from the soldiers and were soon on the road to Lockstadt. Just before reaching it we stopped for lunch at a lovely little spot where the pine trees opened out and a small river ran by a grassy bank. We cooked potatoes and ate them with hard-boiled eggs given us at the farm at Brugge. A flask of milk stood cooling in the river and the prospect of a nap after lunch made life seem rather good. Some Russian officers interrupted us and we had a hectic and almost completely garbled conversation with them. Having been rudely awakened we decided to set off again, but didn't get very far. A kilometre or so down the road we struck a Russian road barrier at Tacken. Maybe this was what those officers had been talking about.

However the Russian NCO in charge of the guard at the barrier contacted a man who we took to be the officer in charge. He staggered us by giving us not only water but full written instructions (in Russian) of an alternative route to Perleberg. Originally we had planned to skirt this relatively large town, but armed with this letter and we hoped its authority, we decided to try going right through. But that was for tomorrow. For we found an ideal barn close by in Strigleben and we soon settled down for the night.

It was 9 kilometres to Perleburg and we boldly approached the town centre, deliberately turning a blind eye to a sign saying Centre d'accueil Francais and Anglo-American Information Centre. We literally bounced our way over Perleburg's cobbled streets onto the Wittenberge road. There was quite a thrill of anticipation as we neared our target destination.

There followed a long, fast, hard march along this straight, tree lined cobbled road for Wittenberge – and we hoped, the American Army. In sight of Weisen (about 5 kilometres short of Wittenberge), back axle trouble manifested itself. A constant rubbing and wobble of the right rear wheel, finally came to a head. Just as I turned to Howard to say, "I think the metal of the axle is getting soft", Barbara emitted a squeak and a groan and rolled over. Poor Barbara! It seemed her days were to be cut short. So we stopped to consider – and have lunch.

Howard went to a nearby house for water and information and having unpacked all our belongings from the cart, I attacked it with pliers and the axe. Soon the front wheels and the long handle became a new cart in embryo and a bit of rope completed the job. So Barbara passed on and after drinking our brew, our new two-wheel "Babs" trundled behind, loaded with our now considerably reduced worldly goods, for we had donned our khaki uniform trousers and dumped the ex-SS shorts and spare boots in the woods.

Now we were on the last stretch of our trek to Wittenberge and beyond was the Elbe – the river that was, to us, 'the be all and end all of all rivers'. Within a hundred metres of the riverbank we were halted and delayed for quite some time by Russian guards. But after distribution of American cigarettes and the explanation that we were English, we were allowed to proceed to the water's edge. At this point I suppose the river was about 200 metres wide. There was a launch in mid-stream with a noisy outboard motor with some Americans in it, obviously enjoying themselves. Impatiently we waited, 10 minutes – 20 minutes – half an hour. It grew cooler, darker. We were in sight of the finishing post after a journey of over 100 kilometres and were considering swimming, when praise be – across the water we heard a Yankee voice hail the launch. "Ask those guys if they want to come across!"

We needed no second asking. Soni, for she was still with us, stood hopefully alongside us. Fortunately the Americans asked no questions, whipped us all aboard and hey presto, we were on our way – back to civilization. Standing in the waist of the boat as it quickly ploughed its way over I was conscious of incredible excitement, while Howard's shoulders bounced up and down as they always did when he chuckled deeply. But Soni, unable to contain her exuberant spirits, laughed, gurgled and literally jumped for joy. It can't have been pleasant to be a German woman east of the Elbe in the early days of the Russian occupation.

So our ten day journey came to an end. We had reached our objective. It seemed so strange, ten minutes later, to be sitting in a jeep speeding off to company headquarters and thinking that from now 'transport will be provided'. At last the days of travel being limited to the number of kilometres we could walk before nightfall, were well and truly over. But, come to think of it, I believe both Howard and I had rather enjoyed the walk.

≈≈≈≈≈≈≈≈≈≈≈

Chapter 18

DDT and TLC

Once we had returned under the wing of military authority in the form of the American Army, things moved pretty swiftly. We were remarkably well treated by the detachment we had suddenly descended upon. Although 10 days of sun, exercise and lots of milk and dairy products had done wonders for our physical fitness, we were still rather gaunt specimens. The Americans took us straight into their field kitchen – a wonderland of ranges, steamers, ovens, long stainless steel serving benches and vast numbers of rectangular pans, about 50cms long, 30cms wide and 12 to 15cms deep. I couldn't be sure whether they were oil fired or electric. Electricity was a possibility as there was a large generator humming away not far from the entrance.

We were ushered in and invited to help ourselves from the hot food that appeared from nowhere in these large metal pans. Everything seemed to be there at once. Meat, vegetables, bread – and even a choice of two or three desserts, but we were at a loss as to how we were to serve ourselves for there were no plates. The sergeant-driver of the jeep guessed our dilemma and indicated the large metal trays provided. These trays had several compartments of slightly varying sizes. The cooks (or should I call them chefs?) wore white cooks clothes and some had the traditional chef's hat. The sergeant held his tray out: "Ah'll have the ham, some corn, sweet pickle and three hot-cakes and maple syrup."

A generous serving of ham descended into one compartment of his tray, a large ladle of sweet corn went into another, the pickle into a smaller one. The hotcakes, were removed from the top of one of the ranges and placed on the right hand side of the tray and alongside them a large spoonful of maple syrup. It was quite a startling introduction to American Army food and Howard and I were very cautious and unambitious in our choices. It took six to eight weeks to recover a proper appetite and small meals at short intervals suited us very much better.

The young lieutenant who had first questioned us as we came across the river, had said something about asking us into the officers' mess that evening for a drink to celebrate our freedom. We didn't take the invitation too seriously at the time but he was true to his word. And that evening, two scruffy British soldiers who had done their best to shake the dust out of their uniform trousers (I had no tunic), rub up boots that hadn't seen polish for months and wash and shave carefully, were ushered into the Mess. The American officers were very pleasant and thoughtful in that they produced a bottle of Scotch whisky – when I am sure they would have preferred Bourbon. Now I do not like whisky – certainly not the Johnny Walker they were offering, but politeness dictated that I accept a glass. We were asked about our journey, what we had seen, exactly where we had come from – all the usual questions. It was a friendly evening and as the young lieutenant said, "It certainly beats the hell out of sitting in a barn!" But if they had expected a riotous booze-up by the pair of us, they must have been sadly disappointed.

Next morning, after a breakfast limited only by what we could eat, we were driven north to a rather lovely country house. It was probably a brigade or divisional headquarters of the American Army and here we were interrogated again, more skillfully and incisively this time, into what we had seen and where we had seen it. Their interest was clearly in the strength and disposition of the Russians in the zone to the east of the River Elbe.

On leaving this HQ we were driven north and west to Luneburg and finally handed over to the British Army. The reception was quite dramatic and decidedly startling. A door was opened for us and commands were barked out: "Stand there! Feet wide apart! Arms straight and extend out to the side! Keep still!"

A nozzle like a suction pipe of a vacuum cleaner was thrust up each of our trouser legs in turn and a strong blast of air loaded with DDT powder distended our trouser legs up to the waist. Then the procedure was repeated at each wrist, the nose-tickling powder being forced up each sleeve until it emerged around the collar band. A quick inspection of our hair satisfied them that we had no 'fellow travellers'.

199

An orderly took us to our accommodation block. We were in a German Army barracks, very big, solidly built and completely soulless. However it had beds and blankets and pretty good showers, but we were tactfully prevented from washing off the DDT immediately by being conducted first to a QM Stores where we got some very necessary basic equipment such as new towels, soap, razor blades etc. Then it was time for a meal – which our presence immediately contaminated so that it smelt and tasted of DDT. Only then, as it was getting on towards evening, were we allowed some time to ourselves and both of us promptly dived for the showers.

Next morning it was off to another army set-up, probably an intelligence unit. Before we were questioned, there was a repeat performance of the DDT pantomime and this was to continue almost everywhere we went over the next two days. It reached the point that on entering a strange room, we would halt, spread our legs astride, hold our arms straight out to the sides and wait for the puff of the deadly powder.

As to the interrogation, I began to wonder whether our previous replies were being transported with us and we were being checked for consistency and truth. However we seemed to satisfy them and we were told that they would try to get us back to England "to-morrow". What a wonderful sound those words had! It was a strange, very limited world we were living in. We didn't belong to a unit. We had no army pay books for identity. We had no money. Although not confined to barracks, we couldn't go beyond our barracks limits without some means of identification. Roll on to-morrow and England!

Sure enough, next morning we were transported out to Luneburg Heath where an airfield had been brought back into service. For some time we sat around. Realising our penniless state, the canteen offered us tea or coffee and periodically orderlies and NCOs came to check name, rank, serial number and what units we had been in. Eventually we walked out to a plane and climbed aboard. We sat and sat there with a few other soldiers who were in the same boat as us. The wait would have been boring but for a lovely little scene as a sergeant-pilot of the RAF cajoled, wheedled, argued and pleaded to be allowed to stow his little bit of loot aboard and take it back to England. The aircrew gave in in the end and managed to manhandle his German Army DKW motorcycle aboard. Then came anticlimax. The plane was to take off but would only fly us as far as Brussels, where another plane would have to be arranged for the rest of the journey.

It was a short quick flight to Brussels and on arrival the ground staff seemed rather more conciliatory than their Luneburg Heath counterparts. They established us in a rather pleasant open air section of a canteen, provided refreshments and invited us to watch the planes for a while as there might be some delay; the weather wasn't good over southern England. Shortly after we had finished our coffee, an army lieutenant strolled up and said it looked as though the weather was closing in over there. He said he would fix us up with some accommodation in Brussels and we could go and enjoy ourselves in the city. Howard and I led the chorus of: "How do we enjoy ourselves without any money?"

He saw the point, said he would contact the services pay office on the airfield and arrange it. Broad smiles at the thought of a night in Brussels – England wouldn't mind waiting for us just one more day.

The lieutenant was gone about 20 minutes. We stood up eagerly only to be told that the weather was now improving and we would be flying out in about half an hour. I really think we might have been disappointed. But not for long. Once airborne and over the Channel, noses pressed against the little windows, the excitement boiled over as we saw the Kentish coast come in sight. Was this really Kent? We flew on over a fine looking moated building – and I recognised it. It was Leeds Castle!

I have no idea which airfield we landed at, but it was almost certainly in Kent or Sussex. The airfield seemed to have been organised to receive ex-prisoners of war. As we climbed down the steps from the plane, willing hands took our small packs or whatever we had to carry and walked with us to the reception centre.

They had a number of semi-reclining couches set up, a little like dental chairs without the adjustable head rest. We were invited to sit down and this time the injections of DDT into trousers and shirtsleeves were done without our having to stand like a starfish!

Once that was over, the reception was kindness itself. WVS ladies descended upon us. Could they send a message to our families to tell them that we were safely home in England? What was the name and address? Did we want to include a short message to anyone in particular? It was overwhelming.

The next stage was new clothing and kit. We literally stepped out of what we were wearing and donned new underwear, shirts and uniform. Teams of volunteer workers armed with needle and thread sewed stripes and regimental badges on sleeves of uniforms and they even found two parachute badges for Howard and me. Being issued with new kit was rather like joining up for the first time – in a very much kindlier atmosphere. Among the kit issued to me that day, were two boot cleaning brushes, one to apply polish and one to do the polishing, a truly magnificent brush! It was stamped with the broad arrow insignia of the services and the date 1944. It is still very serviceable over 60 years later.

Newly kitted out, we were driven in buses to an army hut type camp, which I suppose was a sort of reception station. Here, there was a strong medical contingent and we were checked over very thoroughly. Some of the POWs were far from well. Many were placed on a light diet until such time as they were fit enough to eat a more normal one. To our surprise and joy there were many of the fellows who had been in our camp at Neubrandenburg and there were tales to tell and to hear as we compared our respective journeys. Some of our particular friends pulled our legs, saying we should have waited to be transported home – for they had arrived a day earlier than we had. But we were to have the last laugh. It turned out that the medical officers were more than pleased with our general fitness – although we were still underweight. What prison camp had we been in? They found it hard to believe that we too, had been in Neubrandenburg just like the others. We explained that we had walked nearly 100 miles, that we had been given lots of milk while on this walk and had generally eaten pretty well for the last 14 days or so. We were told we could proceed on leave just as soon as documentation was completed – but our POW companions who had waited for transport to be provided must now wait to be declared fit to go home.

The London stations seemed as drab as usual, except that now that blackout precautions were lifted, more light percolated down onto the platforms. After Leicester, with only 17 more miles to go, I became so impatient that I felt I could have run faster than the train. I can't remember if anyone met me at the station, probably not as they would not have known what train I would be on. Anyway, it was a short very familiar walk from the station to a family reunion. Father hugged me and hurried away, possibly very close to tears. We all were. Mother, an inveterate cigarette smoker, hastily lit up with trembling hands after our first embrace. Then the talk began, so fast, so many subjects all at once, that her cigarette smoked itself quietly away, unnoticed on the edge of the mantelpiece.

It came as a shock that 76 Market Street was no longer my home. Mother had bought Lorne Hill House in Wood Street, about 150 yards further up the hill. This was such an unexpected development for me that it took some time to adjust, but I consoled myself that I had several weeks leave to get used to the idea.

Another surprise was to find that Eddie had been invalided out of the Land Army suffering badly from chemically induced eczema of her hands, and was now working as receptionist at the rather fine Royal Hotel in Ashby. We promptly picked up our old friendship and saw quite a lot of each other. We had always enjoyed each other's company. Her memory differs from mine on what followed. I remember one summer's evening when we were out walking, and I insist that I asked her, "Does it have to be Charles?" Charles, of course was the chap she was engaged to, but Eddie doesn't recall me posing that particular question. And I can't remember whether I got an answer at that moment, but she wrote to me about the difficulty she had in writing a letter to Charles to break it off. A week or so later we seemed to be engaged and talking about a September wedding. If my question 'Does it have to be Charles?' was my only form of proposal, then it must be the weakest ever! But Eddie does admit to falling for my lean and hungry look when I returned after eight months as a prisoner-of-war.

One little snippet of information made me realise how very difficult it must be for families to bear the pressures of uncertainty, of not knowing what had happened. We had gone into action on 17th September and for days the papers were full of the scraps of information that filtered out. At first there was hope for a great triumph, then a realisation of the price being paid and finally, after some 10 days, the knowledge that the battle was over and that the 1st Airborne Division had failed in a gallant attempt to seize the bridge at Arnhem. In company with thousands of others I was posted 'Missing'.

The Quartermaster of the Field Ambulance, Lieutenant Webster, did a wonderful thing. He drove hundreds of miles all over England returning personal effects (including my beloved bicycle) to the families of the missing men. This was in early November, and still all my parents had was the War Office telegram about my missing status. Jim Webster knew a little more than the War Office could reveal. From 'evaders', men who, often with the help of the Dutch Underground, had evaded capture and slowly made their way back to Allied lines, Jim heard that a good number of 16th Para Field Ambulance had been captured in Arnhem at the St. Elizabeth Hospital. It was almost certain that I was one of them. His message to my parents was that I was probably a prisoner.

On Christmas Eve, 1944, my parents received a post-card written by me. It was an official POW card that the German authorities permitted us to fill in and it was then dispatched through Red Cross channels. In actual fact we had filled it in soon after arriving at Neubrandenburg in late September. It is possible that the Germans had caused a deliberate delay, the thinking being that the tardy release of information relating to prisoners would lower morale in Britain. Be that as it may, my parents said that it was the best Christmas present they had ever had! It cheered me immensely and made me realise just how much anxiety they must have suffered during those three long months of uncertainty.

I soon recovered my appetite and I think my parents were glad of the double ration card I had been issued. As yet I couldn't eat a big meal comfortably, but enjoyed food little and often. My mother said she had direct evidence of this from the four knives she found left on the cheese dish in the pantry!

Howard came to spend a few days with us in Ashby and I was to have gone and spent some time with him at his home in Weston-super-Mare, but that never happened and I'm not sure that he has ever forgiven me! Howard went into the Kenya Police Force and we were to lose contact – a circumstance I regret every time I think of those days with Barbara and Soni.

With about 10 days leave still remaining I received an official letter. I was to report on completion of my leave to a Rehabilitation Centre way up in Northeast England at Sedgefield, just north of Stockton-on-Tees. This was new country to me and I can't say that it had very much appeal. However, I duly went of course and was cheered to find that Howard was there and also Brian Miller who had occupied the bottom third bunk beneath us when in Neubrandenburg.

Slowly the purpose of this rehabilitation became apparent. Our physical fitness was being assessed and improved. We didn't always get on well with the NCO who chased us up on the cross-country runs to make sure we finished within a certain time limit. The trick was to finish just within the time limit (a) to avoid having to repeat it and (b) to ensure that we didn't get 'promoted' to a more competitive group!

Another facet of this centre was the psychological examination. There were three full time psychiatrists in the camp and we all saw them at least once. Poor Brian Miller was seen three or four times. It turned out that Brian had been married and had a son. Both his wife and son had been killed in an air raid on Liverpool. Brian had volunteered for parachute duties almost immediately after this tragedy. The psychiatrists, presumably, were trying to ensure that no suicidal tendencies had motivated Brian's volunteering. I very much doubt it, but he certainly didn't take much care of his health. Although he had a stomach ulcer he ate and drank like a fish and survived at least for as long as we managed to maintain contact.

205

After firmly informing the authorities that I did NOT want to volunteer for more overseas service (in Palestine) to ensure my return to the Airborne Division, I was posted to the Shaftesbury Military Hospital in Dorset. I didn't enjoy that experience and was rather relieved when I was moved out to one of their satellite hospitals at Bovington, particularly so when I found two of my 16th Field Ambulance friends already stationed there. It took me some little time to adjust to the office work of a very stationary military hospital after the life and duty required in a highly mobile field ambulance. I had just about come to grips with the process when to my surprise I was recalled to Shaftesbury Hospital and told I was being posted to London, to work in the Returned Army Medical Stores Depot in Woolwich.

Finally I began to understand what was going on – a kindly lieutenant-quartermaster on the hospital staff explained. The position of chief clerk to the hospital was vacant and it carried the rank of Warrant Officer Class II. The position was being filled on a temporary basis by a corporal. They would have liked to promote him immediately to fill this vacancy but couldn't do so while I was on their roll, as I was senior in rank and service. The solution was to post me off the strength of Shaftesbury Hospital. That was why I had been buried at Bovington and had now been resurrected for posting to the depot at Woolwich. I could have appealed the decision and probably stayed on at Shaftesbury, but the work didn't interest me greatly and anyway, I now calculated I had only about another 6 months to serve. So I went quietly.

A few days later I was standing on the platform of Shaftesbury Station with all my kit at my feet. On my head was the Red Beret we all were so justly proud of. There had been arguments over that. Sections of the hierarchy back at Shaftesbury Hospital had tried to deprive me of my beret and return me to the relatively  anonymous ranks of the cheese-cutter brigade. The hospital's lieutenant quartermaster didn't support this move – and told me so. So I kept my beloved beret. As the train pulled out of Shaftesbury I had few regrets to be moving on to pastures new. There had been one real highlight in my stay there. I had been given a reasonable period of leave to get married – I had finally won my girl having wrested her from the arms of the Air Force!

The second highlight – and I had been provided with a new uniform for this – was to go to London for an investiture and to be presented with a medal by King George VI at Buckingham Palace! My mother and Eddie, my recently acquired wife were both there to watch and I was proud but very nervous.

Now I was on my way to the Woolwich Returned Army Medical Stores, very conscious that I was on the 'home straight'.

Demobilisation was getting nearer and nearer every day. Roll on Civvy Street!

≈≈≈≈≈≈≈≈≈≈≈≈

Chapter 19

Café 76

It was summer 1946, and my demob leave extended into September, a great help because my Army pay continued until that time and we needed it. When called up in June 1940 my home had been 76 Market Street, where my parents lived and had their business for about 30 years. On my return the shop was still there, but their home was now Lorne Hill House, at 54 Wood Street. It was a tall, three-storey brick building, standing on the crest of a small rise. Wood Street was the easterly extension of Market Street, and immediately past Lorne Hill, Wood Street became the Nottingham Road.

Of course I had used Lorne Hill on my leaves since returning to England. It had been from there that I had walked the few yards to the lovely old parish church of St. Helens, where Edna Banks and I were married on the 19th September 1945. My mother temporarily solved our housing problem, by renting us a pleasant little house that had been the retirement home of my grandparents. The house was called 'Rowena', as is our elder daughter, and both owe their names to the associations Ashby has with the Lady Rowena in Sir Walter Scott's novel Ivanhoe. It was to be a very temporary solution because my mother sold the house virtually over our heads a few weeks later!

Since my demobilisation I had continued to pester local government for approval to open a catering establishment at 76 Market Street. Memories of the hours of talking and planning with Brian in the POW camp kept flooding back. In our half-starved state, we tended to concentrate on the menus we would offer in all their variety, in fact it became almost a form of self-inflicted torture. Now I was forced to realise that there were much more mundane hurdles to overcome before we could think of opening to the public. I contacted Brian – his home was in Norwich but he was away working temporarily on some scheme or other. Brian had been a student at the Slade School of Art in Oxford and was a talented artist. He came to Ashby as soon as he was free and laboured with us on our fledgling project.

There were three partners in the enterprise; my new brother-in-law Jim Gartland, Brian and myself. Jim was my sister Audrey's second husband. Nick, her first, was a workaholic almost from their honeymoon onwards. He spent all his time and energy deeply involved in the work that was his life. When he returned from army service, Audrey and he agreed to divorce and it was while she was living once again in Ashby that she met Jim Gartland – and a year or so later, married him. Although Jim's parents were English, he had been brought up in America. He had a soft American accent and a good business head. And of course Audrey and Eddie were in it up to their necks!

The long awaited local government approval for a catering establishment in the premises at 76 Market Street was finally given. Café 76 was on its way, though not without difficulties. A number of building deficiencies had to be made good. The floor of the front part of the shop was suspect and we were told to get it fixed. To obtain building materials was very difficult at that time. It was only through the good graces of a cousin of Eddie's, a timber merchant, that we obtained floorboards and joists to repair the floor.

In the interests of economy we undertook all the unskilled labouring that we could ourselves. This included removing the floorboards in the shop, and finding to our horror that most of the joists were also rotting because they had been placed in direct contact with the earth. Not only did we need to replace the floor; we also had to excavate about a foot to 18 inches of earth from beneath most of it to provide the necessary air space. We started digging out immediately, removing the soil by wheelbarrow loads. The task was a long and heavy one. A pneumatic tyred barrow was borrowed from Eddie's father, who had been a builder. This enabled us to work well into the night without disturbing the neighbours, for we had already found that a steel tyred wheelbarrow made a deafening noise in the confined space of the narrow passage way running between us and the next door property.

Repairing or making good part of a floor was one thing, laying a completely new floor so that the public were expected to walk in safety, was quite another. With difficulty we found a carpenter who would undertake the job in his spare time. He was a railway carpenter and came to us immediately his official working day ended. We were his assistants, helping him position, level and support the new floor joists. Soon the day came when new floorboards began to go down, almost half of the floor was complete when there was a railway accident up north somewhere and our carpenter was whisked away to repair and renew timberwork broken in the accident. We couldn't find another carpenter in our area and much of our 30 days grace that the license allowed us before opening had expired. In desperation, Brian and I took over, having closely watched the technique our carpenter had used to cramp and nail the boards in position.

The floor was completed and is still going strong in the 2000s – fair enough for very amateur carpenters. Eddie's father and his brother, Ernest, helped by repairing the ageing plaster on the walls, no easy job as in one area old plaster had to be cut away. It looked strangely greasy, refused to wash clean and paint wouldn't adhere to it. We found hooks in the wall above this greasy area and guessed that hams or bacon had been hung there a hundred years ago or even longer.

During our struggle to get the place open by the due date, the help and encouragement we received from everyone was incredible. Local business people dropped in, literally, when we had no floor, to wish us luck and tell us this was just what the town needed, and to promise to be our first customers.

Catering equipment was almost impossible to obtain. Tables, chairs, table linen, cutlery – wartime shortages persisted and we had to search widely and also improvise. I saw an advertisement for 'sturdy square tables with detachable legs'. I made enquiries and found that they came from a café in a good area of London. We asked for twenty and were lucky to be allocated twelve. On arrival we found that they were very sturdy, well made in America and had been used in a café frequented by American servicemen. This fact was confirmed by the inch thick layer of used chewing gum parked underneath the tabletops! Slowly and laboriously removing it was just one more task that we had not reckoned on.

The deadline opening date approached all too quickly. I can't remember clearly what day it was, very probably a Thursday, for it was certainly mid-week. To plan our menus, we had collected our meat ration from the butcher a couple of days ahead. It was a huge joint of beef, which virtually consumed our meat allowance for the whole week. We had not seen anything like it in our homes since before the war. We stood, rooted to the spot and stared admiringly at its beautiful marbled texture. Our butcher had done us proud, and we were confident that our acting chef, my sister Audrey, would cook it to perfection.

Then came the burning question – how many could we expect for lunch on our first day? We had small bets on it. A number of locals had said they would come along to give us a start, but we had done no advertising and the less optimistic amongst us said 7 or 8. The bolder, more ambitious went into double figures; and we laughed at the supreme optimist who said more than 20.

Came noon, time to start, and everything seemed ready, the cooking totally under control. We just hoped that everything else was. About 15 minutes later a small handful of diners were seated, and we had served them soup, and were cruising happily and smoothly. It was then that the coach going to the Nottingham Races pulled up. About 30 racegoers wanted lunch. Panic set in! As we took orders out in front we returned to the back and hastily peeled extra potatoes. Additional tables were set up, and we even had to unpack items like mustard pots, washing off the fragments of packing straw before filling them. The large roast of beef was rapidly dwindling and people were kept waiting inordinately long periods. But amazingly, no one became irritable – except the harassed staff!

There was one beautiful moment when in the midst of taking order after order for roast beef, one quietly spoken client asked Brian Miller for beans on toast. Brian (who had studied at the Slade School of Art) possessed a rounded Oxford accent. He used it in the kitchen when he gave his order. In polished tones he said rather loudly, "Some bloody fool wants beans on toast!"

212

Despite the mad rush on main meals, somehow beans on toast were produced and Brian returned to his customer to be greeted with a quietly spoken, "This bloody fool heard you!"

During the weeks and months that followed, Eddie and I moved into part of No. 76 as our home, and we began living on the job. The hours we worked were quite unbelievable. Initially we were open 7 days a week, and for several weeks both Eddie and I clocked up about 96 working hours a week.

It wasn't just the hours that we were open, but also the work that had to be done outside these times. Both of us became expert in the art of making fatless sponge cakes because cooking fats were so very closely rationed. Dried egg was freely available at this time, and liberal use of dried egg, sugar and flour produced small fatless sponge cakes which we made in batches of 50 or 60 at a time and always after the café had closed down and we were on our own. They had to be iced the following morning and that was done after the fires had been re-stoked and the pavement in front swept or washed clean.

Shortly after our opening, the annual Statutes Fair was due. Henry III signed a 'statute' in 1219 in favour of Roger de la Zouch for his services abroad, conferring a license on his community to hold a fair. Originally observed on the feast of St Helen, it was also a hiring and firing market. Ashby's annual event falls due on the first Monday on or after the 21st September, and through the years it had grown to embrace the preceding Saturday and the following Tuesday. The large rides and the sideshows were all set up in the main street, totally devastating all through traffic. It was only the fact that Ashby was fortunate enough to have two minor streets in North Street and South Street running parallel to Market Street (the main street through the town) that permitted this traffic disruption to continue to the present day.

The rides and stalls erected the preceding Friday made things equally chaotic. For the five days that the Fair blocked the main street, North Street became a one way only for all eastbound vehicles, and South Street was similarly reserved for westbound traffic. Every year, before the war, the Fair had been set up down the south side of Market Street. This meant that we were subjected to the blank grey canvas backs of sideshows, and there was rumbling of noisy rides, to the accompaniment of the raucous mechanical organs sited almost on people's doorsteps.

For the period of the Fair, trade for those vendors on the south side of Market Street was virtually non-existent. But pressures from the affected businesses had finally convinced the Council to decree that the Fair would occupy the other side of the street on alternate years. For years our ears had reverberated to the sounds of the noisy rattles that the showmen used so vigorously to attract attention, and the startling clang of the steel plates hung behind the target coconuts when the hard wooden balls hit them. It was much more bearable to have them to be on the other side of the wide street — and very much better for business.

As far as our café was concerned the Statutes weekend meant a lot more to us than "Which side of the street is it this year?" We had high hopes that we would reap financial rewards that would help to offset the expenses incurred in opening. In the event we were certainly busy, but it was a different sort of trade and a different clientele. Our tea, coffee and cakes and snack meals were well up on normal, but our midday meal take was down. This was probably due to the total absence of through traffic.

On the Friday when the rides and sideshows were being put up, a rather unprepossessing individual came in to eat. He was obviously a manual worker; hands and clothes impregnated with grease and grime. He must have had an accident to one side of his weather-beaten face for his right eye fixed its gaze straight ahead, with both eyelids on that side drawn back, making it look disconcertingly larger than its neighbour. Before sitting down at a table he came to the counter and asked me whether we objected to his using our café. When I assured him we didn't, he sat down and spread a fair sum of money on the table indicating that whatever he asked for he would pay for. He ordered a substantial meal and appeared to enjoy it. Refusing 'afters' he surprised me by asking for the same again. He explained that he worked very hard physically, and had time for only one meal a day. He added that he would very probably like a third meal after this if I didn't mind! To my

214

amazement and the kitchen staff's total disbelief, he duly ate his third full sized meal.

This man brought fellow workers. They were equally scruffy, but sat and ate quietly and quickly and gave us absolutely no cause for complaint. Since childhood, I have had a 'soft spot' for itinerant fair people and as a young boy I got to know one or two travelling families and would look out for them each year, and this particular year, my acquaintance with 'odd eye' was to bear unexpected dividends.

The Monday was traditionally the night that the local Ashby residents patronised the fair. On the Saturday it was predominantly the surrounding villagers who came, and on the Tuesday it was anyone and everyone who had any money left. Well, on the Monday night I was doing the rounds and was tempted to go on the Cake Walk, a rather old fashioned ride that had not been included in the last few pre-war years. As I got on, I noticed that our daily diner was assisting the running of the ride and had just been relieved from the pay desk. 'Odd eye' spotted me and beamed all over his disfigured face and I was carefully guided to one side, other riders were gently propelled past me, and it looked as though my ride was going to last forever! Eventually I indicated that someone was waiting for me in the crowd, and I was allowed to descend – but despite the noise of the mechanical organ making conversation quite impossible, it was clear that one satisfied client was inviting me to return at any time – on the house.

The Café continued to prosper despite many unforeseen difficulties. One of these was a dramatic shortage of potatoes. Bad weather in the potato growing areas had flooded the clamps where potatoes were stored for winter use, and now the shortage was acute. We were even forced to buy a bag of seed potatoes (at a grossly inflated price of course) to keep our regular customers happy.

In early 1947, the Midlands suffered an exceptionally heavy snowfall. Villages were cut off, roads were closed and the busy main road from Birmingham to Nottingham, the A453 in those days, passed right through Ashby. For some days this important trunk road was blocked between Ashby and Nottingham by huge

215

drifts. Ashby was the nearest town to this newsworthy blockage and reporters from all the London daily newspapers descended upon us. Café 76 was just one of the centres they chose to use as a base. Our local pubs were also popular. But for three or four days we had a fraternity of newsmen sitting in the relative warmth, drinking interminable cups of coffee and making very frequent use of our telephone to report to their London offices on the progress, or rather the lack of it, in reopening the road. They always paid generously for their phone calls, and if we had had a license to sell cigarettes we could have done even better.

During this cold spell, Eddie and I had a little time off and set off for a walk into the white world surrounding our town. A mile along the road to Burton-on-Trent, on Ingles Hill, a snowdrift had closed the road where it passed between two hedge-topped banks. Strong winds had kept the adjacent field virtually free from snow, and by getting off the road into the fields we were able to continue on past the deep drifts. Our discovery of a roadside Bus Stop sign, all but buried by the snow, gave an excellent idea of its depth, for these signs stood 7 or 8 feet above ground. The inevitable thaw followed, the blocked road was opened and traffic was once more back to its usual noisy hum along the highway. The once white and sparkling snow gave way to cold wet slush and the newspaper reporters melted away even more quickly than the snow.

Spring came and the weather improved, but unfortunately not the relationships of the working partners. Perhaps it was because Brian and I were both ex-service men and still had some of the attitudes that become entrenched after five or six years of army life. Jim Gartland, not accepted for medical reasons, had been an air raid warden in Birmingham. I must say the two nights I had in Birmingham while on leave, rapidly convinced me that warden service in the city was a darn sight more dangerous than much of the time spent in the army.

Matters came to a head when our young waitress didn't turn up for two or three days, throwing a much heavier load on all of us. When she did appear (as if it was the accepted thing to do), Brian and I were so very glad to see her back that we accepted her absence as the irresponsibility of youth. Not so Jim. He told her to get her coat, and he firmly escorted her home to the Bull Inn, literally straight across the street.

Brian and I were upset by this – after all nothing was yet quite back to normal. This girl, raised in wartime, reminded me of the Returned Medical Stores where I had worked before being 'demobilised', an exceedingly boring job. There were about 60,000 field dressings stored in a huge warehouse and we were supposed to verify the count. Few of the staff were of much real help. There were three young RAMC servicemen picked as potential clerks because of their 'better educational background'. But when I learnt first hand of their bombed schools and school sharing, one school in the morning, another in the afternoon, and disturbed nights in bomb shelters – just how much education could we expect from them? There were also three ATS girls. One typist could type so long as every word was neatly written, another was supposed to be a typist but I never actually saw her prove it. Fortunately the third was a gem at work, and also, in a totally different way, after work hours. She and her boyfriend introduced me to good music in London. We went to the Albert and Wigmore Halls for symphony concerts and one time we sat in a box. A patron who couldn't attend the concert told the ticket office to give the box to 'two or three service personnel in uniform'.

Thinking about all this made me rather restless. Relations at the café had become badly strained, particularly for Eddie and Audrey. Brian was not so closely involved, but he decided to pull out anyway. And as the whole plan – our plan – had been worked out in the camp, I became less than enthusiastic. So after Eddie and I had discussed it, we too decided that it was time to call it quits. After further discussion with the others a settlement was worked out that managed to satisfy everyone.

It was the end of my very close association with No. 76, but it was far from the end of the business. Jim and Audrey between them ran it most successfully for a number of years. Eventually they sold out, ending an association of over 80 years in which the Tunnicliffe or Bellamy families had owned, lived in and loved 76 Market Street. But Café 76 lived on for quite some time under that same name, and it is, as far as I know, still operating in the 21st century.

≈≈≈≈≈≈≈≈≈≈≈

Chapter 20
Birmingham University

For several months I worked in a milk bar. The proprietor had various business interests and I was really much more interested in his printing and publicity involvement than I was in the actual milk bar and catering. Although I didn't find the work very congenial, it did provide much needed cash for the birth of our first child was imminent. This urgent need for extra income landed me in the doghouse with my mother-in-law!

An upper room at the milk bar was in need of redecoration. My employer asked me whether I would like to earn a bit extra by painting the walls, but that this must be undertaken after closing time. He obtained paint and brushes and I started on the job that same evening – without letting them know at home that I would be late getting back. I had no real fixed time of return because I was using my bicycle daily for the 5 mile journey between Ashby and Coalville.

When I did eventually get home, around 10 pm I think, I was very much in hot water, scolded by my mother-in-law who wanted to know where I had been – because Eddie had been rushed off to hospital and had produced a fine baby boy, David John. Fortunately, her sister Beryl, a nurse at the hospital, was able to slip me in to see mother and son despite the late hour. And I was again firmly reprimanded, this time by Eddie and Beryl!

I must say that at the time I felt aggrieved by this reception. After all I was only trying to earn a little extra largely because of this birth, after a week of waiting for it to eventuate. Of course I should have telephoned to say what I was doing, but when I left that morning, there had been no indication that Eddie was likely to be popped off to hospital that afternoon.

During this period in the milk bar, I had heard of a government scheme for further education for ex-servicemen and women. I duly went off to Nottingham for an interview, having filled in numerous application forms for a grant under this Further Education and Training Scheme (FETS).

219

In Nottingham, I was advised that the only vacancies were in Teacher Training or Dentistry. If I was accepted I would get this government grant and we calculated we could just manage on that. I was given a list of universities offering dental courses and advised that immediate application was essential. My first choice was the University of Birmingham and I wrote off at once and also to Leeds and Liverpool. Dentistry was a course where my medical knowledge might be an advantage and so of the two, I chose that.

When I received a reply from the Birmingham Faculty of Dentistry, the heading on the notepaper intrigued me. It showed that the Director of Dental Studies was a man called Humphrey Humphreys and it listed a number of military decorations after his name as well as several degrees in dentistry and medicine. Mulling it over, I deduced that with these degrees and decorations, he would almost certainly have been in the Royal Army Medical Corps and quite probably had commanded a military hospital.

The day of the interview arrived. The 'Midland Red' bus took me to Birmingham and I was early for my appointment. I shared the waiting room in the Dental faculty office with another would-be dentist, Colin Duckworth, a young fellow from Lancashire. He was to become a good friend during the years of study, but at that moment he was worried that his comparative youth (he was not ex-service) would count against him and that ex-servicemen like me had every advantage. I was hopeful that he was right, but not nearly so sure about this as Colin seemed to be.

When my turn came, Professor Humphreys quickly put me at my ease and opened proceedings by asking what I had been doing in the services. I replied very much off the cuff and rather daringly: "I believe I was in the same corps as you, sir, but in a very different capacity."

"Oh? How do you make that out?" He put me on the spot.

"From your degrees you would almost certainly have been in the RAMC and from your decorations you probably commanded a general hospital."

"Remarkably accurate," he conceded. "Now what was so different about your own service?"

"Well, sir, I was in a Parachute Field Ambulance with the 1st Airborne Division for most of my active service."

He asked a few questions as to where and in what capacity I had served and seemed interested in my replies. Then he followed up with questions on my educational background.

Finally he said he must see the next applicant, but he would recommend that I be accepted. He warned me that the lists were already nearly full – however he would see what he could do. On my return home, I felt sufficiently encouraged to refrain from posting further completed applications to Leeds and Liverpool Dental Schools – at least until I had heard from Birmingham.

About ten days later a letter arrived – I was in – instructed to present myself in early October, 1947. So, at the age of 28, it looked as though I was about to return to school. It was a real shock to the system. Fortunately I was not alone in feeling this way. About 35 of the 40 or so students doing Year 1 Dentistry were a motley collection of ex-servicemen. This first year was a course in the basic sciences. Physics, Chemistry and Biology were to stretch our minds quite painfully for the next few months.

There was no gentle introduction to the course. A short cautionary talk by the Professor of the Chemistry Department warned us of the need for a full and sustained effort and that there would be, as he put it, an inevitable thinning of our ranks after the examinations in June of the coming year. He hoped that he would not have to see any of us before that time for disciplinary reasons, as this too, could mean an earlier departure than might otherwise be expected. The message was loud and clear. Ex-service members who were recipients of Further Education and Training Scheme grants would require a satisfactory progress report at the end of each term, both in work and in attitude. Otherwise this none too generous grant might be withheld for a term while 'work and behavioural attitude attain a satisfactory level'. This was a sword of Damocles held over our heads, particularly for married men with young families.

The Professor's cautionary tale took about 10 minutes and ended a little prematurely by a sudden dramatic increase in strength of a strange odour that permeated the whole of the chemistry department. We were to learn that the smell emanated from the Prof's latest research baby – the production of oil and fluoride compounds. A year or two later these became known as Teflon coatings.

The Professor left and one of the Chemistry tutors took over. In minutes we were floundering with the names of elements, compounds, periodic tables, valency – and the mystery of 'free ions'!

The coffee break seemed a long, long time in arriving. Shortly afterwards we were back, this time in the Physics Department lecture theatre, being welcomed by a quietly spoken professor, Martin Johnson. I liked him immediately and found his introductory talk so brilliantly clear that some of the fears I had been harbouring about the physics course evaporated.

A noisy lunch break followed in the Uni refectory, like being let out of school. During the break we discussed what we thought of it all so far and what was to come in the afternoon session. We were rather pleased to discover that recent school leavers were no more confident than us ex-servicees, but we had much greater responsibilities making it absolutely vital to succeed.

Our programme for the afternoon was listed as 'Biology' and we learned immediately at the introductory talk that the whole of the first term would consist of 'Botany'. Amongst our group, we had a couple of ex-army officers, a naval officer and I believe a squadron leader from Bomber Command. On receiving the news about botany there were snorts of disgusted disbelief. Biology we could appreciate as being necessary to our course, but botany! They might just as well have said 'knitting' for the reception it received.

But Professor Twyman, head of the Botany Department, wasted no time in pleasantries or apologies. In his dry, rather flat voice, he announced, "Today is October 6th. Your only examination in this subject will be on January 8th next year. By then you will be expected to have reached Inter B.Sc standard in Botany. It cannot be done in the time available – so we will commence immediately!"

He dictated copious notes at a phenomenal pace and Ershadi, our Iranian student, found his English just could not cope. Prof.

Twyman was aware of this and at the end of each lecture gave Ershadi the lecture notes. He did this right up to the end of term. The upshot was that many of us befriended 'Farouk' Ershadi at odd times so that we could check the accuracy of our hastily scribbled notes against the master copy in his possession.

Few of us found it easy to take to study after so long a break and there were one or two who fell by the wayside before the end of the first year. Almost at once I settled on a system that seemed to suit me. Despite my bleak lodgings and the attractions of the University Club night life, I stayed in and worked solidly every evening from Monday to Friday and the weekends were then my own, to return home to Ashby and Eddie and David.

Mention of 'my lodgings' reminds me that my very first 'digs' in Birmingham were instrumental in changing my name. As long as I could remember I had been known as 'Jack'. There was no option when I came to lodge with Miss O'Leary in Calthorpe Road near the Five Ways in Birmingham as already several university students were in residence there – and three of them were Jacks. When Miss O'Leary asked my first name I said, "Jack, although I was christened John".

"Well you'll have to be John," she said. "We already have three Jacks!"

Somehow you didn't argue with Miss O'Leary.

The house in Calthorpe Road was a survivor of houses that had been built long ago in this road close to Broad Street and within walking distance of the city centre. My room was reasonably large, a bit drab and there were two built in cupboards on either side of a fireplace. It never saw a fire in my time.

Cleaning out the upper shelf of one of these cupboards I found a book that had been pushed right to the back. It had the strange title The Mycology of the Mouth. Although I was puzzled by the title as I thought 'mycology' had something to do with mushrooms, I found the diagrams of teeth and their supporting tissues interesting and thought it might be of use later on in my studies so I kept it. By an amazing coincidence, my first appointment as a qualified dentist took me to Market Drayton, to join a practice run by Dr. Charles Cartledge. He too was a Birmingham graduate who had used Miss O'Leary's lodgings years earlier – and Mycology of the Mouth was his book!

Christmas was approaching rapidly and the FETS grant was dwindling even more rapidly. Times were hard, so I stayed on in Birmingham after the official end of term and worked sorting the Royal Mail in the Birmingham GPO to earn a little extra cash. There were a number of final year dental students doing the same thing – exalted beings we knew only by name and repute. At times, during the long hours of the night shift, they would be approached by one of the uniformed, full time postal workers and there would be a huddled conversation. Two students and the postal worker would then disappear from the sorting room for 20 minutes or so.

It was some time before I learned what was going on. The National Health Service had not yet been implemented and these final year students were doing a fine trade in illicit extractions, denture repairs, custom made mouth guards for the amateur boxers and even the provision of dentures for patients who lived near enough to make a home visit feasible. Sometimes a post office official smiled on the unofficial use of his office as a temporary surgery, at other times it was the washroom or even the toilet that had to serve as surgery. A second student assisted in many ways, but chiefly by providing his hands and chest as a suitable headrest to support the patient's head during the more strenuous moments of an extraction.

On a good night, working in tandem, each student could make more than we mail sorters made for a full week's work.

We knew from the beginning that the long summer vacation enjoyed by students in other disciplines would only apply to us in our first year. After that, in pre-clinical and clinical years, we were allowed just four weeks leave.

After some hectic and very anxious waiting, all but two of the students of our year were deemed fit to continue the course. The high proportion of ex-servicemen created some interesting situations. One of the assistant tutors in the Biology Department demonstrated that oxygenated blood was bright red and that de-oxygenated blood was not. He did this by alternately administering pure oxygen and then pure carbon dioxide to an anaesthetised and bleeding cat. He was quite astonished at the reception his demonstration received. He was hissed and hounded off the rostrum by students who felt strongly that the sacrifice of a cat's life to demonstrate something that we already knew and accepted without question was totally unjustified.

Later, we used our own blood – just drops at a time of course. It was obtained by the use of a spring loaded needle which was aimed at a finger or thumb near its extremity. Release the trigger and bingo – one small blob of blood. On one occasion I had used this device on my thumb, just a millimetre or two from the nail and had achieved a very good result. To my amusement I discovered that if I held my thumb straight the blob grew only very slowly, but when I bent the last joint over as far as I could, instead of a blob I got a very fine jet of blood about 6 inches high. Rather taken by this effect, I tapped my nearest fellow student on the shoulder and said "Look!" and bent the thumb joint vigorously. He fainted – slumping down between the bench and the high laboratory stools we were perched on. I felt genuinely sorry about it but must admit that I joined in the laughter.

Exam time came in early May and after Biology and a gap of a few days revision we suffered two successive days of agony. There were two 3-hour Physics examinations – 'Properties of Matter and Heat' in the morning, followed by 'Light and Electricity' in the afternoon. At 5 pm we all staggered out to be faced next day by two more 3-hour sessions – Inorganic Chemistry in the morning and Organic Chemistry in the afternoon. Organic Chemistry was, I believed, my weakest subject. I succeeded in passing but I think I used an exam technique rather than true grasp of the subject.

First I read through the question paper carefully and completely. 'Attempt any 5 of the 10 questions' were the instructions. I saw two where I had some knowledge and there were three questions that were nothing more than calculations. I knew that in these set calculations the answer almost invariably was a whole number – if you finished up with something running to five places of decimals – forget it! I did these calculations first and finished with a whole number each time. Reckoning that was about

60% of the marks, two other waffle questions should see me through. I passed.

There was a gap of two blissful weeks before we had to sit our practical biology exam and I joined a group of University Ramblers for a few days walking in the Dove Dale area of Derbyshire. Another student, Hans Cohen (not a Dental) who planned to go on this ramble, also had an exam on the same Saturday morning that my practical biology was due. He had a small car and we estimated that by leaving north Derbyshire early in the morning we could easily be in Birmingham for our 10 am exams.

When we were two days into this trip, Hans decided that he wouldn't bother to sit his exam. Instead, he would accept the 'repeat' he would have to face later in the year. This was a catastrophe for me as it meant he would not be returning to Birmingham on that crucial Saturday.

On the Friday we had walked through Mill Dale in glorious summer weather, hot and exhausting at times and we had finally arrived at Hartington Youth Hostel. It was only then that Hans decided he would not front up for tomorrow morning's exam. It was too late for me to get transport out, so I spent the night there and left at 5 am next morning, hoping to hitch my way into Ashbourne in time to catch the early bus to Derby, where I could get a train to Birmingham.

One solitary vehicle passed my hitching thumb that morning – and it didn't stop. So I alternately ran and marched with my rucksack bouncing madly on my back, measuring my efforts by the distances between telegraph posts. Some years later I checked the mileage from Hartington to Ashbourne in a car – it is 9 miles and as I ran down the steep hill into Ashbourne Market place I was just in time to see the Derby bus departing. The next one was more than an hour away, far too late for my rail connection, but I pressed on, eventually hitching a lift to Derby outskirts and so on to the station. Checking the train times, I discovered that at the very best, I would be an hour late in arriving at the University. I telephoned the Biology Department and told them of my whereabouts and predicament. They said come in and report immediately to the department office on arrival.

Pausing only for a drink of water and a very hurried wash, I pulled the bottoms of my rambling trousers down over my army boots, combed my hair and presented myself, far from confidently, to the office. I was ushered into Professor Medawar's office – the GREAT MAN HIMSELF – who we had seen only from a distance – and I wondered what sort of reception I would get.

"I understand you have had some transport difficulties," he said. "Go and sit the examination and mark your paper '2 hours only'. Hurry along – and good luck!" What a gentleman!

Dr. Edney handed me the paper and a large tray covered with a cloth under which, of all things, was a dog-fish! 'Dissect out the Cranial Nerves' stated the label pinned to the fish. I had already done that during the term time over a full 3 hours – and made a botched job of it. Putting a bold face on it, I murmured quietly to Dr. Edney, "I don't think I need have bothered to come!"

"I shouldn't really tell you this, but you did a good theory paper. Do your best with the dissection and the spotter questions and you should be all right." Since then I have been firmly convinced that there are gentlemen and there are guardian angels!

Heaven was even more firmly on my side that morning as one of the bones that I had to identify in the spotter exam was familiar. We had picked up a rabbit's pelvic bones on the ramble and I had discussed their similarities and differences from a human pelvis with a young qualified doctor in our party. It's not brains you need – just Lady Luck!

That first study year is etched into my mind, but the one long vacation was to be even more memorable. For a start I had applied for work at the 1948 London Olympic Games through a student agency and was accepted. The pay was poor, but the glamour of being in the same camp as these Olympians was tremendous. The athletes were housed in ex-services accommodation (remember this was the first Olympiad since World War II). Much of London still showed Blitz damage and the accommodation provided was a far cry from the luxurious standards for modern Olympic contestants.

I had to report to the West Drayton ex RAF Training Centre – not an airfield, but a place where RAF personnel had received specialised training that they then applied at the nearby airfield.

During the war this airfield was a hotchpotch of miscellaneous hangars, runways and workshops. I think it was known as RAF West Drayton then, but it is now somewhat better known as Heathrow!

The workload in that camp was very variable. It could be hard and fast at times but very quiet between. Ours was a camp of mixed nations and it was intended that it should house the European countries. Mostly Central and Eastern European as it turned out, while the nations of the Commonwealth were housed near Kingston-on-Thames. But then, quite out of the blue, we scored the South Africans and later discovered the reason why. Their team and managers had initially been allocated accommodation in the Commonwealth camp at Kingston – but this had been declined when their managers realised that this camp would also have coloured athletes sharing the same accommodation. So at the last moment they were transferred to our European camp and it meant a lot of work to get their quarters organised quickly. Due to difficulties of plumbing at another camp we had also acquired some South American teams, including quite a large contingent from Brazil. This included not only their equestrian team of Army Officers, all Colonels or above that rank and all very pukka Spanish style gentlemen, but also other athletes and support staff, who could best be described as being of coal black hue. Their presence severely upset the South African team managers, but to their credit, I never heard one of their team athletes utter a critical word.

At this time I was still a very keen cyclist and had cycled the 100 miles or so from Ashby down to the West Drayton camp and because of my interest in the sport, I soon became friendly with the South African cycling team. Their road racing team asked me to accompany them on their gentle training runs – purely as a guide to ensure that they got back to the camp. As I was a complete stranger in this part of England it was very much the blind leading the blind. But working on the principle of always turning left at suitable intervals – and hoping that I would arrive back near something I could recognise – I got them back to camp each time.

They rode very gently, just easing the tensions their long flight had created in their muscles.

One of the team, George Estman, delighted me by asking me to be his official feeder at the Road Race event held in Windsor Great Park. What a thrill that was! Made even greater when their team manager lined me up with the other three helpers when the Duke of Edinburgh visited our trackside station and chatted to us about the team's chances and progress.

The pay for our work may have been poor, but the perks were excellent. On one marvellous day spent in Wembley Stadium I watched some memorable athletics. I recall seeing Fanny Blankers-Koen, the Dutch sprinter, who won both the 100 and 200 metre events at the '48 Olympics. And from very close range, I also watched the shot put, where an American, whose name I think was O'Brien, won the event with a record throw in the most casual relaxed attitude imaginable.

There was also a wonderful afternoon and evening spent at Herne Hill at the Track Cycling events. I watched my hero Reg Harris lose the final of the individual sprint event to the Italian competitor, but compensation was forthcoming when Reg and his partner triumphed in the tandem sprint event. For me, no subsequent Olympic Games, however spectacular, could ever approach the 1948 London Olympiad.

There was still more to come in that very special vacation. Our university rambling organisation had arranged a Youth Hostel trip in the Western Highlands of Scotland and on the Isle of Skye. My contacts with Scotland had been limited to the cold, dark winter months of early Army training at Newbattle Abbey near Dalkeith and the few damp misty days in October of 1942 when we waited in the Clyde for our convoy to sail. I knew that the Highlands were different, but I was to discover just how different in the next few weeks. They proved to be absolutely magical. Those midge-infested wet days of August and September were the start of a lasting love affair with Scotland.

ΝΝΝΝΝΝΝΝΝΝΝ

Chapter 21
The end and the beginning

The second year of our course started slightly less tempestuously than the first. There were not so many dire warnings of retribution to follow if we didn't give our utmost attention to the various branches of the science of dentistry that were now unfolding before us. The exhortations took on a different slant. We were often reminded that we would benefit in our future work by applying the principles demonstrated in that day's lecture or practical exercise and it was usually easy to visualise circumstances where this would obviously be true. The subjects now looming ahead of us – anatomy, physiology and biochemistry – seemed so much more relevant to our needs.

Whereas that first year of general science had been very much a make or break year for mature students, with an ultimatum to pass this section of the course or seek other employment, subsequent years and exams were cushioned by provision for 'repeats' and periods of 'further study'. As a result I felt the tests I had to pass leading to our Finals were single steps on a long staircase to ultimate success. There were no further long holiday vacations to punctuate our progress. We were all permitted to take a fortnight's break sometime during the August-September period, but such holidays had to be individually applied for and sanctioned by the authorities to ensure that a vital part of the training was not missed.

In this second year some younger students joined us – students whose school studies were sufficient to gain them exemption from the first year course we had just survived. They brought our class up to 45 and among the newcomers were three female students – Gloria, Hazel and Joy. One of the male students joining us at this time was Charles Piff, the only one of our year to obtain a distinction in the Medical theory examination. His excellent memory was later put to use on the stage as the actor, Charles Kay.

For much of the time devoted to physiology and biochemistry we worked alongside the medical students. But for anatomy we were segregated and had our own dissecting tables at the far end of the vast room. This anatomy room was cool at all times and well lit, but the immediate overpowering impression on first entry was the strong smell of formalin. Initially this made the eyes water, but some were more successful than others in adjusting to it. I think smokers had an advantage. I never could bend over the cadaver and concentrate for more than a few minutes without my eyes filling with tears.

The Dissection Room was a 'Holy of Holies' and we had been advised, indeed cautioned, to have a respectful attitude. This was fair enough. The bodies lying under their white sheets on the stainless steel tables had been donated for the express purpose of the advancement of science.

We worked under an American tutor, from Princeton, I think. He had a history of being a brilliant embryologist, but as a teacher he was decidedly unpredictable and certainly one of the oddest characters one could ever meet. It was alleged that on occasion he would cook his breakfast in the preparation room where the cadavers were prepared for dissection, and he darned his socks with elastoplast. How true or false these allegations were we never actually demonstrated but they were circulated with enthusiasm.

There was also another anatomy tutor, Dr. Deryk Darlington, who seemed to take the dental students very much under his wing. As a lecturer he was terrific. I can still recall his initial lecture on the mandible. Simply by a superb discourse on the bone, he made us all wonderfully aware not only of its shape, but of the importance of its surface textures and of the modifications of these and the nature of the bone itself in response to its function. He drew our attention to the various ridges, depressions and roughened areas and linked these indivisibly with the soft tissues that surrounded the bone in life. Indivisibly yes, indelibly in our memories? No, not quite – it took many hours of poring over diagrams and textbooks for us to become familiar with all these new names and terms. My very basic Army Medical Corps anatomy training was only useful at this level in that I had heard many of the names and terms before. At least it made note taking simpler.

Anatomy viva voce tests and 'spotters' were held at intervals and also a nervewracking test called a Brain Spotter. In these spotters, anatomical specimens were laid out at well-spaced intervals on long workbenches. Each specimen had two or three small numbered paper flags mounted on toothpicks. These were inserted into various organs or tissues. Each student had a clipboard with a sheet of foolscap paper bearing 30 or so numbers down its left hand margin. There was a loudly ticking clock that gave an imperious ring every minute. Students lined up opposite one of the specimens and while the clock ticked you were required to identify and accurately name the flagged tissue or structure. On the stroke of the bell you had to move on to the next specimen and exactly one minute later the harrowing procedure was repeated. Grown men were almost reduced to tears by the mind-blocking frustration this test could create and this was only the half of it!

The so-called brain spotter was an identically set-up test with the difference that every one of the 30 or 40 specimens set out was of, or related to, sections of the brain and spinal cord. With perhaps 2, 3 or 4 'flags' to identify in each specimen this test could be an absolute horror session! For the medical students a pass mark was set at or around 60% and anything over 70% was considered outstanding. For dental students the pass was set around 48 – 50% and to get over 60% was deemed worthy of congratulation. Our year of 1948 provided some surprises. For a start, several dental students managed to get well over the 60% mark and a number of medicals were in the high 70%s, but two overseas students, one from Nigeria and one from Senegal amazed us all by getting 97% and 96% respectively. Such brilliant results had never previously been achieved.

Although these tests seemed designed to bring on early nervous breakdowns they undoubtedly served the useful purpose of preparing us for the all important anatomy viva at the end of the term when external examiners were brought in. In this final viva we encountered such people as Professors 'Solly' Zuckerman and 'Sammy' Green together with our own incomparable Birmingham representative, Charlie Smout. There was a widely held belief that the two examiners designated for you to see was some advance indication of your final result. If you went to both external examiners you had the possibility of a distinction – or a failure. But if you went to Professor Smout and one other examiner, then you were probably safely through the examination, but at a level that left little chance of a distinction. I went to both external examiners – and I still don't know to which end of that equation I was headed.

A number of different tutors and lecturers took us for Physiology, perhaps too many for I didn't seem to gain a lot from the series of lectures. My clearest recollection is of the help derived from a textbook, The Living Body by Winton and Bayliss. I found this book remarkably easy to read and understand. In retrospect this aspect of our course could probably have received more attention. Since my time at university, I know that giant steps have been made in the teaching of physiology to medical and dental students.

Professor E.B. Manley was the principal lecturer in the Dental Anatomy and Histology Course and Dr. Edward Marsland, a recently qualified young man, very ably supported him. Despite a crippling illness, Marsland was to have a brilliant academic career and this led to his becoming Director of the Dental School and finally Vice-Chancellor of the University.

Our year was the first one where the Birmingham syllabus didn't include masses of Comparative Dental Anatomy, for which, having seen what previous years of students were subjected to, we were very truly grateful. For the uninitiated, Comparative Dental Anatomy is the study of the teeth and jaws of animals and as the name implies, comparison of them with those of human beings.

We sat the second Batchelor of Dental Surgery examination in June 1949 and at once went into the Prosthetics laboratory for an introductory course in elementary dental mechanics. There was also the Junior Operative course, teaching the theory and practice of restorative dentistry. By cutting cavities in extracted teeth we could learn how to make them suitable for retaining a variety of filling materials. For example, a cavity prepared in a molar tooth for an amalgam filling had fundamental differences from a cavity prepared for fitment of a gold inlay. Preparations for silicate fillings that closely matched the colour of the natural tooth were different from either amalgam or gold inlay cavities. There was no end to the variety of the procedures that we had to master and to this point there had been no mention of elaborate work involving production of crowns and bridges and the requirements of root fillings.

This part of the course was both exciting and exacting. Our tutor R.J. Smith (known familiarly as Roger) demanded tremendously high standards. We worked hard but for the most part happily. Some had greater natural manual dexterity and achieved good results more quickly than others. Two members of our year who were already qualified dental mechanics had started on this Preliminary Operative well ahead of us because they had been excused from the mechanics course we lumbered through. They were now working on advanced procedures and were about to start on their Local Anaesthesia course preparatory to work on real patients. At this stage such activities were just wistful dreams for the rest of us.

There were moments of fun and failure in those weeks of the Junior Operative. We cut cavities in extracted teeth for restoration with amalgam, at first simple cavities and fillings, but getting more complicated as we progressed. Cavities in anterior teeth were usually cut for restoration with tooth-matching material and had to be designed to take in as little of the front face of the tooth as possible. If the cavity involved the incisal or biting edge of the tooth, a gold inlay might be required and this implied the cutting of a lock or keyway on the back of the tooth. One student left our wonderful tutor at a loss for words – and that, we had thought, was an impossibility. The student, a cocoa coloured African little more than four feet tall, had to prepare a tip inlay for a front central tooth. Instead of carefully cutting the keyway on the back of the tooth where it is unseen, he had boldly cut it straight across the front of the tooth where it was clearly visible. Horrified to see this keyway on the front of the tooth, tutor Roger remonstrated at some length with student Baal. Finally, he said with patient understatement, "Baal, whatever would your patients say if you did this to them?"

Little Baal drew himself to his full 4 feet 2 inches, looked squarely up at Roger and said with complete conviction, "My patients would not mind, sir." Which was almost certainly absolutely true – and Roger knew it and for once was at a loss for words.

We cast our own inlays using 'B' metal as a substitute for gold. There was one mechanical centrifugal casting machine, but it was often difficult to get to use it and use of the hand operated 'swinger' device continued – and not without some danger to any student in the vicinity. Hot metal had been known to fly!

There was a large gas fired oven or muffle that was used to heat and burn out the wax from refractory investment materials of inlays or crowns before casting. It stood on a bench in a side room. It was nearly 2 feet high, about the same in depth and a little less in width. Its effective interior oven space was small, little more than a six-inch cube. The reason for this was the thickness of insulation used to ensure that any casting ring placed in the oven reached extremely high temperatures. The gas jets around the oven core were awkwardly placed and it was not easy to ignite them. On one occasion, my friend David Bowles had been unable to light them and after trying for some time had sought the help of Roger. Our dauntless tutor reassured David, saying that he would do it. Unfortunately, David had left the gas turned on and by the time Roger reached the scene, the whole oven was filled with gas. The match, skillfully applied to just the right spot, produced an instant reaction. There was an almighty boom! And the whole heavy oven jumped about 6 inches vertically in the air, thrusting the long straight vertical chimney pipe the same distance through the ceiling. The thick insulated door, with its double refractory-glass window, detached itself from its hinges and flew between an awestruck David and a shocked Roger. There was a measurable period of silence before Roger, in a shaky voice, requested David to turn the gas off at the main tap. The oven was unusable for some considerable time before repairs were done. Life in Preliminary Operative was never dull – only a little unpredictable.

Our year of students was the last to use foot engines to operate dental drills in the cutting of cavities. These treadle-operated machines required the operator to pedal with one foot while standing on the other. At the same time your balance had to be such that you could use the drill handpiece with great accuracy. It would be close to impossible now to find patients with personal experience of a treadle operated dental drill. If you should chance to encounter an elderly person who has had such experience, they will surely narrate a tale of horror. The noisy vibration experienced on the tooth would have been earth-shaking. I would add that it was not all beer and skittles on the pedaling end of the procedure either. All your weight was borne on one leg, while the other worked vigorously (at times furiously) to keep the drill spinning as rapidly and smoothly as possible. At the end of a long afternoon of such activity, walking out of the dental hospital to catch a bus home could be hazardous. The pedaling leg would continue its rhythmic up and down movements for hours after work had finished for the day.

Not all of our time was spent on this very practical training. We were concurrently attending lectures on dental pathology and learning the intricacies of local and general anaesthesia. Every day we were getting nearer and nearer to working with real live patients. Some were really eager to do so; others, less confident, were rather dreading that first encounter with the public.

When it came, individual reactions were very varied. Many of us did innumerable examinations and chartings followed by scaling and polishes before daring to load the drill with a cutting bur instead of a polishing brush. When, almost trembling with anxiety, we dared to cut tooth tissue with a slowly rotating bur, the very simplest cavity took hours to prepare. Those patients were magnificent, calmly tolerating our nerves and reluctance to plough on with the job.

At the end of a month figures were published showing what our work output had been during that period. To our amazement, male chauvinists that we were, one of the three young women in our group had got off to a flying start. Perhaps Joy would forgive me for saying she had not so far shown herself to be the most confident student at any stage of the course, but here she was leading us all. After the regulation examinations, scales and polishes that we were required to undertake, she had quickly started cutting cavities and completing amalgam fillings, whereas many of us kept deferring this by doing ever more and more scales and polishes.

Joy's example showed us what could be done and maybe small hands were an advantage.

There were sighs of relief when the time came to do a conversion course to electrically operated drills. We were eternally grateful for this – and I am sure that our patients were even more gratified.

Meanwhile our course in dental mechanics continued concurrently with the Junior Operative. Here again we were entering a different world from past dental mechanics courses. The use of vulcanite for denture making was very much on the way out, being replaced by the more modern and very preferable acrylic resins. One of our tutors, Mr. Kitchen, was an expert in handling vulcanite, but it was Maurice Aspin and his co-tutors who really demonstrated the possibilities of the new acrylic materials.

Quite outside the scope or the needs of our dental training, but perhaps more interesting because of that, was Maurice Aspin's fascinating work in the construction of artificial eyes. He was to be involved through the Queen Elizabeth Hospital in provision of acrylic implants for patients unfortunate enough to have lost an eye. His work was truly an art form. The shaping and colouring of the iris, the reproduction of the tiny flecks and vessels all of which he reproduced closely matching a colour photograph of the patient's surviving eye, were quite wonderful. We could also only marvel at the smoothness he achieved in the fitting surface of the replacement eye. When Maurice had cause to castigate me for shoddy work, I at least had the satisfaction of knowing that he was a perfectionist and practised what he preached.

Herbert Rott and Gordon Hodgetts, the qualified dental mechanics in our year, raced ahead at this point and began work constructing dentures for real patients. Meanwhile we toiled with wax knives and bunsen flame on interminable 'set-ups' of full dentures for mythical patients – and almost all our efforts seemed doomed to fail to satisfy the tutors. It was often very hot in the Prosthetics Laboratory during that summer and patience and tempers were taxed to the limit. Maurice Aspin, now Senior Tutor, made it very plain that he was in charge and kept our noses firmly to the grindstone.

Eventually we followed in Rott and Hodgett's footsteps and were actually dealing with human beings. Very closely supervised at each stage, we took our first impressions on real live patients.

The first impressions were taken using 'composition', a heat-softened material, forgiving and simple to use and producing a reasonably accurate impression. We used these impressions to make carefully cast models of our patients' mouths and on these impressions we made 'Special Trays'. These were impression trays specifically made to conform to the shape of the patient's mouth and designed to leave just enough space for a uniformly even and adequate depth of the final alginate impression material. Every stage was closely and carefully supervised, and slowly, with the help and hints of our kindly tutors, our confidence grew and with it so did our expertise.

Those patients in the Prosthetic (dentures) Department were nearly always edentulous – i.e. toothless. Sometimes we had a patient who had his or her own teeth in one jaw and required a full replacement in the other, but this was rare.

There were patients requesting full dentures who, in many cases, could well have retained some of their own natural teeth. Conservative dentistry, that is timely fillings, and improvement in oral care and hygiene, were not generally popular among the patients who sought treatment in the United Kingdom at this time. The National Health Service, providing free or financially assisted dental treatment, had not yet been introduced and treatment offered by dental training schools was often far and away the best the public could find. However there were many more patients requesting and in many cases urgently needing full upper and lower dentures than the Dental Hospital service could provide, so that we students were never short of volunteer patients.

The continual close supervision ensured that the standard of work was excellent, but things did go wrong from time to time. I had a male patient, a pleasant middle-aged working man, who required new upper and lower dentures. I followed the procedures laid down and took composition impressions. I cast plaster of paris models of his jaws and made two 'Special Trays' and these were used at the following appointment to take the final impressions in alginate material. There followed the 'bite' taking procedure, in which the relationship between the two jaws is recorded and the size and shape of teeth to be used is decided. Then the try-in. In this the teeth to be used were set up on wax-based dentures and these were then tried in on the patient who looked in a mirror – and approved or otherwise.

My patient really liked the look of his new teeth and said they were a great improvement on his old ones. He decided the lower teeth looked better and more regular than his own teeth had ever been! We went ahead and processed them and all went well until I was doing the final polish with brush and linen mop on the polishing lathe. Carelessly I used a coarse polishing slurry on the brush when working on the lower front teeth. The fine detail of shape and surface markings were immediately scored and damaged. As much as I 'fine polished' in desperation, I couldn't restore them to their pristine shape and shine.

Miserably I awaited the return of my patient. I feared that I would have to repeat the whole procedure – 5 more visits for him with loss of work time on each occasion. He sat in the chair and I tried in the upper set. Spot on! Pretty good retention and the appearance was excellent. Then the lowers – always the problem for patients – and dentists. These too fitted really well. But oh – the awful appearance of those lower incisors – I could see the brush marks on the tips of the teeth sticking out a mile! There was no way the supervising dentist was going to pass them.

Nervously I approached the supervisor and asked him to look at my result. His sharp eye spotted the lower incisors immediately and he took me on one side – and hit the roof! He knew just what I had done and said so in no uncertain terms and added that they would have to be re-made. We returned to the chair and the waiting patient and the demonstrator said, "Let's just have a look at these a moment, Mr. –"

He was about to break it gently to the man that the whole procedure would have to be done all over again. But first he removed the upper and asked were there any sore spots? Was it pinching anywhere? The patient shook his head. The demonstrator went to remove the lower denture, but it seemed to resist his

239

efforts. With a slight frown he gripped it more firmly and lifted it – and up it came very reluctantly with a slight sucking sound. He frowned at me. "Have you put denture adhesive on this?" he asked.

"No, nothing at all," I replied.

Perhaps he didn't believe me, for he took the offending denture over to the sink and washed it vigorously under the cold tap before returning and re-trying it in the mouth. Again, it clung to that lower jaw like a limpet! The demonstrator shook his head and said, "I don't know how on earth you have managed to get such good retention. You've messed up those lower anteriors and the mark you're going to get will reflect that, but I'm not going to tell you to re-make them because I don't believe you will ever get another lower denture retaining as well as this one, however long you try!"

He was absolutely right – I don't think I ever did. But I only got 3 out of 10 for my efforts on that occasion. The patient came to the rescue of my ego. He was sitting in the chair looking at his new teeth in the hand mirror "You know," he said, "these look a lot more like my own teeth than they did when you tried 'em in last week!"

In between sessions in the Prosthetic Department and working on the dentures we were making, we were also taking a course in Local Anaesthetics. This really did seem to indicate we were making progress. The course involved a lot of revision of facial anatomy with special reference to the 'Muscles of Mastication' and of primary importance, the course of the nerve supply to the various teeth and their surrounding soft tissues. Although local anaesthetics were sparingly used for the cutting of cavities, we had to rely on the tutors to give our injections for us.

When we did the practical part of the local anaesthetics course, we did it in pairs. Two of us would report to Mr. Brown, our usual instructor, in the room specifically allotted for this purpose. This was the very first time we had been called upon to give an injection into the mouth. A decidedly nervous patient fronted up and on top of that, after a reasonable wait for the local to work, the procedure was to extract the tooth that was the cause of the trouble. As there were always at least two surgeries in daily use for casual patients needing urgent relief of pain, it was possible to make some minor selection of suitable cases to be 'steered' towards the absolute beginners – us! Two senior students in their final year usually manned the second surgery – still under supervision of course. This permitted the simpler cases to be directed to the two of us who were the absolute beginners. Despite this pre-selection of cases, we were often as nervous as the patients themselves.

There were some wonderful moments, most of which were funny afterwards but almost heart-stopping at the time. One such moment was caused by one of our senior student colleagues who was operating next door and passed through our waiting room where two already injected patients awaited their extractions. One of them was a jittery patient who asked a crucial question of this senior colleague.

"This is the first time I've ever had a tooth extracted – so – are they any good at the job?"

Of course our senior friend could not resist making use of a hoary old dental joke: "Don't worry! You've never had a tooth out before – and that dentist has never extracted one either! You'll be fine!" Amazingly, he was!

Another moment was the time when I thought I had drawn the short straw. I was faced with the task of an extraction of a large lower molar tooth from an outsize navvy or builder's labourer. He was big and powerful and obviously had teeth and bones to match. I was concerned as to whether I could physically manage the extraction. I gave the necessary injection to the best of my ability and our instructor Mr. Brown checked that it had worked properly when the patient returned to the dental chair after the usual 10 minutes wait outside. 'Father' Brown, as we called our well liked instructor, said, rather more loudly than I thought necessary, "You have achieved very good anaesthesia, very good indeed." Then he added, almost in a whisper, "Don't rush it. You know what you should do. If you can't feel any movement desist and I'll take over."

I think the patient must have heard him, for I saw his huge hands grip the arm rests of the chair as I approached with the appropriate molar forceps. With my left hand supporting his great jaw extra firmly – praying that he wouldn't bite my fingers or thumb by now inserted round the troublesome molar – then I began. Following the usual practice, I eased one beak of the forceps down the tongue side of his tooth followed by the other beak on the cheek side. I lifted my elbow a little as I gently squeezed the forceps handles, pushing his tooth towards his tongue. I could see his knuckles whiten out of the corner of my eye as he tightened his grip on the chair, when there was suddenly an audible 'pop' – and bingo! The large tooth was nestling, cradled in my forceps, but safely and cleanly extracted. My patient's eyebrows shot up to his hairline with surprised relief, "Bloody Hell!" he exclaimed before I squeezed the socket firmly together and gave him a cotton pack to bite on to control the bleeding.

Father Brown was chuckling silently in the background, and he said to me afterwards, "There were two very surprised and relieved people in the surgery when the tooth came out like that!'

As we approached our final examinations we were instructed to find a suitable patient for the practical examination. In this we had to cut a cavity in a tooth selected by the examiners. Finding an ideal patient was not easy. You needed someone who was a calm dental patient and moreover, one who could and would attend without fail on the time and date set. I enlisted a medical student whose mouth offered two or more suitable cavities for examination purposes. He was also a good friend of mine (we had climbed together in Snowdonia) and I could rely on him to attend on time and not be too put out by the length of time these final practical examinations took to complete. I duly presented him to my examiners. In turn they looked at his teeth and the state of his oral hygiene (it was good – I had seen to that). They selected an upper left tooth that needed attention and I was asked to cut a cavity for a gold inlay. This I did, very slowly and nervously but without mishap. The examiners watched the work from all angles, a most disconcerting procedure. However my cavity eventually found sufficient favour with the examiners to be passed and I was told to take an impression of the tooth and show the result to them before I put a temporary dressing in and dismissed the patient. I had to make a further appointment for the fitting of the inlay as considerable work and time is required to complete it ready for cementing into the patient's mouth. Fortunately for this final stage I needed only our own Birmingham examiner to check that it was completely satisfactory – the external examiners had by then departed back to their home universities.

There remained only our Final written papers to complete. These were, as usual, a worry. I don't think any of us was totally confident and we all worked exceedingly hard to prepare for them. These final exams were held at the end of the year and it was early in December that we sat the written exams followed almost immediately by the vivas in the separate branches of dentistry. I vividly remember the viva in Orthodontics. Imagine my delight when I came to examine a talkative young patient who not only told me what had caused her badly protruding central teeth but also how it was proposed to treat the condition. Effectively, she had given me the answers to all the questions the orthodontic specialist was to ask me ten minutes later. Bless the young lady – but I wonder – had she been picked as an examination case – purely because she chatted so freely?

After the finals were over there was a very short waiting period before the results were announced. The Board of Examiners made a point of being as quick as possible. A few years earlier one over-anxious student had committed suicide while awaiting the outcome of his finals. By the time we had finished our last interview it was Friday lunchtime and it seemed unlikely that the results would be published before the Monday morning, so I hurried off to catch the bus home some 30 miles away. I arranged with David Bowles, who lived in Birmingham, to phone me if there was any news over the weekend. To my surprise he rang before lunch on Saturday. He quickly put my mind at rest by saying that I had passed – and then added in a rather subdued voice that he had not. I felt absolutely dreadful. He must have found it very difficult to have to make that phone call.

But I wasn't depressed for long. I now had letters after my name and had already obtained an assistantship – subject to my qualification – in Market Drayton, in Shropshire. I telephoned the principal of that practice and told him my good news and he congratulated me and said he would like me to start as early in

January as possible. A mad rush followed – and we moved to Market Drayton on the 31st December 1952.

Christmas with our families around us was wonderful of course – but Eddie and I had so much on our minds relating to our move to Market Drayton that we couldn't give it our full attention. December 31st was a difficult day for us to engage a furniture removal firm. Jack Plant, our local man, managed to employ a driver who was prepared to work on that day but he couldn't find an assistant to go with him..

"We'll get you there," said Jack. "And when you get there – chat up a local bloke who wants to make a quid. Get him to be the assistant!"

Of course when we arrived at the house, there was nobody to be seen for miles around. After all it was the afternoon of New Year's Eve and bitterly cold. So I became the removal assistant for the afternoon. The house was high standing, 3-storey, Victorian built. The ground floor was already a separate flat; but the first and second floors were ours. Eddie and I had been married seven and a half years and I didn't think we had accumulated a great deal of furniture. But by the time I had helped the driver get the bulk of our stuff onto the first floor and a very little on to the second I was convinced we had far too many possessions. That house had high ceilings. High ceilings are pleasant to live under in summer but they also mean long flights of stairs between floors and by the time the empty truck departed we were exhausted.

Market Drayton was an awkward place to get to from Ashby. It had a railway station and in those halcyon days, trains actually stopped there. But if Eddie and David had chosen to come by rail they would have had a terribly roundabout journey via Burton-on-Trent, Birmingham and Crewe with the possibility of waits at each station. Despite the bitterly cold weather we were experiencing, Eddie decided to travel in the removal lorry with David, our 5 year old, while I made my way on my motorcycle. We all arrived safely but Eddie and David were half frozen after their journey in the unheated cab of the lorry. By contrast, I actually fared better on the motorbike.

The flat on the ground floor of 44 Stafford Street was occupied by Bill Knox and his wife Heidi. Bill, a Scot, was senior Dental Technician in the practice. I was to discover that Bill was not only very skilled in his trade but a delightful man and he became a firm friend. But it was his wife Heidi who saw how cold Eddie and David were when they arrived. She invited them into their flat while the driver and Bill and I set about the unloading.

It was dark when we finished and we quickly assembled David's bed and got him into it. Then we made our own bed. Our eyes had barely closed when a loud bell tolled three times. It sounded very close and we waited, and wondered, then sat up in shock as a lusty peel of the eight bells rang out, coming from Market Drayton Parish Church close by. Bells at 10 pm? We lay robbed of sleep while the numerous changes continued until 10.30 when, just as suddenly as they had begun, they stopped and there was this wonderful silence. Hugging each other in relief we settled down for the night. It seemed the bells were not going to continue on till midnight to welcome the New Year in after all.

It must have been one minute to midnight when thunderous peals rang out once more, fortunately only for 15 minutes. With any luck the bellringers would take a well-earned rest and a New Year tot of rum!

Peace reigned. Young David slept through it all and now it was surely our turn – but not just yet. Downstairs, Bill Knox, who had been celebrating Hogmanay by doing the rounds of 'first footing', came home in merry mood. Well – at least the brand new year of 1953 was getting off to a rousing beginning!

This indeed was an end and a beginning. For Eddie, David and me it was the end of a difficult period of managing our lives on the minimum income my student's grant afforded. During this time Eddie had achieved miracles in the way she managed to feed and clothe us. It was the beginning of a vast learning experience for me in practical dentistry and a somewhat more affluent life style for my wife and growing family. Slowly, there also came a realization of the demand there was for dental services the world over. My skills were portable. The need for dental treatment was virtually

245

worldwide. The world was as wide open as the mouths before me – the only question was – where do we go next – and when?

And little did we know that dentistry was to lead us round the globe to Kangaroo Island in South Australia and eventually to Tasmania where we live now.

≈≈≈≈≈≈≈≈≈≈≈
≈≈≈≈≈≈≈≈≈≈≈
≈≈≈≈≈≈≈≈≈≈≈